JOSEPH E. JOHNSTON

CONFEDERATE LIVES

SOLDIERS AND STATESMEN

Gamaliel Bradford, Jr.

Dover Publications, Inc.
Mineola, New York

TO

MARVIN SPRAGUE

"*Est aliquid sacri in antiquis necessitudinibus.*"

Bibliographical Note

This Dover edition, first published in 2005, is an unabridged republication of the work originally published by Houghton Mifflin Company, Boston and New York, in 1914 under the title *Confederate Portraits.*

Library of Congress Cataloging-in-Publication Data

Bradford, Gamaliel, 1863–1932.
Confederate lives : soldiers and statesmen / Gamaliel Bradford, Jr.
p. cm.
Originally published as Confederate portraits: Boston : Houghton Mifflin, 1914.
ISBN 0-486-44414-7 (pbk.)
1. United States—History—Civil War, 1861–1865—Biography. 2. Confederate States of America—Biography. 3. Confederate States of America—Biography—Portraits. 4. Generals—Confederate States of America—Biography. 5. Generals—Confederate States of America—Portraits. 6. Statesmen—Confederate States of America—Biography. 7. Statesmen—Confederate States of America—Portraits. 8. Gettysburg, Battle of, Gettysburg, Pa., 1863. I. Title.

E467.B78 2005
973.7'349'0922—dc22

2005048372

Manufactured in the United States of America
Dover Publications, Inc., 31 East 2nd Street, Mineola, N.Y. 11501

"La critique pour moi, c'est le plaisir de connaître les esprits, non de les régenter."

Sainte-Beuve.

PREFACE

WHAT has impressed me most in revising these portraits is their lack of finality. *Nous sommes des êtres mobiles et nous jugeons des êtres mobiles.* No two men will take the same view of another man. Traits which seem most significant to some, to others seem negligible. Some will overlook a little vice for a great virtue, while to others the little vice makes even the great virtue an object of suspicion.

Again, one may seize justly, yet be led away in the presentation. It is difficult to give various qualities their exact proportion and emphasis. One may stress a marked trait too strongly and so make it too marked and spoil that balance which is everywhere essential to the truth of nature. One may establish one's portrait in a tone which is not perfectly suited to the temper of the subject. Thus, the portraits here given of Johnston and of Stuart are keyed quite differently. I cannot see the two men otherwise. But others may feel that I have struck a false note in one case, or in the other, or in both.

This difficulty, or impossibility, of attaining anything final may make psychography seem a useless and unprofitable art. Such it would be, if finality were its object. It is not. The psychographer does not attempt to say the complete and permanent word about any of his subjects. He knows that such an attempt would be indeed futile. Instead, he aims simply to facilitate to others, even a little, what he has himself found to be the most fascinating and inexhaustible of pursuits, the study of the human soul. In this study, if there were complete finality, if you could exhaust the book, even any one particular book, even your own, and shut it with a snap, half the fascination would be gone. The wisest of us hardly dares say, with the soothsayer in *Antony and Cleopatra*, —

> "In nature's infinite book of secrecy
> A little I can read."

In some of these Confederate portraits there may be thought to be a note of undue harshness. All I can say is that I have endeavored to display and to insist upon the high and fine qualities manifest in every case. To pass over or slight the shadows seemed to me neither just nor wise. As to any partiality in the matter, after careful self-examination, I can discover no motive which could lead me to anything of the sort, unless it were an undue desire to exalt Lee. Of this I am not conscious, and, if I have not been misled by some such influence, I feel that the net result of careful study of Lee's companions in arms is to bring out more than ever the serene elevation of his greatness. Some of them were, perhaps, more brilliant than he, some greater orators, some profounder thinkers, some even as capable soldiers. Not one approaches him in those moral qualities, which, as Mr. Adams has justly pointed out, place him, as they do Washington, far above those who aided him in his terrible struggle.

During my prolonged study of Lee's contemporaries, which compelled me to take note of their various faults and weaknesses, I have also continued my careful watch for similar weaknesses in Lee himself. The suggestion of anything of the kind has been rare enough; but in justice to Johnston and Longstreet and Beauregard I think it right to print the following very curious passage from a letter of General G. W. Smith to Johnston himself, written in the summer of 1862, before Lee had thoroughly established his great reputation. Smith was sore, from neglect, deserved or undeserved, and wide search elsewhere reveals no suggestion of a state of mind like his in any one else. But it must be confessed that just the defects of manner indicated here are what one would look for in a temperament like Lee's, if defects were there at all.

"I came off on a three weeks' leave. Just before it expired I requested Beckham to write to Chilton, for Lee's information, saying that I would not return because not well enough, but was improving. I received yesterday a note from Lee, in answer to Beckham's note to Chilton, first a layer of sugar, three lines, then two lines telling me to forward a certificate, and three more lines of sugar. I shall keep him informed from time to time of the condition of my health. Gaillard is with me, so I feel quite assured of correct information and judgment in the case, and do not propose supplying General Lee with any more surgeon's certificates beyond that upon which the original leave was granted. He took special pains to tell me, when I called to find out about Jackson's movements, in order to judge whether I had better stay in Richmond any longer waiting for a battle, that he could not grant me leave except on surgeon's certificate; that was 'his rule,' he said. I told him I did n't come to ask for leave, but to get information upon which to determine whether I would yield to the advice of the surgeons and leave the city, adding that I had already put it off for ten days or more in anticipation of active operations, and was getting worse, instead of better. In a semi-pious, semi-official, and altogether disagreeable manner, he commenced regretting that I had n't gone sooner; considered that the army had lost my services for ten days unnecessarily—and other like stuff. We 'will bide our time.' All I want is success to the cause; but there is a limit beyond which forbearance ceases to be a virtue, and if provoked much further I will tear the mask off of some who think themselves wonderfully successful in covering up their tracks." (*O. R.*, vol. 108, p. 593.)

Some readers may, perhaps, be surprised, in a volume of Confederate portraits, to find no portrait of either of the two chief Confederates, next to Lee, Davis and Jackson. I have, however, already dealt with these distinguished figures in the chapters on "Lee and Davis" and "Lee and Jackson" in *Lee the American*, and I felt that to introduce them here would simply mean a considerable repetition of the earlier studies.

I wish I could thank in detail the very numerous correspondents who have furnished me with suggestions and corrections. I am especially indebted to Captain Frederick M. Colston, of Baltimore, for most valuable material and comment. Professor Ulrich B. Phillips, of the University of Michigan, has kindly supplied me with advance copies of his excellent *Life of Toombs* and of his forthcoming edition of the Toombs correspondence, which have induced me to modify and considerably enlarge my portrait of that fascinating personage. Honorable Robert M. Hughes, General Johnston's grand-nephew and conscientious biographer, has supplemented his courteous protest against my judgment of the general by the communication of extensive material, on the strength of which that judgment has been somewhat altered, though not, I fear, so much as Mr. Hughes would desire.

Seven of the portraits contained in this volume have been printed in the *Atlantic Monthly*, the portrait of General Beauregard in *Neale's Monthly Magazine*, and the sketch of the battle of Gettysburg in the *Youth's Companion*.

WELLESLEY HILLS, MASS.,
September 19, 1913.

CONTENTS

I. JOSEPH E. JOHNSTON 1

Brief summary of Johnston's military career — judgments of his generalship — his ill-luck — in wounds — in being always too late — Davis a prominent element in Johnston's ill-luck — Johnston's character a prominent element — rashness, producing wounds — the quarrel with Davis — Davis's faulty attitude — Johnston's — his free criticism — his animosity to Davis's favorites — to Davis himself — restraint on both sides during war — bitterness on both sides afterwards — Johnston's book condemns him — admirable and charming elements of his character — his courage — frankness — honesty — simplicity — freedom from ambition — affection for friends and family — devotion of his officers to him — of the country — of his soldiers — two quotations summing up Johnston's character.

II. J. E. B. STUART 33

Stuart's fighting disposition — his early career — capture of John Brown—Stuart's indifference to danger—his mens' trust in him — his comradeship with them — his care for them — his discipline — more than a mere sworder — his self-control — his foresight and calculation — should Lee have given him Jackson's place? — his joy in battle — infectiousness of this — his unfailing spirits — his vanity — love of display — shows in his writing — his laughter — his love of song — and dance — and women — their admiration for him — yet his purity — and temperance — and religion — thorough humanness of his quarrel with Trimble — fortunate in his death.

III. JAMES LONGSTREET 63

Dutch characteristics of character and appearance — fighting qualities — coolness — a marked trait, self-confidence — shows in relations with Lee — their mutual affection — but

Longstreet's advice and patronage — particularly at Gettysburg — Longstreet goes west in 1863 — similar self-confidence with regard to Bragg — with regard to Davis — with regard to Law and McLaws at Fort Loudon — and again with regard to Lee in Richmond campaign — self-confidence also explains Longstreet's conduct after war — Mrs. Longstreet's testimony — other qualities of Longstreet's character — undeniable jealousy and bitterness — towards Lee, Early, Jackson — but Longstreet's fine qualities — his patriotism — his generosity — his love for his men — their love for him — Longstreet dies a Roman Catholic.

IV. P. G. T. Beauregard 93

Beauregard's French origin and temperament — his social charm — his vanity — shown in his love of rhetoric — in his exaltation of his own achievements — in Roman's biography — his vanity a cause of jealousy — this makes difficult relations with Davis — with others — notably J. E. Johnston — Beauregard's ill-feeling restrained during the war, however — his patriotism — his military ability — his coolness — his hold on his troops — and consequent popularity — his fertile imagination — and unlimited planning — value of his plans — none of them effective — dangers of too great imagination — "driveling on possibilities" — the solace of what might have been.

V. Judah P. Benjamin 121

Diversity of Benjamin's career — disbelieves in biography and destroys papers — which does him no good — his professional qualities — oratory — his high character as a lawyer — in politics strong Southerner — his many failures — attorney-general of Confederacy — secretary of war — fails — secretary of state — fails — his connection with the St. Albans raid — not a great statesman — his prominence owing first to business methods — second to knowledge of men — yet this not supplemented by sympathy, as with Lee — Benjamin in private life — his social charm — his smile — his religion — his quick temper — his quarrel with Davis — his love of excitement — his family relations — not an unscrupulous adventurer — nor a mere advocate — genuinely loyal to the Confederacy — but not a great man.

VI. Alexander H. Stephens 151

Contradictions in Stephens's character — his delicate health — his energy of soul — recalls Voltaire — but Stephens had spiritual as well as physical ills — his melancholy — conquers this by effort — by religion — by action — by social interests — his humor — his popularity — his affections — for home — for persons — for animals — his philanthropy — his tolerance and gentleness — essentially an intellectualist — follows his conviction — to the death, if necessary — his intellectualism in business habits — in religion — in law — in politics — no partisan, but follows truth as he sees it — believes in eighteenth century abstractions — his book — Stephens politically ineffectual, but historically significant.

VII. Robert Toombs 183

His impressive physique — a fighter — in law — in politics — delight in opposition — follows own course in all policies — prominent on Southern side before war — speakership contest — Tremont Temple speech — Sumner assault — other qualities besides fighting — humor — love of simple country life — hospitality — domestic affection — professional honesty — balancing qualities and conservatism in politics — opposes even secession till the end — under Confederacy fails politically — fails militarily — cause of failure — lack of discipline — fighting qualities come out again after war — does much of value for Georgia — dies an unrepentant rebel — Milton's Satan.

VIII. Raphael Semmes 217

Romance of *Official Records* — names — Raphael Semmes — not a pirate — in spite of his own views of privateering — general character of Alabama's career — Semmes not romantic adventurer — elderly, respectable professional man — his intelligence — his humanity to prisoners — relations with crew — discipline — their affection for him — his private life — domestic affection — love of nature — religious feeling — Christian virtues — bearing of these upon his public career — his patriotism — his freedom from ambition — but defects — coarse strain in abuse of enemies — something piratical after all — Byronics — described as corsair in appearance — rhetoric — "Rest thee, excalibur."

IX. THE BATTLE OF GETTYSBURG 247

Origin of the war — a five-act drama — act I, alarums and excursions — act II, Southern triumph — act III, Vicksburg and Gettysburg — characters of Lee and of Meade — first day, battle in the village, Reynolds killed, Confederate advantage — second day, Longstreet attacks Round Tops — and fails — third day, Pickett's great charge repulsed — Gettysburg climax of war — act IV, Wilderness and Sherman's march — act V, Petersburg — lessons of Gettysburg.

NOTES 263

INDEX 281

ILLUSTRATIONS

Joseph E. Johnston . . . . *Frontispiece*

J. E. B. Stuart 33

James Longstreet 65

P. G. T. Beauregard 95

Judah P. Benjamin 123

Alexander H. Stephens 153

Robert Toombs 183

Raphael Semmes 219

The portrait of Alexander H. Stephens is from a photograph by Brady in the Library of the State Department, Washington, D.C.; the other portraits are from photographs in the Library of the Military Order of the Loyal Legion of the United States, and are reproduced by the courtesy of Colonel Arnold A. Rand.

CONFEDERATE LIVES

I

JOSEPH E. JOHNSTON

CHRONOLOGY

Born in Prince Edward County, Virginia, February 3, 1807.
Entered West Point in 1825.
Second Lieutenant, 1829.
Engaged in Black Hawk Expedition, 1832.
Indian wars in Florida, 1836.
Captain, 1838.
Indian wars under Worth, 1842.
Married, July 10, 1845, Lydia McLane.
Served in Mexican War, 1846–47.
Lieutenant Colonel, 1847.
Quartermaster-General, 1860.
Resigned U.S. commission, April 22, 1861.
Commanded at First Bull Run, July 21, 1861.
General, 1861.
Commanded at Williamsburg, May 5, 1862.
Wounded at Fair Oaks, May 31, 1862.
Commanded in Tennessee, 1863.
Opposed to Sherman, 1863–1864.
Relieved, July 17, 1864.
Commanded in North Carolina, February 23, 1865.
Surrendered to Sherman, April 26, 1865.
Wrote Narrative of Military Operations, 1874.
Died, March 21, 1891.

CONFEDERATE LIVES

I

JOSEPH E. JOHNSTON

OPINIONS differ as to the quality of Johnston's generalship. Let us have the bare, indisputable facts first. After distinguished service with the United States Army against the Indians and in Mexico, he was the highest officer in rank to join the Confederacy, although he was given only the fourth position among the five Confederate generals. His first command was at Harper's Ferry and in the Shenandoah Valley. Here he outmanœuvred Patterson and appeared at Bull Run in time to assume control during that battle. He himself admits that he believed it inexpedient to follow up the Confederate victory with a march on Washington. In the spring of 1862 Johnston led the Army of Northern Virginia and fought the battles of Williamsburg and Fair Oaks. After this a severe wound kept him inactive through the summer and Lee took his place.

During the first half of 1863 Johnston held a somewhat vague control over the western armies of the Confederacy. Davis hoped that he would defeat Grant and save Vicksburg; but he did neither. After Bragg had been worsted and had become so unpopular that Davis could no longer support him, Johnston was given the command of the Army of Tennessee and commissioned to resist Sherman's advance through Georgia. This he did in slow and careful retreat, disputing every disputable point, inflicting greater losses than he received, and wonderfully preserving the discipline, courage, and energy of his army. The Government was not satisfied, however, and preferred to substitute Hood and his disastrous offensive. Early in 1865, when Lee became commander-in-chief, he restored Johnston, who conducted a skillful, if hopeless, campaign in the Carolinas, and finally surrendered to Sherman on favorable terms.

Unsurpassed in retreat and defense, a wide reader and thinker and a profound military student, Johnston was no offensive fighter, say his critics. Among Northern writers Cox, who admired him greatly, remarks: "His abilities are undoubted, and when once committed to an offensive campaign, he conducted it with vigor and skill. The bent of his mind, however, was plainly in favor of the course which he steadily urged — to await his adversary's advance and watch for errors which would give him a manifest opportunity to ruin him."[1] And on the Southern side Alexander's summary is that "Johnston never fought but one aggressive battle, the battle of Seven Pines, which was phenomenally mismanaged."[2]

Other competent authorities are more enthusiastic. Longstreet speaks of Johnston as "the foremost soldier of the South,"[3] and Pollard as "the greatest military man in the Confederacy."[4] The English observer and critic, Chesney, says: "What he might have ventured had a rasher or less wary commander been before him, is as impossible to say as it would be to declare what would have been the result to Lee had Sherman taken the place of Grant in Virginia. As things were actually disposed, it is not too much to declare that Johnston's doing what he did with the limited means at his command is a feat that should leave his name in the annals of defensive war at least as high as that of Fabius, or Turenne, or Moreau."[5] Among Johnston's enemies, Grant said to Bishop Lay, "When I heard your Government had removed Johnston from command, I was as happy as if I had reinforced Sherman with a large army corps";[6] and to Young, "I have had nearly all of the Southern generals in high command in front of me, and Joe Johnston gave me more anxiety than any of the others. I was never half so anxious about Lee."[7] Sherman, who should have known, declares that "Johnston is one of the most enterprising of all their generals."[8] And in the opinion of Ropes, writing in dispassionate study, "Johnston had as good a military mind as any general on either side."[9]

Yet I confess, I wish the man had achieved something. The skill, the prudence mixed with daring, which held every position before Sherman till the last possible moment and then slipped away, without loss, without disaster, cannot be too much commended. Perhaps Stonewall

Jackson would have done no more. But I cannot help thinking Stonewall Jackson would have tried.

No one understands a man better than his wife. Mrs. Johnston adored her husband. He was her knight, her chevalier, her hero, as he deserved to be. But when he scolded a girl who was attacked by a turkey-gobbler and neither ran nor resisted, saying, "If she will not fight, sir, is not the best thing for her to do to run away, sir?" Mrs. Johnston commented, "with a burst of her hearty laughter, 'That used to be your plan always, I know, sir.'"[10] No doubt the lady was mocking purely. No doubt she would have raged, if any one else had said it. Yet — no one understands a man better than his wife — when she understands him at all.

In short, too much of Johnston's career consists of the things he would have done, if circumstances had only been different.

And here it is urged, and justly urged, that fortune was against him. All his life he seems to have been the victim of ill luck. Lee was wounded, I think, only once. Johnston was getting wounded perpetually. He himself told Fremantle that he had been wounded ten times.[11] General Scott said of him before the war that he "had an unfortunate knack of getting himself shot in every engagement."[12] A shell struck him down at Fair Oaks, just as it seemed that he might have beaten McClellan and saved Richmond.

Nor was it wounds only. Johnston had a vigorous

frame, compact, muscular, energetically martial; yet bodily illness would sometimes hamper him just at a crisis. On the voyage to Mexico Lee was enjoying himself, keenly alive to everything that went on about him. "I have a nice stateroom on board this ship," he writes. "Joe Johnston and myself occupy it, but my poor Joe is so sick all the time I can do nothing with him."[13]

And external circumstance was no kinder than the clayey habitation. "It seemed Johnston's fate to be always placed on posts of duty where extended efforts were necessarily devoted to organizing armies,"[14] writes his biographer. He was always in time for toil, for discipline, for sacrifice. For achievement he was apt to be too late. It is surprising how often the phrase recurs in his correspondence. "It is very unfortunate to be placed in such a command after the enemy has had time to prepare his attack."[15] "I arrived this evening, finding the enemy in full force between this place and General Pemberton, cutting off the communication. I am too late."[16] "It is too late to expect me to concentrate troops capable of driving back Sherman."[17] At the greatest crisis of all, after retreating a hundred miles to draw his enemy on, he at last made his preparations with cunning skill for a decisive stand, which should turn retreat into triumph — too late. For the order arrived, removing him from the command and robbing him once more of the gifts of Fortune.

It was from Davis that this blow came and Davis, or

so Johnston thought, was Johnston's ill luck personified. There are legends of quarrel and conflict even in early days at West Point, laying the foundation of lifelong hostility; but those who knew Johnston best discredit these. At any rate, the two were unfriendly from the beginning of the war, and certainly nothing could be more damaging for a general than to have the head of his Government prejudiced against him. It was for this reason, in Johnston's opinion, that commands were given him when it was too late to accomplish anything and taken away when he was on the brink of achieving something great. It was for this reason that necessary support was denied and necessary supplies given grudgingly, for this reason that his powers were curtailed, his plans criticized, his intentions mistrusted. In the list of Destiny's unkindnesses, as summed up by one of the general's admirers, the ill will and ill treatment of Davis and Davis's favorites figure so prominently that other accidental elements seem of minor account. "If there is such a thing as ill fortune, he had more than his share of it. He never had the chance that Lee had. If he had not been wounded at Seven Pines, a great victory would have crowned his arms with substantial results. If he had not been betrayed at Jackson, he would have joined with Pemberton and captured Grant's army. If he had not been removed at Atlanta, he would almost certainly have defeated Sherman." [18]

When I survey this portentous concatenation of *ifs*, I

ask myself whether, after all, Fortune deserved the full blame in the matter. You and I know scores of men who would have been rich and great and prosperous, if — if — if — And then a little reflection shows us that the *if* lies latent, or even patent, in the character or conduct of the man himself. It would be unjust and cruel to deny that many cross-accidents thwarted Johnston's career, that inevitable and undeserved misfortunes fell between him and glory. Yet a careful, thoughtful study of that career forces me to admit that the man was in some respects his own ill fortune and injured himself.

Take even the mere mechanical matter of wounds. Johnston may have got more than his share of blindly billeted projectiles. But every one agrees that his splendid recklessness took him often into unnecessary danger. One of his aides told Mrs. Chesnut that he had never seen a battle. "No man exposes himself more recklessly to danger than General Johnston, and no one strives harder to keep others out of it." [19] Take also his trumpet words to a young soldier who had lost his horse. "To have a horse killed under one puts a tall feather in his cap. . . . Even at present prices I'd freely give a good horse to the same fate." [20] Such adventurous chivalry in an officer of high rank is noble and lovable, but it is apt to mean ill luck in the matter of damages.

Some of Johnston's other qualities were less noble and, I think, bred ill luck with no adequate compensation. In the original cause of the quarrel with Davis,

Johnston probably had justice on his side. The Confederate generals were to have ranked according to their position in the United States Army. In that army Johnston stood highest. But Davis placed him below Cooper, A. S. Johnston, and Lee. Davis had, as always, ingenious arguments to support this procedure. Johnston thought the real argument was personal preference, and it may be that he was right. At any rate, he did not like it, and said so.

Further, there was a radical difference between president and general as to military policy all through the war. Johnston believed that the true course was concentration, to let outlying regions go, mass forces, beat the enemy, and then easily recover what had been given up. Davis felt that the demoralization consequent upon such a course would more than outweigh the military advantages.

Neither was a man to give up his own opinion. Neither was a man to compromise. Neither was a man who could forget his own view to work out honestly, heartily, successfully, the view of another. "They were too much alike to get along," says Johnston's biographer. ". . . They were each high-tempered, impetuous, jealous of honor, of the love of their friends, and they could brook no rival. They required absolute devotion, without question."[21]

You see that from these adjectives we begin to get a little more insight into Johnston's ill luck. Not that Davis was not also largely at fault. To appreciate both sides, we must look more closely into the written words and comments of each. It is a painful, pitiable study, but absolutely necessary for understanding the character of Johnston.

Davis, then, was ready to interfere when he should not. He had his own ideas of military policy and was anxious to have them carried out. Johnston was not at all inclined to carry out the president's ideas, and, having urged his own at first with little profit, became reluctant to communicate them, especially as he did not feel sure of secrecy, and perhaps even a little reluctant to conceive them. Davis's eager temperament is annoyed, frets, appeals. "Painfully anxious as to the result at Vicksburg, I have remained without information from you as to any plans proposed or attempt to raise the siege. Equally uninformed as to your plans in relation to Port Hudson, I have to request such information in relation thereto as the Government has a right to expect from one of its commanding generals in the field."[22] Again, "I wish to hear from you as to the present situation, and your plan of operations, so specifically as will enable me to anticipate events."[23]

When Johnston's replies are evasive or non-committal, — partly because of his fear of publicity, — Davis's attitude becomes crisply imperative. "The President instructs me to reply," he writes through Cooper, "that he adheres to his order and desires you to execute it."[24] No tact here; no attempt at conciliation or persuasion. Sometimes the tone is injured, hurt, resentful: "While some have expressed surprise that my orders to you were not observed, I have at least hoped that you would recognize the desire to aid and sustain you, and that it would produce the corresponding action on your part."[25] Sometimes it is brusque to roughness: "I do not perceive why a junction was not attempted, which would have made our force nearly equal in number to the estimated strength of the enemy and might have resulted in his total defeat under circumstances, which rendered retreat or reinforcement for him scarcely practicable."[26] The president rates his second in command as if he were a refractory schoolboy. "The original mistakes in your telegram of 12th June would gladly have been overlooked as accidental, if acknowledged when pointed out. The perseverance with which they have been insisted on has not permitted me to pass them by as mere oversights."[27] "It is needless to say that you are not considered capable of giving countenance to such efforts at laudation of yourself and detraction of others."[28] "The language of your letter is, as you say, unusual, its insinuations unfounded, and its arguments utterly unbecoming from a general in the field to his superior."[29] And the head of the Government is said to have gone even so far as, in speaking to Johnston's own former soldiers, to accuse their chief of actual disloyalty.[30]

As I read this sort of thing, I cannot help being

reminded of Captain MacTurk's joyous comment, "Oh, crimini, if these sweetmeats be passing between them, it is only the two ends of a handkercher that can serve the turn—Cot tamn!"

And now, how much reason and excuse did Johnston give for such treatment? Abundant. Really, when I remember Davis's keen and fiery disposition, I am less surprised at the things he did say than at those he did not. It is not so much any one word or speech in Johnston's case, as the constant attitude of disapproval, of fault-finding, of resentment even approaching sullenness.

To begin with, Johnston criticized with the utmost freedom. He criticized even Lee. And if we did not know how deep was the affection between the two, we should be inclined to attribute the criticism to jealousy. "After his operations in the Wilderness, General Lee adopted as thorough a defensive as mine, and added by it to his great fame. The only other difference between our operations was due to Grant's bull-headedness and Sherman's extreme caution, which carried the army in Virginia to Petersburg in less than half the time in which Sherman reached Atlanta."[31] In the same way, according to Fremantle, he criticized Jackson. "General Johnston said that although this extraordinary man did not possess any great qualities as a strategist, and was perhaps unfit for the independent command of a large army; yet he was gifted with wonderful courage and determination. . . .

He was much indebted to General Ewell in the Valley Campaign." [32]

It was natural enough for Johnston to think these things. It would have been better if he had not said them.

When it is a question of Davis's friends and favorites, the criticism becomes manifest irritability. Thus Johnston writes to Randolph, whom he really admired. "Your order was positive and unconditional. I had no option but to obey it. If injustice has been done it was not by me. If an improper order was given it was not mine. Mine, therefore, permit me to say, is not the one to be recalled or modified." [33] He writes to Benjamin, whom he did not admire at all: "Let me suggest that, having broken up the dispositions of the military commander, you give whatever other orders may be necessary." [34] As for Pemberton, who disobeyed him, and Hood, who supplanted him, he has no belief in their capacity nor patience with their blunders.

When it comes to Davis himself, the tone is no more amiable or conciliatory. The long, vigorous, and eloquent letter, written in regard to the question of rank which originated the trouble, deserves to be studied in every line. This was the one which Davis briefly docketed as "insubordinate." It is insubordinate, in spite of its logic and its nobility, and its significance is increased by Johnston's own confession that he waited for a night's reflection before sending it. "If the action against which I have protested is legal, it is not for me to question the expediency of degrading one who has served laboriously from the commencement of the war on this frontier, and borne a prominent part in the only great event of that war, for the benefit of persons [Sidney Johnston and Lee] neither of whom has yet struck a blow for the Confederacy."[35] The spirit is wrong, not such as becomes a man ready to give more than his life, his own self-will, for a great cause.

The same spirit continues and intensifies to the very end. Davis may have provoked it. He did not create it. And who can wonder that it harassed him past bearing? No quotation of a line here and there can give the full effect of the wasp stings which Johnston's schoolboy petulance — I can call it nothing else — was constantly inflicting. "I request, therefore, to be relieved of a merely nominal geographical command."[36] "Let me ask, for the sake of discipline, that you have this rule enforced. It will save much time and trouble and create the belief in the army that I am its commander."[37] "If the Department will give me timely notice when it intends to exercise my command, I shall be able to avoid such interference with its orders."[38]

Doubtless, also, Johnston's attitude reacted upon the officers about him. He was an outspoken man and those who loved him were not very likely to love the president. An exceedingly interesting letter of Mackall's, printed in the "Official Records," gives some insight into the condition of things I refer to. "Pemberton is everything with Davis, the devout," writes Mackall; "his intelligence is only equaled by his self-sacrificing regard for others."[39] And again: "The people won't stand this nonsense much longer. Mr. Davis's game now is to pretend that he don't think you a great general. He don't tell the truth, and if he did, as all the military men in the country differ with him, he will be forced to yield."[40] Any commander who tolerates this sort of thing from a subordinate, tacitly, more than tacitly, admits that he shares the subordinate's opinion.

The sum of the matter is that Johnston had allowed himself to fall into the fatal frame of mind of assuming that Davis's action was constantly dictated by personal animosity towards himself. Such an assumption, whether well founded or not, if dwelt on and brooded over, was sure to breed a corresponding animosity and to paralyze both the general's genius and his usefulness. Nothing shows this attitude better than Johnston's remark to S. D. Lee, when Lee congratulated him on his restoration to command in 1865 and on Davis's promise of support: "He will not do it. He has never done it. It is too late now, and he has only put me in command to disgrace me."[41]

While the war was actually going on, this mutual hostility of president and general was controlled to some extent by the necessary conventions and civilities of official intercourse. It is both curious and pitiable to see the restraints of decency covering such obvious distrust, dissatisfaction, and dislike. Davis was always the more diplomatic. Further, I think he shows a deeper sense of the immense interests involved and the necessity of making sacrifices for them than Johnston does. Indeed, for a long time he was ready to meet Johnston halfway, if Johnston would have gone his half. Even after their preliminary squabble about rank, so late as June, 1862, at the time of Johnston's wound, the president writes: "General J. E. Johnston is steadily improving. I wish he were able to take the field. Despite the critics, who know military affairs by instinct, he is a good soldier, never brags of what he did do, and could at this time render most valuable service."[42] Much later still, real, almost pathetic kindness is mingled with reproof and recrimination: "I assure you that nothing shall be wanting on the part of the Government to aid you in your effort to regain possession of the territory from which we have been driven. . . . It is my desire that you should communicate fully and freely with me concerning your plan of action, that all the assistance and coöperation may be most advantageously afforded that it is in the power of the Government to render."[43]

As for Johnston, he is the military subordinate of this personal enemy of his. He knows his duty. He will be submissive, he will be obedient, he will be respectful, if it costs his own ruin and his country's. The study of his efforts is painfully interesting. Before the rupture had become chronic, they were successful and his tone rises to real nobility. "Your Excellency's known sense of justice will not hold me to that responsibility while the corresponding control is not in my hands. Let me assure your Excellency that I am prompted in this matter by no love of privilege, of position, or of personal rights as such, but by a firm belief that under the circumstances what I propose is necessary to the safety of our troops and cause."[44] Even to the end official respect is preserved, whatever may have been the feelings underneath it. "I need not say, however, that your wishes shall be promptly executed."[45] "That suggestion [of mine] was injudicious. It is necessary, of course, that those should be promoted whom you consider best qualified."[46] "I will obey any orders of the President zealously and execute any plan of campaign of his to the best of my ability."[47] "I beg leave to suggest—most respectfully—that there is but one way by which the Government can, without injury to discipline, give the orders—the mode prescribed by itself—through the officers commanding armies or departments."[48]

Also, it must not be supposed that Johnston ever permitted himself petty complaints to those about him. So late as August, 1863, one who knew him well writes: "In all the many and frequent conversations I have had with General Johnston I have never heard one word escape his lips savoring of any want of personal regard for the President."[49] And even after the general had been superseded by Hood another good observer writes to the same effect: "He bore his trouble with a stoicism which was pathetic, since we, who knew and loved him, were so fully aware of the agony of mind and heart he suffered. But no word escaped his lips, whatever his thoughts may have been."[50]

Then the war came to a disastrous end and everybody was free to abuse everybody else. Davis, in a private letter, afterwards printed, implied pretty directly that Johnston and Beauregard were knaves,[51] and Johnston told a reporter that Davis was "perverse and wrong-headed"; that he was "malignant and utterly unfitted to be at the head of any important movement."[52] Davis and Johnston both wrote books and said what they thought with lamentable outspokenness. Perhaps Davis's individual utterances are more savage than any of Johnston's. Thus, the former writes in his book: "Very little experience, or a fair amount of modesty without any experience, would serve to prevent one from announcing the conclusion that troops could be withdrawn from a place or places without knowing how many were there."[53] And still more forcibly in the very able paper which he prepared for the last session of the Confederate Congress: "My confidence in General Johnston's fitness for separate command was now destroyed. The proof was too complete to admit of longer doubt that he was deficient in enterprise, tardy in movement, defective in preparation, and singularly neglectful of the duty of preserving our means of supply and transportation, although experience should have taught him their value and the difficulty of procuring them."[54]

But, after all, the quarrel with Johnston was but one element in Davis's vast career; and it was the president's great good fortune that in his case patriotism and self-preservation went together and his most earnest and genuine efforts for his country were also for himself.

With Johnston the situation was unhappily different. He was never anything but nobly patriotic in intention. But the ruin of the nation was coincident with the ruin of his own personal enemy, and he brooded so deeply over that personal enmity that it seems as if his narrative were mainly occupied with the attempt to portray his enemy's injustice and consequent failures and mistakes. I have read and reread his book, and every reading deepens the impression of pity for splendid gifts so blighted, for great opportunities, not so much military as moral, thrown away. One, or two, or five quotations are not enough to justify this impression. It springs quite as much from what is unsaid as from what is said. Yet some quotation we must have.

To begin with, Johnston writes admirably, a clear, vigorous, logical style, which makes every point tell, bites, stings, lashes, if necessary. His vigor and brevity give the impression of absolute truth, and no one can suspect him of ever intending anything else. Indeed, his biographer declares that in all his statements he is singularly scrupulous and accurate. Some careful critics have denied this. Thus his deduction of Sherman's losses from the burials in Marietta Cemetery has been shown to be altogether wrong because many of those burials were of soldiers who never belonged to Sherman's army at all.[55] Again, General Palfrey, usually so impartial, declares: "The more I study Johnston's writings, the more cause I find to mistrust them. I like to believe in him; but I cannot do so absolutely, for I find that he permits himself great freedom in asserting what he does not know to be true." [56]

The freedom and looseness of statement spring from Johnston's dogmatic temper, from his energy and decision, his practical incapacity for seeing more than his own side and point of view; and the dogmatism and the energy lend double bitterness to the slurs which he is constantly flinging at the man who had been his leader, for better and for worse, and who — at least, so it seems to me — should have been respected for the sake of a noble cause and a vanished ideal. "Under such circumstances his accusation is, to say the least, very discreditable." [57] "It is not easy to reconcile the increase of my command by the President, with his very numerous disparaging notices of me." [58] "Such an occurrence [explosion of buried shells] must have been known to the whole army, but it was not; so it must have been a dream of the writer." [59] "These are fancies. He arrived upon the field after the last armed enemy had left it, when none were within cannon-shot, or south of Bull Run, when the victory was 'complete' as well as 'assured,' and no opportunity left for the influence of 'his name and bearing.'"[60] "As good-natured weakness was never attributed to Mr. Davis as a fault, it is not easy to reconcile the assertions and tone of this letter with his official course toward me."[61] "I was unable then, as now, to imagine any military object for which this letter could have been written, especially by one whose time was supposed to be devoted to the most important concerns of the Government. . . . As I had much better means of information on the subjects of this paper than its author, it could not have been written for my instruction."[62]

"Oh, Iago, the pity of it, Iago!" Even the non-committal and considerate Lee "instanced Joe Johnston's sensitiveness and how wrong and unwise it was,"[63] while Mr. Rhodes says, "Had Johnston been less sensitive to an affront to his personal dignity, had he been in temper like Lee, and had Davis shown such abnegation of self as did Lincoln in his dealings with his generals, blame and recrimination would not have been written on every page of Southern history."[64]

"No man was ever written down except by himself," said Dr. Johnson. Johnston wrote his book to clear his fame, and behold, it condemns him. One sentence of large forgiveness in face of calamity, one word of recognition that Davis and Seddon, however misguided, however erring, had done their best to serve the same great cause that he was serving, would have achieved more for his lasting glory than all his five hundred pages of bitter self-justification. A large element in Johnston's ill-luck was just simply Joseph E. Johnston.

And now comes the puzzle. It appears that in all ordinary intercourse this man was one of the most amiable, most companionable, most lovable of human beings. Incontestable evidence gives him a list of attractive qualities so long that few can equal it.

That he was brave goes without saying, with a delightful bravery that goes anywhere, and does anything, and makes no fuss. He was always ready to lead a charge or to cover a retreat. He had an enchanting, quiet courage, such as we timid spirits can lean upon, as upon a wall. Read the account of his behavior when he was so severely wounded at Fair Oaks. "Reeling in his saddle, he said: 'Quite extraordinary! It's nothing, gentlemen, I assure you; not worthy of comment. I think we ought to move up a little closer. If a surgeon is within call, and not too busy, at his convenience, perfect convenience, — he might as well look me over.' If some one on his staff had not caught him, the general would have fallen from his horse."[65] Read also his playful confession with reference to kerosene lamps. Only perfect courage can so trifle with itself: "Some kind of a patent kerosene lamp was sent me as a present, and the donor lit it, explaining to me the method of working it. Such was my nervousness, I never knew he was talking to me. Later, after somebody had extinguished the lamp, I tried to reason out to myself what a poltroon I was. We get hardened in time; but I assure you, nothing would ever induce me to light or extinguish a kerosene lamp. I really envy you, madam, as possessing heroic traits, when you tell me you feel no alarm when in the presence of a kerosene lamp. But I am, by nature, an arrant coward. An enemy, armed with kerosene lamps, would drive me off the field. I should be panic personified." [66]

And Johnston was absolutely frank, outspoken, straightforward, too much so for his own good; but charmingly so. He gave his opinion of things and people, so that you knew where he stood, whether you agreed with him or not. How neatly does Colonel Anderson portray him with a touch. "'I think the Scotch the best,' the General quickly rejoined, with that slight toss of the head, with which he sometimes emphasized the expression of an opinion he was ready to do battle for." [67] There was no cant about him, no rhetoric. I would not say, or imply, that the abundance of religious language in Southern reports and orders is ever insincere. But I occasionally tire of it. Johnston is very sparing in this regard. What he does say is evidently solemn and heartfelt.

The general's honesty and uprightness are delightful, also. He was no politician, but his political convictions were as lofty and constant as they were simple. He followed Virginia. That was enough. "Nothing earthly could afford me greater satisfaction than the fulfillment of his good wishes by this army striking a blow for the freedom and independence of Virginia."[68] "I drew it [his father's sword] in the war not for rank or fame, but to defend the sacred soil, the homes and hearths, the women and children, aye, and the men of my mother, Virginia,—my native South."[69] After the war, when he was a candidate for Congress, his standpoint was as elementary—and as honorable. Some of his followers had tried to explain away his tariff attitude, for the sake of winning votes. "Gentlemen," he said, "this is a matter about which I do not propose to ask your advice, because it involves my conscience and personal honor. I spoke yesterday, at Louisa Court-House, under a free-trade flag. I have never ridden 'both sides of the sapling,' and I don't propose to begin at this late day. That banner in Clay Ward comes down to-day or I retire from this canvass by published card to-morrow."[70] Perhaps the finest tribute to his moral elevation comes from a generous enemy. "I recorded at the time," says Cox, writing of the surrender, "my own feeling that I had rarely met a man who was personally more attractive to me than General Johnston. His mode of viewing things was a large one, his thoughts and his expression of them was refined, his conscientious anxiety to do exactly what was right in the circumstances was apparent in every word and act, his ability and his natural gift of leadership showed in his whole bearing and conduct."[71] And in illustration of the scrupulous conscientiousness Cox adds that when the general learned that one of his staff had retained a little cavalry guidon of silk in the form of a Confederate flag, he sent for it at once and passed it over to the Union officers, as the colors were supposed to be surrendered.

Johnston was as simple, too, as he was upright and honest, cared nothing for display, parade, or show, lived with his men and shared their fare and their hardships. "There was only one fork (one prong deficient) between himself and staff, and this was handed to me ceremoniously as the guest," says Fremantle.[72] "While on his journey to Atlanta to assume command of the second army of the Confederacy, he excited universal remark by having an ordinary box car assigned to himself and staff, instead of imitating the brigadiers of the time and taking possession of a passenger coach," says Hughes.[73]

Even as regards Johnston's sensitiveness to personal slights and to the advancement of others, it is curious to note that this does not seem to have been owing to any inordinate ambition. He himself says that he did not draw his sword for rank or fame; and General Gordon tells us that he was not ambitious. This is doubtless exaggerated. All soldiers — all men — like rank and fame, when they can get them honestly. But I find no shadow of evidence that Johnston was devoured by Jackson's ardent fever, or ever dreamed long dreams of shadowy glory and success. His attitude in this connection recalls what Clarendon says of the Earl of Essex: "His pride supplied his want of ambition, and he was angry to see any man more respected than himself because he thought he deserved it more." [74] I believe that Johnston was even capable of the highest, noblest self-sacrifice, so long as it was quite voluntary and not demanded of him by others, and that he was always ready to act upon his own fine saying: "The great energy exhibited by the Government of the United States, the danger in which our very existence as an independent people lies, requires sacrifice from us all who have been educated as soldiers." [75]

What is most winning about Johnston, however, in fact quite irresistible, is his warmth of nature, his affection, his feminine tenderness, doubly charming in a man as strenuously virile as ever lived. His letters, even official, have a vivacity and personal quality wholly different from Lee's. He loved his men, watched over them, cared for them, praised them: "I can find no record of more effective fighting in modern battles than that of this army in December, evincing skill in the commanders and courage in the troops." [76] He had the most kindly words for the achievements of his officers. Of Stuart he writes: "He is a rare man, wonderfully endowed by nature with the qualities necessary for an officer of light cavalry. Calm, firm, acute, active, and enterprising, I know no one more competent than he to estimate the occurrences before him at their true value." [77] And to Stuart: "How can I eat or sleep without you upon the outpost?" [78] Of Longstreet: "I rode upon the field, but found myself compelled to be a mere spectator, for General Longstreet's clear head and brave heart left me no apology for interference." [79] With his equals in other commands he was amply generous, where they did not represent Davis. Thus he writes of Bragg: "I am very glad that your confidence in General Bragg is unshaken. My own is confirmed by his recent operations, which, in my opinion, evince great vigor and skill. It would be very unfortunate to remove him at this juncture, when he has just earned, if not won, the gratitude of the country." [80]

The man is even more attractive in his private friendships. "One of the purest and strongest men I ever knew," says Stiles, "and perhaps the most affectionate." [81] Few more touching letters were ever written than the one he addressed to Mrs. Lee after her husband's death. Less known, but almost equally charming in its frankness is the letter to Wigfall about Lee, written in March, 1865: "What you write me of Lee gratifies me beyond measure. In youth and early manhood I admired him more than any man in the world. Since then we have had little intercourse and have become formal in our personal intercourse. . . . When we are together former feelings always return. I have long thought that he had forgotten our early friendship; to be convinced that I was mistaken in so thinking would give me inexpressible pleasure. Be assured, however, that Knight of old never fought under his King more loyally than I 'll serve under General Lee." [82]

Characteristic of Johnston's friendship was its singular demonstrativeness. He embraced and kissed his male friends as tenderly as if they were women. "I have said he was the most affectionate of men," writes Stiles. "It will surprise many, who saw only the iron bearing of the soldier, to hear that we never met or parted, for any length of time, that he did not, if we were alone, throw his arms about me and kiss me, and that such was his habit in parting from or greeting his male relatives and most cherished friends." [83]

In his domestic relations there was the same tenderness, the same devotion. He adored his wife, and their love was a lifelong idyl, diversified, as idyls should be, by sunny mocking and sweet merriment. He had no children, but his nephews and nieces were as near to him as children. When he was told, in Mexico, of one nephew's death, "the shock was so great that he fell prostrate upon the works. Up to the day of his death, forty-four years later, Johnston kept a likeness of his nephew in his room and never failed to look at it immediately after rising." [84]

With all this, is it any wonder that men loved him and resent bitterly to-day the inevitable conclusions drawn from his own written words? Bragg wrote, in answer to one of Johnston's kind letters: "That spontaneous offer from a brother soldier and fellow-citizen, so honored and esteemed, will be treasured as a source of happiness and a reward which neither time nor circumstances can impair." [85] Kirby Smith wrote: "I would willingly be back under your command at any personal sacrifice."[86] Longstreet wrote: "General Johnston was skilled in the art and science of war, gifted in his quick, penetrating mind and soldierly bearing, genial and affectionate in nature, honorable and winning in person, and confiding in his love. He drew the hearts of those about him so close that his comrades felt that they could die for him."[87]

The country trusted him. "I discover from my correspondence you possess the confidence of the whole country as you do mine," writes a civilian, in December, 1863.[88]

The soldiers trusted him. After weeks of falling back, yielding point after point to an encroaching enemy, the evidence is overwhelming that Johnston's troops were cheerful, eager, zealous, had unbounded belief that he was doing the best that could be done, unbounded regret when they heard that he had been removed. His disciplinary faculty, his grip upon the hearts of men, his power of inspiration were immense and undisputed. He had the greatest gift a leader can have, magnetism. "There was a magnetic power about him no man could resist, and exact discipline followed at once upon his assuming any command."[89] What the general feeling in his army was is nowhere better shown than in the fine letter written to him by Brigadier-General Stevens, after Johnston had been relieved by Hood: "We have ever felt that the best was being done that could be, and have looked confidently forward to the day of triumph, when with you as our leader we should surely march to a glorious victory. This confidence and implicit trust has been in no way impaired, and we are to-day ready, as we have ever been, to obey your orders, whether they be to retire before a largely outnumbering foe, or to spend our last drop of blood in the fiercest conflict. We feel that in parting with you our loss is irreparable . . . and you carry with you the love, respect, esteem, and confidence, of the officers and men of this brigade." [90]

Yet a man so honored, admired, and beloved could write the "Narrative of Military Operations"! What a tangle human nature is!

If I wished to sum up Johnston's character briefly, I should quote two passages, both, as it happens, left us by women. Mrs. Chesnut writes, toward the close of the war: "Afterwards, when Isabella and I were taking a walk, General Joseph E. Johnston joined us. He explained to us all of Lee's and Stonewall Jackson's mistakes. We had nothing to say — how could we say anything?" [91] When one reads this, remembering what Lee's position in the Confederacy was, what Johnston's was, and that he was talking to what must have been one of the liveliest tongues in the Southern States, one appreciates why Johnston did not succeed. When one turns to the remark of an officer to Mrs. Pickett — "Lee was a great general and a good man, but I never wanted to put my arms round his neck as I used to want to to Joe Johnston" [92] — one is overcome with pity to think that Johnston should have failed.

J. E. B. STUART

II

J. E. B. Stuart

CHRONOLOGY

Born in Patrick County, Virginia, February 6, 1833.
Graduated from West Point, 1854.
Second Lieutenant, October 31, 1854.
Married to Miss Flora Cooke, November 14, 1855.
First Lieutenant, December 20, 1855.
Served in Kansas in 1856.
Served against the Indians in 1857.
Served in the West till 1860.
Volunteered under Lee in John Brown Raid, 1859.
Colonel in Confederate Army, July 16, 1861.
Brigadier-General, September 24, 1861.
Major-General, July 25, 1862.
Served with Army of Northern Virginia throughout the war.
Commanded Jackson's corps after Jackson's death at Chancellorsville.
But returned again to cavalry command, May, 1863.
Wounded at Yellow Tavern, May 11, 1864.
Died, May 12, 1864.

II

J. E. B. STUART

STUART was a fighter by nature. When he was at West Point in the early fifties, his distinguishing characteristics, as chronicled by Fitzhugh Lee, were "a strict attendance to his military duties, an erect, soldierly bearing, an immediate and almost thankful acceptance of a challenge from any cadet to fight, who might in any way feel himself aggrieved."[1] The tendency, if not inherited, did not lack paternal encouragement; for the elder Stuart writes to his son, in regard to one of these combats: "I did not consider you so much to blame. An insult should be resented under all circumstances."[2] The young cadet also showed himself to be a fearless and an exceptionally skillful horseman.

These qualities served him well in the Indian warfare to which he was immediately transferred from West Point. His recklessness in taking chances was equaled only by his ingenuity in pulling through. One of his superiors writes: "Lieutenant Stuart was brave and gallant, always prompt in execution of orders and reckless of danger and exposure. I considered him at that time one of the most promising young officers in the United States Army."[3]

Later Stuart took a prominent part in the capture of

John Brown. He himself wrote an account of the matter at the time for the newspapers, simply to explain and justify Lee's conduct. He also wrote a letter to his mother, with a characteristic description of his own doings: "I approached the door in the presence of perhaps two thousand spectators, and told *Mr. Smith* that I had a communication for him from Colonel Lee. He opened the door about four inches, and placed his body against the crack, with a cocked carbine in his hand; hence his remark after his capture that he could have wiped me out like a mosquito. . . . When *Smith* first came to the door I recognized old *Osawatomie Brown*, who had given us so much trouble in Kansas. No one present but myself could have performed that service. I got his bowie-knife from his person, and have it yet."[4]

From the very beginning of the war Stuart maintained this fighting reputation. He would attack any thing anywhere, and the men who served under him had to do the same; what is more, and marks the born leader, he made them wish to do the same. "How can I eat, sleep, or rest in peace without you upon the outpost?"[5] wrote Joseph Johnston; and a noble enemy, who had been a friend, Sedgwick, is reported to have said that Stuart was "the greatest cavalry officer ever foaled in America."[6]

Danger he met with more than stolid indifference, a sort of furious bravado, thrusting himself into it with manifest pleasure, and holding back, when he did hold back, with a sigh. And some men's luck! Johnston was wounded a dozen times, was always getting wounded. Yet Stuart, probably far more exposed, was wounded only once in his life, among the Indians; in the war not at all. His clothes were pierced again and again. According to Von Borcke, the general had half of his moustache cut off by a bullet "as neatly as it could have been done by the hand of an experienced barber."[7] Yet nothing ever drew blood till the shot which was mortal. Such an immunity naturally encouraged the sort of fatalism not unusual with great soldiers, and Stuart once said of the proximity of his enemies, "You might have shot a marble at them—but I am not afraid of any ball aimed at me."[8]

In this spirit he got into scores of difficult places—and got out again. Sometimes it was by quick action and a mad rush, as when he left his hat and a few officers behind him. Sometimes it was by stealth and secrecy, as when he hid his whole command all night within a few hundred yards of the marching enemy. "And nothing now remained but to watch and wait and keep quiet. Quiet? Yes, the men kept very quiet, for they realized that even Stuart never before had them in so tight a place. But many a time did we fear that we were betrayed by the weary, hungry, headstrong mules of the ordnance train. Men were stationed at the head of every team; but in spite of all precautions, a discordant bray would every now and then fill the air. Never was the voice of a mule so harsh!"[9]

The men who had watched and tried and tested him on such occasions as these knew what he was and gave him their trust. He asked nothing of them that he would not do himself. Therefore they did what he asked of them. Scheibert says that "he won their confidence and inspired them by his whole bearing and personality, by his kindling speech, his flashing eye, and his cheerfulness which no reverse could overcome."[10] Stuart himself describes his followers' enthusiastic loyalty with a naïveté as winning as it is characteristic. "There was something of the sublime in the implicit confidence and unquestioning trust of the rank and file in a leader guiding them straight, apparently, into the very jaws of the enemy, every step appearing to them to diminish the very faintest hope of extrication."[11] Yet he asked this trust and they gave it simply on the strength of his word. "You are about to engage in an enterprise which, to ensure success, imperatively demands at your hands coolness, decision, and the strictest order and sobriety on the march and in the bivouac. The destination and extent of this expedition had better be kept to myself than known to you."[12]

The men loved him also because, when the strain was removed, he put on no airs, pretense, or remoteness of superiority, but treated them as man to man. "He was the most approachable of major-generals, and jested with the private soldiers of his command as jovially as though he had been one of themselves. The men were perfectly unconstrained in his presence, and treated him more like the chief huntsman of a hunting party than as a major-general."[13] His officers also loved him, and not only trusted him for war, but enjoyed his company in peace. He was constantly on the watch to do them kindnesses, and would frolic with them — marbles, snowballs, quoits, what not? — like a boy with boys.

And Stuart loved his men as they loved him, did not regard them as mere food for cannon, to be used, and abused, and forgotten. There is something almost pathetic in his neglect of self in praising them. "The horseman who, at his officer's bidding, without question, leaps into unexplored darkness, knowing nothing except that there is danger ahead, possesses the highest attribute of the patriot soldier. It is a great source of pride to me to command a division of such men."[14] Careless of his own danger always, he was far more thoughtful of those about him. In the last battle he was peculiarly reckless, and Major McClellan noticed that the general kept sending him with messages to General Anderson. "At last the thought occurred to me that he was endeavoring to shield me from danger. I said to him: 'General, my horse is weary. You are exposing yourself, and you are alone. Please let me remain with you.' He smiled at me kindly, but bade me go to General Anderson with another message."[15]

Any reflection on his command arouses him at once to its defense. "There seems to be a growing tendency to abuse and underrate the services of that arm of the service [cavalry] by a few officers of infantry, among whom I regret to find General Trimble. Troops should be taught to take pride in other branches of the service than their own." [16]

It is very rare that Stuart has any occasion to address himself directly to the authorities at Richmond. Fighting, not writing, was his business. But when he feels that his men and horses are being starved unnecessarily, he bestirs himself, and sends Seddon a letter which is as interesting for nervous and vigorous expression as for the character of the writer. "I beg to urge that in no case should persons not connected with the army, and who are amply compensated for all that is taken, be allowed more subsistence per day than the noble veterans who are periling their lives in the cause and at every sacrifice are enduring hardship and exposure in the ranks." [17]

And the general's care and enthusiasm for his officers was as great as for the privates. It is charming to see how earnestly and how specifically he commends them in every report. Particularly, he is anxious to impress upon Lee that no family considerations should prevent the merited advancement of Lee's own son and nephew. Even on his deathbed one of his last wishes was that his faithful followers should have his horses, and he allotted them thoughtfully according to each officer's needs.

The general did not allow his feelings to interfere

with subordination, however. His discipline "was as firm as could be with such men as composed the cavalry of General Lee's army," writes Judge Garnett. "He never tolerated nor overlooked disobedience of orders."[18] Even his favorites, Mosby and Fitz Lee, come in for reproof when needed. Of the latter's failure to arrive at Raccoon Ford when expected he writes: "By this failure to comply with instructions not only the movement of the cavalry across the Rapidan was postponed a day, but a fine opportunity was lost to overhaul a body of the enemy's cavalry on a predatory excursion far beyond their lines."[19] His tendency to severity in regard to a certain subordinate calls forth one of Lee's gently tactful cautions: "I am perfectly willing to transfer him to Paxton's brigade, if he desires it; but if he does not, I know of no act of his to justify my doing so. Do not let your judgment be warped."[20] There were officers with whom Stuart could not get along; for instance, "Grumble Jones," who perhaps could get along with no one. Yet, after Stuart's death, Jones said of him: "By G——, Martin! You know I had little love for Stuart, and he had just as little for me; but that is the greatest loss that army has ever sustained except the death of Jackson."[21]

From these various considerations it will be surmised that Stuart was no mere reckless sworder, no Rupert, good with sabre, furious in onset, beyond that signifying nothing. He knew the spirit of the antique maxim, "Be bold, and evermore be bold; be not too bold." He had learned the hardest lesson and the essential corrective for such a temperament, self-control. To me there is an immense pathos in his quiet, almost plaintive explanation to Lee, on one occasion: "The commanding general will, I am sure, appreciate how hard it was to desist from the undertaking, but to any one on the spot there could be but one opinion—its impossibility. I gave it up."[22] On the other hand, no one knew better that in some cases perfect prudence and splendid boldness are one and the same thing. To use again his own language: "Although the expedition was prosecuted further than was contemplated in your instructions, I feel assured that the considerations which actuated me will convince you that I did not depart from their spirit and that the bold development in the subsequent direction of the march was the quintessence of prudence."[23] Lee always found the right words. In one of his reports he says of Stuart [italics mine]: "I take occasion to express to the Department my sense of the boldness, *judgment*, and *prudence* he displayed in its execution."[24]

But one may have self-control without commanding intelligence. Fremantle's description of Stuart's movements does not suggest much of the latter quality. "He seems to roam over the country at his own discretion, and always gives a good account of himself, turning up at the right moment, and hitherto he has not got himself into any serious trouble."[25] Later, more studious observers do not take quite the same view. One should read the whole of the Prussian colonel Scheibert's account of Stuart's thorough planning, his careful calculation, his exact methods of procedure. "Before Stuart undertook any movement, he spared nothing in the way of preparation which might make it succeed. He informed himself as exactly as possible by scouts and spies, himself reconnoitred with his staff, often far beyond the outposts, had his engineer officers constantly fill out and improve the rather inadequate maps and ascertain the practicability of roads, fords, etc. In short, he omitted no precaution and spared no pains or effort to secure the best possible results for such undertakings as he planned; therefore he was in the saddle almost as long again as his men." [26] Similar testimony can be gathered incidentally everywhere in Stuart's letters and reports, proving that he was no chance roamer, but went where he planned to go and came back when he intended. For instance, he writes of the Peninsular operations: "It is proper to remark here that the commanding general had, on the occasion of my late expedition to the Pamunkey, imparted to me his design of bringing Jackson down upon the enemy's right flank and rear, and directed that I should examine the country with reference to its practicability for such a movement. I therefore had studied the features of the country very thoroughly and knew exactly how to conform my movements to Jackson's route." [27]

On the strength of these larger military qualities it has

sometimes been contended that Stuart should have had an even more responsible command than fell to him and that Lee should have retained him at the head of Jackson's corps after Jackson's death. Certainly Lee can have expressed no higher opinion of any one: "A more zealous, ardent, brave and devoted soldier than Stuart the Confederacy cannot have."[28] Johnston called him "calm, firm, acute, active, and enterprising, I know of no one more competent than he to estimate occurrences at their true value."[29] Longstreet, hitting Jackson as well as praising Stuart, said: "His death was possibly a greater loss to the Confederate army than that of the swift-moving General Stonewall Jackson."[30] Among foreign authorities Scheibert writes that "General von Schmidt, the regenerator of our [Prussian] cavalry tactics, has told me that Stuart was the model cavalry leader of this century and has questioned me very often about his mode of fighting."[31] And Captain Battine thinks that he should have had Jackson's place.[32] Finally, Alexander, sanest of Confederate writers, expresses the same view strongly and definitely: "I always thought it an injustice to Stuart and a loss to the army that he was not from that moment *continued in command of Jackson's corps.* He had *won* the right to it. I believe he had all of Jackson's genius and dash and originality, without that eccentricity of character which sometimes led to disappointment. Jackson's spirit and inspiration were uneven. Stuart, however, possessed the rare quality of being always *equal to himself at his very best.*"[33]

This is magnificent praise, coming from such a source. Nevertheless, I find it hard to question Lee's judgment. There was nothing in the world to prevent his giving Stuart the position, if he thought him qualified. It is not absolutely certain how Stuart would have carried independent command. I can hardly imagine Davis, even early in the war, writing of Jackson as he did of Stuart: "The letter of General Hill painfully impresses me with that which has before been indicated—a want of vigilance and intelligent observation on the part of General Stuart."[34] Major Bigelow, who knows the battle of Chancellorsville as well as any one living, does not judge Stuart's action so favorably as Alexander. And Cooke, who adored Stuart and served constantly under him, says: "At Chancellorsville, when he succeeded Jackson, the troops, although quite enthusiastic about him, complained that he led them too recklessly against artillery; and it is hard for those who knew the man to believe that, as an army commander, he would have consented to a strictly defensive campaign. Fighting was a necessity of his blood, and the slow movements of infantry did not suit his genius."[35]

May it not be also that Lee thought Stuart indispensable where he was and believed it would be as difficult to replace him as Jackson? Most of Stuart's correspondence has perished and we are obliged to gather its tenor from letters written to him, which is much like listening to a one-sided conversation over the telephone. From one of Lee's letters, however, it is fairly evident that neither he nor Stuart himself had seriously considered the latter's taking Jackson's place. Lee writes: "I am obliged to you for your views as to the successor of the great and good Jackson. Unless God in his mercy will raise us up one, I do not know what we shall do. I agree with you on the subject, and have so expressed myself."[36]

In any event, what his countrymen will always remember of Stuart is the fighting figure, the glory of battle, the sudden and tumultuous fury of charge and onset.

And what above all distinguishes him in this is his splendid joy in it. Others fought with clenched fist and set teeth, rejoicing, perhaps, but with deadly determination of lip and brow. He laughed and sang. His blue eye sparkled and his white teeth gleamed. To others it was the valley of the shadow of death. To him it was a picnic and a pleasure party.

He views everything by its picturesque side, catches the theatrical detail which turns terror and death into a scenic surprise. "My arrival could not have been more fortunately timed, for, arriving after dark, the ponderous march, with the rolling artillery, must have impressed the enemy's cavalry, watching their rear, with the idea of an immense army about to cut off their retreat."[37] He rushed gayly into battle, singing, "Old Joe Hooker, won't you come out of the Wilderness?" or his favorite of favorites, "If you want to have a good time, jine the cavalry." When he is riding off, as it were into the mouth of hell, his adjutant asks, "How long?" and he answers, as Touchstone might, with a bit of old ballad, "It may be for years and it may be for ever." [38] His clear laughter, in the sternest crises, echoes through dusty war books, like a silver bell. As he sped back from his Peninsular raid, the Union troops were close upon him and the swollen Chickahominy in front, impassable, it seemed. Stuart thought a moment, pulling at his beard. Then he found the remains of an old bridge and set his men to rebuild it. "While the men were at work upon it, Stuart was lying down on the bank of the stream, in the gayest humor I ever saw, laughing at the prank he had played on McClellan." [39]

It is needless to enlarge on the effect of such a temper, such exuberant confidence and cheerfulness in danger, on subordinates. It lightened labor, banished fatigue, warmed chill limbs and fainting courage. "My men and horses are tired, hungry, jaded, but all right," [40] was the last despatch he ever wrote. So long as he was with them, they were all right. His very voice was like music, says Fitz Lee, "like the silver trumpet of the Archangel." It sounded oblivion of everything but glory. His gayety, his laughter, were infectious and turned a raid into a revel. "That summer night," writes Mosby of the McClellan expedition, "was a carnival of fun I can never forget. Nobody thought of danger or sleep, when champagne bottles were bursting and wine was flowing in copious streams. All had perfect confidence in their leader. . . . The discipline of the soldiers for a while gave way to the wild revelry of Comus." [41]

And this spirit of adventure, of romance, of buoyant optimism and energy, was not merely reserved for occasions of excitement, was not the triumphant outcome of glory and success. It was constant and unfailing. To begin with, Stuart had a magnificent physique. "Nothing seemed strong enough to break down his powerful organization of mind and body," [42] says his biographer; and Mosby, "Although he had been in the saddle two days and nights without sleep, he was as gay as a lark." [43] When exhaustion finally fell upon him, he would drop off his horse by the roadside, anywhere, sleep for an hour, and arise as active as ever. Universal testimony proves that he was overcome and disheartened by no disaster. He would be thoughtful for a moment, pulling at his beard, then seize upon the best decision that presented itself and push on. Dreariness sometimes crushes those who can well resist actual misfortune. Not Stuart. "In the midst of rainstorms, when everybody was riding along grum and cowering beneath the flood pouring down, he would trot on, head up, and singing gayly." [44]

The list of his personal adventures and achievements is endless. He braved capture and death with entire indifference, trusting in his admirable horsemanship, which often saved him, trusting in Providence, trusting in nothing at all but his quick wit and strong arm, curious mainly, perhaps, to see what would happen. On one occasion he is said to have captured forty-four Union soldiers. He was riding absolutely alone and ran into them taking their ease in a field. Instantly he chose his course. "Throw down your arms or you are all dead men." [45] They were green troops and threw down their arms, and Stuart marched the whole squad into camp. When duty forbids a choice adventure, he sighs, as might Don Quixote: "A scouting party of one hundred and fifty lancers had just passed toward Gettysburg. I regretted exceedingly that my march did not admit of the delay necessary to catch them." [46]

I have sometimes asked myself how much of this spirit of romantic adventure, of knight-errantry, as it were, in Stuart was conscious. Did he, like Claverhouse, read Homer and Froissart, and try to realize in modern Virginia the heroic deeds, still more, the heroic spirit, of antique chivalry? In common with all Southerners, he probably knew the prose and poetry of Scott and dreamed of the plume of Marmion and the lance of Ivanhoe. He must have felt the weight of his name, also, and believed that "James Stuart" might be aptly fitted with valorous adventure, and knightly deeds, and sudden glory. It is extremely interesting to find him writing to Jackson: "Did you receive the volume of Napoleon and his Maxims I sent you?" [47] I should like to own that volume. And in his newspaper account of Brown's raid he quotes

Horace, horribly, but still Horace: *Erant fortes ante Agamemnona.*

Yet I do not gather that he was much of a student. He preferred to live poems rather than read them. The spirit of romance, the instinct of the picturesque, was born in him and would out anywhere and everywhere. Life was a perpetual play, with ever shifting scenes, and gay lime-light, and hurrying incident, and passionate climax. Again and again he reminds me of a boy playing soldiers. His ambition, his love of glory, was of this order, not a bit the ardent, devouring, frowning, far-sighted passion of Jackson, but a jovial sense of pleasant things that can be touched and heard and tasted here, to-day. He had a childlike, simple vanity which all his biographers smile at, liked parade, display, and pomp and gorgeousness, utterly differing in this from Jackson, who was too proud, or Lee, who was too lofty. Stuart rode fine horses, never was seen on an inferior animal.[48] He wore fine clothes, all that his position justified, perhaps a little more. Here is Fitz Lee's picture of him: "His strong figure, his big brown beard, his piercing, laughing blue eye, the drooping hat and black feather, the 'fighting jacket' as he termed it, the tall cavalry boots, forming one of the most jubilant and striking figures in the war." [49] And Cooke is even more particular: "His fighting jacket shone with dazzling buttons and was covered with gold braid; his hat was looped up with a golden star, and decorated with a black ostrich plume; his fine buff gauntlets reached to the elbow; around his waist was tied a splendid yellow sash, and his spurs were of pure gold." [50] After this, we appreciate the biographer's assertion that Stuart was as fond of colors as a boy or girl, and elsewhere we read that he never moved without his gorgeous red battle-flag which often drew the fire of the enemy.[51]

As to the spurs, they were presented to the general by the ladies of Baltimore and he took great pride in them, signing himself sometimes in his private letters, K.G.S., Knight of the Golden Spurs.[52]

This last touch is perfectly characteristic and the Stuart of the pen is precisely the same as the Stuart of the sword. He could express himself as simply as Napoleon: "Tell General Lee that all is right. Jackson has not advanced, but I have; and I am going to crowd them with artillery."[53] But usually he did not. Indeed, the severe taste of Lee recoiled from his subordinate's fashions of speech: "The general deals in the flowery style, as you will perceive, if you ever see his reports in detail." [54] But I love them, they ring and resound so with the temper of the man, gorgeous scraps of tawdry rhetoric, made charming by their riotous sincerity, as with Scott and Dumas. "Their brave men behaved with coolness and intrepidity in danger, unswerving resolution before difficulties, and stood unappalled before the rushing torrent of the Chickahominy, with the probability of an enemy at their heels armed with the fury of a tigress robbed of her whelps." [55]

Could anything be worse from Lee's point of view? But it does put some life into an official report. Or take this Homeric picture of a charge, which rushes like a half-dozen stanzas of "Chevy Chase": "Lieutenant Robbins, handling it in the most skilful manner, managed to clear the way for the march with little delay, and infused by a sudden dash at a picket such a wholesome terror that it never paused to take a second look. . . . On, on dashed Robbins, here skirting a field, there leaping a fence or ditch, and clearing the woods beyond."[56]

When I read these things, I cannot but remember Madame de Sévigné's fascinating comment on the historical novels of her day. "The style of La Calprenède is detestable in a thousand ways: long-winded, romantic phrases, ill-chosen words, I admit it all. I agree that it is detestable; yet it holds me like glue. The beauty of the sentiments, the violence of the passions, the grandeur of the events, and the miraculous success of the hero's redoubtable sword—it sweeps me away as if I were a child."

And Stuart's was a real sword!

Then, too, as in Shakespearean tragedy or modern melodrama, the tension, in Stuart's case, is constantly relieved by hearty, wholesome, cheery laughter, which shook his broad shoulders and sparkled in his blue eyes. See what a strange comedy his report makes of this lurid night scene, in which another might have found only shadow and death: "It so far succeeded as to get possession of his [General Bartlett's] headquarters at one o'clock at night, the general having saved himself by precipitate flight in his nether garments. The headquarters flag was brought away. No prisoners were attempted to be taken, the party shooting down every one within reach. Some horses breaking loose near headquarters ran through an adjacent regimental camp, causing the greatest commotion, mid firing and yelling and cries of 'Halt!' 'Rally!' mingling in wild disorder, and ludicrous stampede which beggars description." [57] Can't you hear him laugh?

It must not be concluded from this that Stuart was cruel in his jesting. Where gentleness and sympathy were really called for, all the evidence shows that no man could give more. But he believed that the rough places are made smooth and the hard places soft and the barren places green and smiling by genial laughter. Who shall say that he was wrong? Therefore he would have his jest, with inferior and superior, with friend and enemy. Even the sombre Jackson was not spared. Once he had floundered into winter-quarters oddly decorated. Stuart suggested "that a drawing of the apartment should be made, with the race-horses, gamecocks, and terrier in bold relief, the picture to be labelled: 'View of the winter-quarters of General Jackson, affording an insight into the tastes and character of the individual.'" [58] And Jackson enjoyed it.

When it came to his adversaries, Stuart's fun was

unlimited. Everybody knows his telegraphed complaint to the United States Commissary Department that the mules he had been getting lately were most unsatisfactory and he wished they would provide a better quality. Even more amusing is the correspondence that occurred at Lewinsville. One of Stuart's old comrades wrote, addressing him by his West Point nickname. "My dear Beauty,—I am sorry that circumstances are such that I can't have the pleasure of seeing you, although so near you. Griffin says he would like to have you dine with him at Willard's at 5 o'clock on Saturday next. Keep your Black Horse off me, if you please. Yours, etc., Orlando M. Poe." On the back of this was penciled in Stuart's writing: "I have the honor to report that 'circumstances' were such that they could have seen me if they had stopped to look behind, and I answered both at the cannon's mouth. Judging from his speed, Griffin surely left for Washington to hurry up that dinner." [59]

I had an old friend who adored the most violent melodrama. When the curtain and his tears had fallen together, he would sigh and murmur, "Now let's have a little of that snare-drum music." Such was Stuart. "It might almost be said that music was his passion," writes his biographer.[60] I doubt, however, whether he dealt largely in the fugues of Bach. His favorites, in the serious order, are said to have been "The dew is on the blossom," and "Sweet Evelina." But his joy was the uproarious "If you get there before I do"; or his precious

"If you want to have a good time, jine the cavalry." He liked to live in the blare of trumpets and the crash of cymbals, liked to have his nerves tingle and his blood leap to a merry hunts-up or a riotous chorus, liked to have the high strain of war's melodrama broken by the sudden crackle of the snare-drum. His banjo-player, Sweeney, was as near to him as an aide-de-camp, followed him everywhere. "Stuart wrote his most important correspondence with the rattle of the gay instrument stunning everybody, and would turn round from his work, burst into a laugh, and join uproariously in Sweeney's chorus." [61]

And dance was as keen a spice to peril as song and laughter. To fight all day and dance all night was a good day's work to this creature of perfect physique and inexhaustible energy. If his staff officers could not keep pace with him and preferred a little sleep, the general did not like it at all. What? Here is—or was—a gay town, and pretty girls. Just because we are here to-day and gone to-morrow, shall we not fleet the time carelessly, as they did in the golden world? And the girls are got together, and a ball is organized, and the fun grows swifter and swifter. Perhaps a fortunate officer picks the prettiest and is about to stand up with her. Stuart whispers in his ear that a hurried message must be carried, laughs his gay laugh, and slips into the vacant place. Then an orderly hurries in, covered with dust. The enemy are upon us. "The officers rushed to their weapons and called for their horses, panic-stricken fathers and mothers endeavored to collect around them their bewildered children, while the young ladies ran to and fro in most admired despair. General Stuart maintained his accustomed coolness and composure. Our horses were immediately saddled, and in less than five minutes we were in rapid gallop to the front." [62] Oh, what a life!

You divine that with such a temperament Stuart would love women. So he did. Not that he let them interfere with duty. He would have heartily accepted the profound doctrine of Enobarbus in regard to the fair: "It were pity to cast them away for nothing; yet between them and a great cause they should be esteemed as nothing." Stuart arrested hundreds of ladies, says his biographer, and remained inexorable to their petitions. Cooke's charming account of one of these arrests should be read in full: how the fair captives first raved, and then listened, and then laughed, and then were charmed by the mellifluous Sweeney and the persuasive general, and at last departed with kissed hands and kindly hearts, leaving Stuart to explain to his puzzled aide, who inquired why he took so much pains: "Don't you understand? When those ladies arrived they were mad enough with me to bite my head off, and I determined to put them in good humor before they left me." [63]

But Cooke dresses his viands. I prefer the following taste of Stuart and girls and duty, as we get it unspiced from the rough-spoken common soldier: "General Lee would come up and spend hours studying the situation with his splendid glasses; and the glorious Stuart would dash up, always with a lady, and a pretty one, too. I wonder if the girl is yet alive who rode the general's fine horse and raced with him to charge our station. When they had reached the level platform, and Stuart had left her in care of one of us and took the other off to one side and questioned the very sweat out of him about the enemy's position, he was General Stuart then, but when he got back and lifted the beauty into the saddle and rode off humming a breezy air . . . he was Stuart the beau."[64]

And the women liked Stuart. It was a grand thing to be the first officer in the Confederate cavalry, with a blue eye and a fair beard, and all gold, like Horace's Lydia, from hat to spurs. When he rode singing and laughing into a little town, "by river or seashore," they flocked to meet him, young and old, and touched his garments, and begged his buttons and kissed his gloved hands, until he suggested that his cheeks were available, and then they kissed those, young and old alike.[65] They showered him with flowers also, buried him under nosegays and garlands, till he rode like old god Bacchus or the queen of May. What an odd fashion of making war! And the best I have met with is, that one day Stuart described one of these occurrences to his great chieftain. "I had to wear her garland, till I was out of sight," apologized the young cavalier. "Why are n't you wearing it now?" retorted Lee. Is n't that admirable? I verily believe that if any young woman had had the unimaginable audacity to throw a garland over Lee, he would have worn it through the streets of Richmond itself. [66]

You say, then, this Stuart was dissipated, perhaps, a scapegrace, a rioter, imitating Rupert and Murat in other things than great cavalry charges. That is the curious point. The man was nothing of the sort. With all his instinct of revelry, he had no vices, a very Puritan of laughter. He liked pretty girls everywhere; but when he was charged with libertinism, he answered, in the boldness of innocence, "That person does not live who can say that I ever did anything improper of that description"; [67] and he liked his wife better than any other pretty girl. He married her when he was twenty-two years old and his last wish was that she might reach him before he died. His few letters to her that have been printed are charming in their playful affection. He adored his children also; in short, was a pattern of domesticity. He did, indeed, love his country more, and telegraphed to his wife, when she called him to his dying daughter's bedside, "My duty to the country must be performed before I can give way to the feelings of a father"; but the child's death was a cruel blow to him. With his intimates he constantly referred to her, and when he himself was dying, he whispered, "I shall soon be with my little Flora again." [68]

"I never saw him touch a card," writes one who was very near him, "and he never dreamed of uttering an oath under any provocation, nor would he permit it at his headquarters." [69] We are assured by many that he never drank and an explicit statement of his own on the subject is reported: "I promised my mother in my childhood never to touch ardent spirits and a drop has never passed my lips, except the wine of the communion." [70]

As the last words show, he had religion as well as morals. He joined the Methodist church when he was fifteen; later the Episcopal. When he was twenty-four, he sent money home to his mother to aid in the building of a church. He carried his Bible with him always. In his reports religion is not obtrusive. When it does occur, it is evidently sincere. "The Lord of Hosts was plainly fighting on our side, and the solid walls of Federal infantry melted away before the straggling, but nevertheless determined, onset of our infantry columns." [71] "Believing that the hand of God was clearly manifested in the signal deliverance of my command from danger, and the crowning success attending it, I ascribe to Him the praise, the honor, and the glory." [72] He inclined to strictness in the observance of Sunday. Captain Colston writes me that when twelve struck of a Saturday night Stuart held up his hand relentlessly and stopped song and dance in their full tide, though youth and beauty begged for just one more. He was equally scrupulous in the field, though, in his feeling of injury because the enemy were not, I seem to detect his habitual touch of humor: "The next morning being the Sabbath, I recognized my obligation to do no duty other than what was absolutely necessary, and determined, so far as possible, to devote it to rest. Not so the enemy, whose guns about 8 A.M. showed that he would not observe it." [73]

I have no doubt that Stuart's religion was inward as well as outward and remoulded his heart. But, after all, he was but little over thirty when he died, and I love to trace in him the occasional working of the old Adam which had such lively play in the bosom of many an officer who was unjustly blamed or missed some well-deserved promotion. Stuart's own letters are too few to afford much insight of this kind. But here again we get that one-sided correspondence with Lee which is so teasingly suggestive. On one occasion Lee writes: "The expression 'appropriated by the Stuart Horse Artillery' was not taken from a report of Colonel Baldwin, nor intended in any objectionable sense, but used for want of a better phrase, without any intention on my part of wounding." [74] And again, after Chancellorsville: "As regards the closing remarks of your note, I am at a loss to understand their reference or to know what has given rise to them. In the management of the difficult operations at Chancellorsville, which you so promptly undertook and creditably performed, I saw no errors to correct, nor has there been a fit opportunity to commend your conduct. I prefer your acts to speak for themselves, nor does your character or reputation require bolstering up by out-of-place expressions of my opinion."[75]

But by far the most interesting human revelation of this kind is one letter of Stuart's own, written to justify himself against some aspersions of General Trimble. With the right or wrong of the case we are not concerned; simply with the fascinating study of Stuart's state of mind. He begins evidently with firm restraint and a Christian moderation: "Human memory is frail I know." But the exposure of his wrongs heats his blood, as he goes on, and spurs him, though he still endeavors to check himself: "It is true I am not in the habit of giving orders, particularly to my seniors in years, in a dictatorial and authoritative manner, and my manner very likely on this occasion was more restive than imperative; indeed, I may have been content to satisfy myself that the dispositions which he himself proposed accorded with my own ideas, without any blustering show of orders to do this or that. . . . General Trimble says I did not reach the place until seven or eight o'clock. I was in plain view all the time, and rode through, around, and all about the place soon after its capture. General Trimble is mistaken."[76] Nay, in his stammering eagerness to right himself, his phrases, usually so crisp and clear, stumble and fall over each other: "In the face of General Trimble's positive denial of sending me such a message, 'that he would prefer waiting until daylight,' or anything like it, while my recollection is clear that I did receive such a message, and received it as coming from General Trimble, yet, as he is so positive to not having sent such a message or anything like it, I feel bound to believe that either the message was misrepresented or made up by the messenger, or that it was a message received from General Robertson, whose sharpshooters had been previously deployed." [77]

A real man, you see, like the rest of us; but a noble one, and lovable. Fortunate, also, in his death as in his life. For he was not shot down in the early days, like Jackson and Sidney Johnston, when it seemed as if his great aid might have changed destiny. He had done all a man in his position could do. When he went, hope too was going. He was spared the long, weary days of Petersburg, spared the bitter cup of Appomattox, spared the cruel domination of the conqueror, spared what was perhaps worst of all, the harsh words and reproaches which flew too hotly where there should have been nothing but love and silence. He slept untroubled in his glory, while his countrymen mourned and Lee "yearned for him." His best epitaph has been written by a magnanimous opponent: "Deep in the hearts of all true cavalrymen, North and South, will ever burn a sentiment of admiration mingled with regret for this knightly soldier and generous man." [78]

III

James Longstreet

CHRONOLOGY

Born in Edgefield District, South Carolina, January 8, 1821.
Graduated at West Point, 1842.
Second Lieutenant, July 1, 1842.
Served in Texas during 1845–46.
Served in Mexican War, 1846–47.
First Lieutenant, February 23, 1847.
Married Maria Louise Garland, March 8, 1848.
Served in West till 1861.
Captain, December 7, 1852.
Major, July 19, 1858.
Major-General in Confederate Army, 1861.
Served with Army of Northern Virginia till April, 1863.
Independent command south of James River, April, May, 1863.
With Army of Northern Virginia till autumn of 1863.
Served in Tennessee till January, 1864.
With Army of Northern Virginia till close of war.
After war became a Republican.
Minister to Turkey, 1880.
Married Helen Dortch, September 8, 1897.
Died, January 2, 1904.

JAMES LONGSTREET

III

JAMES LONGSTREET

LONGSTREET had half New Jersey blood and probably part Dutch. It shows in him. He is far more the modern, practical nineteenth-century American than most of his fellows. What Southern romance he has sits awkwardly and is mixed with mocking. He reminds you again and again of Grant and Sherman in his bulldog pugnacity and tenacity, his brusque, sharp fashions of hitting right out at men and measures. Southern easy-going ways and shiftlessness vexed him: "Our people have been so accustomed to having things at their hands that they seem at a loss for resources when emergencies arise. 'Where there is a will there is a way' of overcoming all human obstacles. It is left for us to find it out."[1]

He was hard-headed, solid, stolid; and he looked it. "A thick-set, determined-looking man,"[2] says Fremantle. And Pollard describes his appearance as "not engaging. It was decidedly sombre; the bluish-gray eye was intelligent, but cold; a very heavy brown beard was allowed to grow untrimmed; he seldom spoke unnecessarily; his weather-stained clothes, splashed boots, and heavy black hat gave a certain fierce aspect to the man."[3] His health, vigor, power of supporting fatigue were remarkable. "The iron endurance of General Longstreet is most extraordinary: he seems to require neither food nor sleep."[4]

As a fighter he was superb, the best fighter in the Army of Northern Virginia, the soldiers called him. This perhaps refers more to character than to brains, as it is admitted that he was no great student at West Point or anywhere else. In Mexico he fought most creditably, side by side with Grant and other contemporaries. From Bull Run to Appomattox he was always where the fighting was hottest. His soldiers believed in him and trusted him. He spoke straight out to them, as if he meant it. Sometimes it was with a heavy sarcasm, as at Gettysburg, to an officer who complained of not being able to bring up his troops: "Very well, never mind, then, General; just let them remain where they are; the enemy 's going to advance, and will spare you the trouble."[5] More often he gave them sound, direct, practical advice, of the kind to put heart into a man: "Let officers and men, even under the most formidable fire, preserve a quiet demeanor and self-possessed temper. Keep cool, obey orders, and aim low. Remember, while you are doing this, and driving the enemy before you, your comrades may be relied upon to support you on either side, and are in turn relying upon you."[6]

Such advice coming from the War Department might not have amounted to much. Coming from a man who was as cool in battle as in a ballroom, it must have been almost as if he laid a hand on your shoulder. How imperturbable he was is shown by many witnesses, notably Fremantle: "No person could have been more calm or self-possessed than General Longstreet under these trying circumstances [after Gettysburg], aggravated as they now were by the movements of the enemy, who began to show a strong disposition to advance. I could now appreciate the term bulldog which I had heard applied to him by the soldiers. Difficulties seem to make no other impression upon him than to make him a little more savage." [7] He may not have felt the dancing ecstasy with which Stuart charged and which Longstreet himself admirably describes in another: "He came into battle as gayly as a beau, and seemed to receive orders which threw him into more exposed positions with peculiar delight." [8] But he was always ready to face any exposure — too ready. "Every one deplores that Longstreet *will* expose himself in such a reckless manner. To-day he led a Georgian regiment in a charge against a battery, hat in hand and in front of everybody." [9]

The same imperturbable coolness that distinguished Longstreet in actual fighting characterized him as a leader. He was never anxious, never flurried. Victory could not over-excite him with triumph, nor defeat with confusion. He made every preparation, took every precaution, was ready for difficulties and indifferent to dangers. Unfortunately, however, consummate generalship requires something more than imperturbability. It requires brains and speed. Had Longstreet these? His work as an independent commander suggests some doubt. Intelligence of a certain order, the solid, firm, Dutch grasp of a situation, and common sense in the handling of it, can never be denied him. But quick insight, long penetration, the sudden conception of what is daring to be done and not too daring, — in short, a brain like Jackson's, I do not think he had. As to speed there will be less question. Even Lee is said to have remarked, "Longstreet is the hardest man to move in my army." In every case the general was able to give a good reason for not arriving in time. But Jackson, when at his best, arrived in time in spite of good reasons.

Both these defects and many of Longstreet's excellences are intimately bound up with one strongly marked trait which is often an excellence but runs into a defect too easily; I mean a singular, an unfailing, an almost unlimited self-confidence. Self-confidence does nearly all the great things that are done in the world. "Trust thyself," says Emerson; "every heart vibrates to that iron string." Doubt of one's powers, doubt of one's nerve, dread of responsibility — these weaknesses will paralyze the keenest perceptions, the finest intelligence. But self-confidence, to achieve the highest, must be tempered with insight and sympathy. A man must trust himself, but he must trust others. Before he decides, resolves, executes, he must listen. His own judgment must prevail with him; but it must be his own judgment qualified, enriched, by the judgment of those wiser, or even less wise. No one can impose his own personality, however solid and sturdy, on the whole world.

This is what Longstreet tried to do, with exquisite and naïve unconsciousness. And this quality of an immense self-confidence runs through his whole career with a steadiness which is very peculiar, very instructive — and very unfortunate. Note that Johnston's trouble was an over-sensitive pride. This is not Longstreet's main trouble; nor was he largely stirred by wounded ambitions. "I am not prompted by any desire to do, or to attempt to do, great things. I only wish to do what I regard as my duty — give you the full benefit of my views."[10] And again: "If there is no duty to which I can be assigned on this side of the Mississippi River without displacing an officer, I will cheerfully accept service in the trans-Mississippi Department."[11] Note also that it is not a foolish conceit, or pig-headed pride of opinion. Once convince the man that he was in the wrong and he would have been perfectly ready to say, "All my fault," and begin over again. But you never could convince him that he was wrong. There was one way to see the question in hand and that was the way he saw it, one way to act and that was the way he acted. Other ways and other views were incomplete, or unenlightened, or simply stupid. No single quotation can sum up this attitude, naturally. It will, I think, appear in overwhelming significance, as we go on. Page after page of Longstreet's book is stamped with it. But perhaps one paragraph near the beginning is as characteristic as any. "Speaking of the impending struggle [spring of 1861], I was asked as to the length of the war, and said, 'At least three years, and if it holds for five you may begin to look for a dictator,' at which Lieutenant Ryan, of the Seventh Infantry, said, 'If we have to have a dictator, I hope that you may be the man.'"[12] No doubt, for the good of the country, Longstreet himself hoped that he would be the man.

It is in his relation to Lee that this stolid self-confidence of Longstreet manifests itself most interestingly. The two men loved each other. Lee showed his affection for his second in command more frankly and directly than for almost any one else, even Jackson. "My old war-horse," he called him, perhaps characterizing the subordinate more fully than he meant. If so, Longstreet was quite oblivious of it and refers to the phrase with proud complacency, as he does to another point which most of us are inclined to view a little differently, that is, the fact that "on his march he [Lee] usually had his headquarters near mine."[13] Lee has other words, however, of a less equivocal nature. Thus, he writes to the general in the West: "I think you can do better than I could. It was with that view I urged your going."[14] But he longs to have him back: "I missed you dreadfully and your brave corps. Your cheerful face and strong arm would have been invaluable. I hope you will soon return to me."[15]

Longstreet's love for his great chief was equally fervent. Speaking of him after the war he says: "The relations existing between us were affectionate, confidential, and even tender, from first to last. There was never a harsh word between us."[16] Writing to Lee from the West he expresses feeling as evidently deep as it is genuine: "All that we have to be proud of has been accomplished under your eye and under your orders. Our affections for you are stronger, if it is possible for them to be stronger, than our admiration for you."[17] And Fremantle, who had observed both men closely, corroborates these words in the most charming manner: "It is impossible to please Longstreet more than by praising Lee. I believe these two generals to be as little ambitious and as thoroughly unselfish as any men in the world."[18]

But Longstreet did not propose to allow judgment to be hoodwinked by affection. Not for him was the attitude so passionately expressed by Jackson: "General Lee is a phenomenon. I would follow him blindfold." On the contrary, the commander of the First Corps was keenly aware of his chief's defects and has recorded them mercilessly for posterity. "In the field his characteristic fault was headlong combativeness. . . . In the immediate presence of the enemy General Lee's mind, at all other times calm and clear, became excited."[19] These defects it was naturally the duty of an affectionate lieutenant to watch for and remedy in every possible way. And Longstreet watched.

From the first day Lee took command we have his subordinate's delightful accounts of the way in which he advised, suggested, as some might almost say, dictated. It was Longstreet who conceived the plan by which Jackson was to be called from the Valley that McClellan might be driven from the Peninsula; and if Jackson had been at all equal to the occasion, a great triumph would have been achieved.[20] It was Longstreet who found Lee hesitating about going into Maryland on account of lack of supplies. "But I reminded him of my experiences in Mexico, where sometimes we were obliged to live two or three days on green corn. . . . Finally he determined to go on." [21] It was Longstreet who pointed out to his commander the folly of the Harper's Ferry scheme and supposed it was abandoned. But he could not be on the watch all the time and the pestilent Jackson took advantage of his absence to impose on a mind always too easily led.[22] Later Longstreet did his best to remedy a bad state of things. "Lee listened patiently enough, but did not change his plans, and directed that I should go back the next day and make a stand at the mountain. After lying down, my mind was still on the battle of the next day, and I was so impressed with the thought that it would be impossible for us to do anything at South Mountain . . . that I rose and, striking a light, wrote a note to General Lee, urging him to order Hill away and concentrate at Sharpsburg. To that note I got no answer." [23] Do you wonder why?

But Gettysburg is the best of all. And observe, I take no part in the controversy as to what Longstreet actually did. It does not become an outsider and a civilian to do so. His judgment as to possibilities before and as to events after may have been wise, may have been correct. What interests me solely is Longstreet's character as displayed in Longstreet's own words.

To begin with, then, he is opposed to the campaign from the start, believing that the main operations should be carried on in the West. However, finding Lee unwilling to agree to this, Longstreet permits his commander to enter upon his project. "I then accepted his proposal to make a campaign into Pennsylvania, provided it should be offensive in strategy, but defensive in tactics." [24] Judge of his disgust when they found themselves at Gettysburg and the commander ventured to overstep the lines which his mentor had laid down for him. "I suggested that the course seemed to be at variance with the plan of the campaign that had been agreed on before leaving Fredericksburg. He said, 'If the enemy is there to-morrow, we must attack him.' . . . I said that it seemed to me that if, during our council at Fredericksburg, we had described the position in which we desired to get the two armies, we could not have expected to get the enemy in a better position for us than he then occupied. . . . He, however, did not seem to abandon the idea of attack on the next day." [25]

And they attacked and failed all along the line, because Longstreet's heart was not in it, say his enemies, because success was impossible, says Longstreet himself.

And the scene was renewed again the day following, Lee deciding, ordering, Longstreet protesting, with imperturbable confidence in his own judgment, and snubbed in a fashion made tenfold more dramatic by its being Lee who did it and Longstreet who recorded it, apparently without the dimmest perception of what it meant [italics mine]: "I said: 'General, I have been a soldier all my life. I have been with soldiers engaged in fights by couples, by squads, companies, regiments, divisions, and armies, and should know as well as any one what soldiers can do. It is my opinion that no 15,000 men ever arrayed for battle can take that position,' pointing to Cemetery Hill. *General Lee in reply to this ordered me to prepare Pickett's division for the attack.*" [26]

When everything was over, Lee declared, with divine humility, that it was all his fault. "Fine," says Longstreet, in effect, "especially as it was."

In the autumn of 1863 Longstreet went West. He had long felt that he was needed there and he finally prevailed on Davis and Lee to let him go. It would be impossible to surpass the serene confidence with which he viewed this undertaking. Note also that he disclaims, and no doubt sincerely, all thought of personal ambition in the matter [italics mine]: "If my corps cannot go West, I think that we might accomplish something by giving me Jenkins, Wise, and Cooke's brigades, and putting me in General Bragg's place, and giving him my corps. . . . *We would surely run no risk* in such a change and we might gain a great deal. I feel that I am influenced by no personal motive in making this suggestion; and will most cheerfully give up, when we have a fair prospect of holding our Western country. I doubt if General Bragg has great confidence in his troops or himself either. He is not likely to do a great deal for us." [27]

He was not put in Bragg's place, however, but under Bragg's orders, and therefore naturally was unable to accomplish all the great things that he had counted on. If he had found it difficult to place much reliance on Lee, how was it to be expected that he should place any on Bragg? He did not, and said so. Here again, I do not think there was any set purpose of malice or mischief-making. Bragg was wrong. Longstreet was right. This must be so obvious to every one that outspoken comment could hardly make it any plainer. The effect, however, was not happy; witness Mackall, who was no friend to Bragg: "I think Longstreet has done more injury to the general than all the others put together. You may understand how much influence with his troops a remark from a man of his standing would have to the effect that Bragg was not on the field and Lee would have been." [28]

This sort of thing seems incredible in a man of Longstreet's age, training, and soldierly habits; but the language of his own letters shows abundantly what his attitude was. He writes to Buckner: "As every other move had been proposed to the general and rejected or put off till time made them more convenient, I came to the conclusion that this was to be the fate of our army — to wait till all good opportunities passed, and then, in desperation, to seize upon the least favorable one." [29]

And here again, as at Gettysburg, we can ask nothing more characteristic than the little scene that the general paints for us, apparently quite unconscious of its significance, but depicting himself and a dozen men of similar type that we all know, as effectively as Rembrandt might have done: "The only notice my plan received was a remark that General Hardee was pleased to make: 'I don't think that is a bad idea of Longstreet's.' . . . I repeated my ideas, but they did not even receive notice. It was not till I had repeated them, however, that General Hardee even noticed me." [30] Unconscious self-interpretation like this, as with Pepys, amounts to genius.

No one could attack Bragg without attacking Davis, and to Longstreet, Davis — when he was wrong — was no more than Bragg. Twice, at least, in full and formal military council, the general offered his advice to the President — and was snubbed. The first time was early in the war before the Peninsular campaign. "From the hasty interruption I concluded that my opinion had only been asked through polite recognition of my presence, not that it was wanted, and said no more." [31] The second time was in connection with the movements of Bragg and Johnston in the West and involved Lee as well as Longstreet. As described by the latter, it is a singularly impressive and characteristic incident. He had given his views in regard to the situation at some length, and assumes that Lee agreed with them. The President did not. "General Lee wore his beard full, but neatly trimmed. He pulled at it nervously, and more vigorously as time and silence grew, till his nervousness was conquered. The profound quiet of a minute or more seemed an hour. When he spoke, it was of other matters, but the air was troubled by his efforts to surrender hopeful anticipations to the caprice of empirics. He rose to take leave of the august presence, gave his hand to the President, and bowed himself out of the council chamber. His assistant went through the same forms, and no one approached the door to offer parting courtesy." [32] Even after this Longstreet could not get the responsibility of the matter off his mind. On returning to the West, "it occurred to me to write to the President, and try to soften the asperities of the Richmond council. . . . In reply the President sent a rebuke of my delay." [33]

The most significant element of all in Longstreet's Western campaign is his dealings with his own subordinates, McLaws, Law, and Robertson. The dramatic genius of Sophocles could not have devised a finer climax than that situation. At Gettysburg, just before, as second in command to Lee, the general had thoroughly disapproved of his chief's action and had not hesitated to say so. Likewise, he had failed to carry out his chief's wishes, through either indifference or inability. Lee, with supreme generosity, intent on the future, not on the past, had accepted the latter solution and found no word of fault with his lieutenant's motives in any way whatsoever.

Then Longstreet goes West and is placed in charge of the Knoxville expedition. His second in command, McLaws, disapproves of the assault on Fort Loudon, exactly as Longstreet disapproved of the assault at Gettysburg. Hear McLaw's own words: "I object to being put forward as a blind to draw attention away from the main issue, which is the conduct of the campaign in East Tennessee by General Longstreet. I assert that the enemy could have been brought to an engagement before reaching Knoxville; that the town, if assaulted at all, should have been on the first day we arrived or on the next at furthest; that when the assault was made on Fort Loudon it was not called for by any line of policy whatever."[34]

If he had been endowed with divination, could he have anticipated more perfectly Longstreet's later attitude with regard to Gettysburg?

But how different was Longstreet's treatment of his subordinate under these circumstances from Lee's! As soon as he suspects disaffection, he writes sharply through his aide, "I am directed to say that throughout the campaign on which we are engaged you have exhibited a want of confidence in the efforts and plans which the commanding general has thought proper to adopt, and he is apprehensive that this feeling will extend more or less to the troops under your command."[35] When the assault is imminent, he insists that previous conviction of failure is the surest road to it. "Please urge upon your officers the importance of making the assault with a determination to succeed. If the assault is made with that spirit, I shall feel no doubt of its success."[36] And again: "If we go in with the idea that we shall fail, we will be sure to do so. But no men who are determined to succeed can fail. Let me urge you not to entertain such feelings for a moment. Do not let any one fail, or any thing."[37] Imagine how Lee would have liked to say that to Longstreet on the morning of July 3, and if he had, what Longstreet would have answered.

When all is over, the general does, indeed, admit to the War Department that it may have been his fault: "It is fair to infer that the fault is entirely with me, and I desire, therefore, that some other commander may be tried."[38] This does not mean, however, that he forgets or forgives, so far as his subordinates are concerned. He prefers charges against McLaws, Law, and Robertson.

They are tried by a court martial, which only partially sustains the commander, and even this insufficient verdict is reversed by the Richmond authorities. "The proceedings, finding, and sentence of the court are disapproved. Major-General McLaws will at once return to duty with his command." [39] Longstreet rebels and receives an even harsher snub from Davis: "General Longstreet has seriously offended against good order and military discipline in re-arresting an officer who had been released by the War Department, without any new offense having been committed." [40] Longstreet has a final word on the matter in his book, whether to his own advantage or disadvantage, I leave to the reader's judgment. "Confidence in the conduct of the war was broken, and with it the tone and spirit for battle further impaired by the efforts of those in authority to damage, if not prevent the success of work ordered in their own vital interest." [41]

It might be supposed that, after these varied experiences, the general would have returned to Lee's supremacy with a saddened and a chastened spirit. I do not find this indicated. Through the spring of 1864 and later, when he returned to duty after his Wilderness wound, he was always cheerfully ready to patronize his commander and to give abundant advice, when it was asked for and when it was not. "I am pleased at all times to have any suggestions that you may make, and am gratified to find that you in your numerous duties do not lose sight of these small matters," [42] is the usual tone. Perhaps the most curious suggestion offered is that the military authorities should "impress" all the gold in the country and use it for the necessities of defense.[43] Unfortunately most of Lee's replies to his subordinate's exhortations are lost. We have his comment on this gold matter, however, — a gentle reminder that the specie is not accumulated in chests which troopers can walk off with, but is scattered and hidden all over the Confederacy. Longstreet, perfectly unconcerned, insists as before: "The gold is in the country, and most of it is lying idle. Let us take it at once and [use] it to save Richmond and end the war." [44]

Finally, in considering Longstreet's conduct after the war was over, I think we shall find the best excuse or explanation for it in this same trait of overmastering self-confidence. Here we should turn to Mrs. Longstreet. It is worth observing that the lives of three of the most prominent Southern leaders — Davis, Jackson, and Longstreet — have been written by their wives with loving eulogy, and that in each case these ladies furnish — quite unintentionally — the most striking testimony as to their husbands' weaknesses and defects. It is a notable illustration of the old poet's remark, —

> "Those have most power to hurt us that we love;
> We lay our sleeping lives within their arms."

Thus, when Mrs. Longstreet insists that her hero, in joining the Republican party and accepting government office, sacrificed personal advantage to a spirit of lofty patriotism, much as did Lee at the beginning of the war, she makes him ridiculous. Her own naïve account of the activities and the luxury of his last years emphasizes this, and the swelling phrases of her affectionate enthusiasm require no comment: "I love best to think of him, not as the warrior leading his legions to victory, but as the grand citizen after the war was ended, nobly dedicating himself to the rehabilitation of his broken people, offering a brave man's homage to the flag of the established government, and standing steadfast in all the passions, prejudices, and persecutions of that unhappy period. It was the love and honor and soul of the man crystallized into a being of wonderful majesty, immovable as Gibraltar." [45]

Verily, "those have most power to hurt us that we love." Yet, as to the substance, I think Mrs. Longstreet is right, and the many Southerners who accuse her husband of mere place-hunting, of flattering the conqueror for his own aggrandizement, are totally wrong. He was patriotic. He did believe that he was doing the best for his country. He was a practical American. The war was over. The Union must be restored. The sooner it was restored, the better. And the more good men that took hold to restore it, the better still. The sentiment of lost causes, and fallen flags, and consecrated graves was—sentiment. Those who were to make the future had no time for it. That was his view. And, as all his life, he could not imagine that there could be any other. He acted on it at once — and found himself, among thousands of old comrades, all alone.

And now, surely, we are eager to probe the "wonderful majesty" of this "immovable Gibraltar" for what was human under it, to thrust below the stolid Dutch phlegmatic surface of grim work and rocklike confidence and find the emotions of mortality.

They were there. Let us take the unsightly ones first and be rid of them. They had a grip on the man's soul that forbids us to pass them by. He was jealous, he was harsh, he was bitter to his enemies. Much there was, undoubtedly, to bring out these feelings in him. But others have borne as much in a different spirit.

To begin with his attitude towards Lee — or Lee's admirers. Immediately after Gettysburg, perhaps under the influence of Lee's example, he wrote the noble letter to his uncle in which he says: "As we failed, I must take my share of the responsibility. In fact, I would prefer that all the blame should rest upon me. As General Lee is our commander, he should have all the support and influence we can give him. If the blame, if there is any, can be shifted from him to me, I shall help him and our cause by taking it." [46] But this mood did not last. On which side the fault-finding began is disputed, but it soon grew into bitter recrimination. Longstreet's course, justly or unjustly, was condemned by many, and he retorted with the utmost acridity, in the Philadelphia "Times" articles, in "Battles and Leaders," and finally in his book. The lofty determination to exonerate Lee at his own expense was gradually transformed into assertions—before quoted—that his old chief was not a master of offensive battle;[47] that "in the field his characteristic fault was headlong combativeness";[48] that "in the immediate presence of the enemy General Lee's mind, at all other times calm and clear, became excited";[49] and that the fighting at Gettysburg had to go on until "blood enough was shed to appease him."[50]

But Longstreet's attitude towards some of his comrades in arms shows even more unpleasant features than his attitude towards his beloved commander. And let me repeat that these things must be insisted on because they indicate such a fatal and such an instructive flaw in a nature of unusual depth and power. The proposed duel with A. P. Hill early in the war, if it really was proposed, sprang from pride in his troops as much as in himself.[51] No such excuse will avail for his cruel language towards Early. It is true that Early had criticized him; but just here Longstreet's weakness comes out most. Early, in explaining his criticisms later, says with noble and Christian charity, "You will observe that in my article there is some causticity of expression, which was provoked by the character of the article I was replying to. I now sincerely regret the necessity which called forth the personal strictures contained in my replies, and would be glad if they could be eliminated."[52] Yet Longstreet, writing his book much later still, could express himself in this venomous fashion: "There was a man on the left of the line who did not care to make the battle win. He knew where it was, had viewed it from its earliest formation, had orders for his part in it, but so withheld part of his command from it as to make coöperative concert of action impracticable. He had a pruriency for the honors of the field of Mars, was eloquent, before the fires of the bivouac and his chief, of the glory of war's gory shield; but when its envied laurels were dipping to his grasp, when the heavy field called for bloody work, he found the placid horizon, far and beyond the cavalry, more lovely and inviting." [53]

This spirit is even more apparent in Longstreet's remarks about Jackson and Virginia. Here again one should read Colonel Allan's noble expression of Virginia's opinion about Longstreet.[54] This only emphasizes such remarks as the following, in regard to Harper's Ferry: "Jackson was quite satisfied with the campaign, as the Virginia papers made him the hero of Harper's Ferry, although the greater danger was with McLaws, whose service was the severer and more important"; [55] or this other, when Jackson declined Longstreet's assistance in the Valley: "I had been left in command on the Rapidan, but was not authorized to assume command of the Valley district. As the commander of the district did not care to have an officer there of higher rank, the subject was discontinued." [56] These things make one recur to

Mrs. Longstreet's eulogy and to her quotation of her husband's appeal to his countrymen at the outbreak of the Spanish War: "If I could recall one hour of my distant but glorious command, I would say, on the eve of battle with a foreign foe, 'Little children, love one another.' "[57]

The most characteristic, most important, and most unfortunate of all Longstreet's writings about his old companions is the deliberate close of his article in the second volume of "Battles and Leaders." I do not think the most ardent admirer of Lincoln can approve either the feeling or the taste with which his name is introduced here. "I cannot close this sketch without reference to the Confederate commander. When he came upon the scene for the first time, General Lee was an unusually handsome man, even in his advanced life. He seemed fresh from West Point, so trim was his figure, and so elastic his step. Out of battle he was as gentle as a woman, but when the clash of arms came, he loved fight, and urged his battle with wonderful determination. As a usual thing he was remarkably well balanced—always so, except on one or two occasions of severe trial when he failed to maintain his exact equipoise. Lee's orders were always well considered and well chosen. He depended almost too much on his officers for their execution. Jackson was a very skillful man against such men as Shields, Banks, and Frémont, but when pitted against the best of the Federal commanders, he did not appear so well. Without doubt the greatest man of rebellion times, the one matchless among forty millions for the peculiar difficulties of the period, was Abraham Lincoln." [58]

But who could leave Longstreet so? It is incontestable that, with all these marked and disastrous defects, the man was immensely lovable and had not only force, but charm. Under the stolid exterior there were kindly emotions as well as sharper ones. Socially he is said to have been quiet and undemonstrative, yet at times he showed a tenderness and affection which were all the more appreciated.

There can be no doubt that his patriotism and devotion to the cause he served were strong and genuine. "While we weep with the friends of our gallant dead, we must confess that a soldier's grave, in so holy and just a cause, is the highest honor that a man can attain." [59] "For myself," he says, after Vicksburg and Gettysburg, "I felt that our last hope was gone, and that it was only a question of time with us." [60] Yet he fought on as steadily, as bravely, as persistently as ever, and declared, in January, 1865, "We are better able to cope with the enemy now than we have ever been, if we will profit by our experience and exert ourselves properly in improving our organization." [61]

He was as thoughtful in his sympathy for noncombatants as he was hardy in fighting. Thus after Fredericksburg he directs a subscription to be taken up for the inhabitants and describes their sufferings and their devotion with the most evident tenderness.[62]

I have cited many bitter things that he wrote of his enemies. Alas, they are in print, set solid in history, and injure him far more than those he attacked. But we should weigh against them the kindly, charitable things which Mrs. Longstreet describes him as saying. When Gordon, who had uttered harsh words as to Gettysburg, was reported ill, Longstreet inquired, with touching concern, about his condition.[63] Judge Speer and the general had had disagreements. When asked how he would receive the judge, Longstreet answered: "As I would receive any other distinguished American. And as for our past differences, that has been a long time ago, and I have forgotten what it was all about."[64] General Hampton felt bitterly as to Longstreet's politics and would not meet him. Mrs. Longstreet commented on the matter with some harshness. But her husband said: "There was not a finer, braver, more gallant officer in the Confederate service than Wade Hampton."[65] Most touching also is Mrs. Longstreet's picture of her husband's yearning for the lost esteem of his fellow-Southerners. "General Longstreet said nothing, but his eyes slowly filled. While he bore unjust criticism in silence, he was visibly moved by any evidence of affection from the Southern people."[66]

And he is said to have been most deeply touched by the enthusiasm shown for him by his old followers at the unveiling of the Lee Monument.

Indeed, if one wishes to forget the general's unamiable peculiarities, one must turn to his relation with his soldiers, and one cannot fail to appreciate what a really great heart he had. He loved his men, sympathized with them, laughed at and understood their failings, saw their needs and strove with all his might to remedy them. When he found troops altering the works for better security, although the engineers objected, he approved, saying, "If you save the finger of a man's hand, that does some good." [67] When the cavalry leaders were inclined to scoff at the infantry, he rebukes them: "The commanding general regrets that you entertain the impression that your forces are fighting for the bread of the infantry. Your troops are in the service of the Government, and are battling for a common cause and a common country. The infantry of this army have fought too many battles to be told that their bread is earned by the cavalry." [68]

And better even than Longstreet's love for his men is his men's love for him. The immense collection of testimonial letters printed in Mrs. Longstreet's book goes far beyond mere conventional eulogy. It shows a devotion and a regret which can only have been bred by something great. Concretely these feelings are best illustrated by the old soldier who brought his gray jacket and his enlistment papers to be buried in his general's grave: "I 've served my time, and the General, he 's served his time, too. And I reckon I won't need my uniform and papers again. But I 'd like to leave them with him for always."[69] Beside which should be put Stiles's striking account, well-paralleled by another instance in Fremantle,[70] of the behavior of the officers at the time of Longstreet's wound: "The members of his staff surrounded the vehicle, some on one side and some on the other, and some behind. One, I remember, stood upon the rear step of the ambulance, seeming to desire to be as near him as possible. I never on any occasion during the four years of the war saw a group of officers and gentlemen so deeply distressed. They were literally bowed down with grief. All of them were in tears. One, by whose side I rode for some distance, was himself severely hurt, but he made no allusion to his wound and I do not think he felt it. It was not alone the general they admired who had been shot down — it was rather the man they loved."[71]

To inspire devotion like that a leader must, indeed, have noble qualities; and, morever, it confirms one in the belief that a round self-confidence, backed by tried capacity, is a trait men cling to, as much as to anything, in the hour of trouble.

Towards the end of his life Longstreet joined the Catholic Church. This forms such a remarkable close to his career that it cannot be passed over. Mrs. Longstreet, with another of those shrewd blows that come most stingingly from those we love, says he did it because his former Episcopal associates would not sit in the same pew with him after his political conversion and he wanted a church that had more charity.

I cannot suppose that he was a man of naturally religious bent. Such references as he makes to the subject have an excess of unction which I would not for a moment call insincere, but which suggests an excursion into paths not habitually traveled; and these references have a rhetorical turn which appears in almost all his attempts to express unusual emotion. Thus, he writes of General Jenkins's death: "In a moment of highest earthly hope he was transported to serenest heavenly joy; to that life beyond which knows no bugle call, beat of drum, or clash of steel. May his beautiful spirit, through the mercy of God, rest in peace! Amen!"[72] He himself closes his book with a little anecdote which strongly confirms my opinion as to this phase of his character. He visits an old servant long after the war. "'Marse Jim,' says the negro, 'do you belong to any church?' 'Oh, yes, I try to be a good Christian.' He laughed loud and long, and said,—'Something must have scared you mighty bad, to change you so from what you was when I had to care for you.'"[73]

Yet this man became a Roman Catholic! This man who had all his life trusted nobody, who had placed his own judgment above that of every other, took the Church which substitutes authority for individual judgment, treats kings and commanders and babes and sucklings alike! It may have been for this very reason.

If he was to make the surrender, he may have preferred to make it absolute, and where the Lees and Jacksons would have had to make it too. Nevertheless, I find a singular piquancy in the image of him who is said to have jeoparded great battles by his stiff-necked self-will becoming as a little child again, of him who had rejected the generalship of Lee submitting his soul to the guidance of a ghostly confessor.

IV

P. G. T. Beauregard

CHRONOLOGY

Born in Louisiana, May 28, 1818.
Graduated at West Point, 1838.
Second Lieutenant, July 1, 1838.
Served in Mexican War, 1846–47.
Superintendent at West Point, January 23–28, 1861.
General in Confederate Army, 1861.
Commanded at Charleston, spring of 1861.
Commanded at Battle of Bull Run, July, 1861.
Commanded in West, Battle of Shiloh, spring of 1862.
Commanded at Charleston during 1863.
Commanded south of James River, spring of 1864.
Died at New Orleans, February 20, 1893.

P. G. T. BEAUREGARD

IV

P. G. T. BEAUREGARD

WE are apt to feel that at the time of the Civil War the South was more homogeneous, more typically Anglo-Saxon than the North. Yet among the Confederate leaders we find Longstreet the Dutchman, Benjamin the Jew, and Beauregard, who was French as if from Paris.

Born in French Louisiana, Beauregard carried his French traditions and manners to West Point and through the Mexican War, in which he served with distinguished gallantry. He was a small, dark man, of French physique, justly proud of great muscular strength, compact, alert, thoroughly martial. For the most part, his face was grave and quiet, but in battle it lighted up with a splendid glory. During the war his hair grew suddenly gray. This was attributed by some to overwhelming anxiety, by others, ill-naturedly, to the scarcity of imported Parisian cosmetics.

He had too much real genius to ape any one. Yet being a Frenchman and a soldier, he could not but dream nightly and daily of Napoleon, and that overshadowing influence modeled, perhaps unconsciously, a good many of his habits and methods. "He possesses large concentrativeness and vivid perception; and having once formed his determinations, is inflexible in his purpose. In appearance and habits of life he resembles the first Napoleon, and like him eats but frugally. At supper I have frequently observed him only partake of a small portion of biscuit and a glass of water."[1] Whether Napoleonic or not, temperance, almost complete abstinence, from stimulants and tobacco marked Beauregard through life.

Chivalrous and courteous in all things, he was a devoted admirer of women. "Like many of our other distinguished soldiers, especially of his race," says Wise, "he was fond of the gentler sex, and at his best when in their company."[2] This is severe, but Wise is inclined to be satirical. Cooke's account of the general's social relations is more just. With both men and women he was polite and kindly, "wholly free from affectation and assumption." And the biographer tells a pretty story of the presentation of a bouquet from some young ladies, which the general received "stammering and blushing like a girl."[3]

Persons of a different race will perhaps consider as a Gallic trait in Beauregard his singular, simple, outspoken, ever-present vanity, not so much a high conceit of self as an instinctive desire, unrepressed and irrepressible, to occupy the centre of the stage, no matter what is going on.

Note that in Beauregard's case, as in D'Artagnan, in Dumas, for that matter in Napoleon himself, this vanity is quite compatible with genius, with real greatness, even with a certain sort of modesty; at any rate, simplicity. Beauregard is large enough at moments to get outside the blur of his own egotism: "My duty is to defend Charleston and Savannah; hence I may think them more important than they really are."[4] When he drops his rhetoric, he has words so simple as to approach grandeur. Thus, some one complained of the name Bull Run as unrefined. Beauregard said, "Let us try to make it as great a name as your South Carolina Cowpens."[5]

But, for the most part, the general takes himself, his army, his gifts, his plans, and all his doings in a very serious manner and never shows the least disposition to underrate their importance. He has French talents of speech, and even in the lavish military rhetoric which the war produced on both sides his stands out with proud preëminence. How he does luxuriate in large language to his soldiers: "Soldiers, untoward events saved the enemy from annihilation. His insolent presence still pollutes your soil, his hostile flag still flaunts before you. There can be no peace so long as these things are."[6] What pleasure he must have taken in writing the celebrated "beauty and booty" proclamation! "All rules of civilized warfare are abandoned, and they proclaim by their acts, if not on their banners, that their war-cry is, 'Beauty and booty.'"[7] What greater pleasure in the accidental publicity which distributed it both South and North! Less critical than Captain Dugald Dalgetty, he urges that weapons are indifferent. "Come with pikes and scythes, so you come." And Victor Hugo might have been glad to own the sonorous call for church bells to be melted into cannon.

Even an official report seemed a pleasant medium for bestowing phraseology on word-thirsty millions, and over the head of the staid Cooper this eager warrior speaks far out to the adoring Confederacy. "O my country! I would readily have sacrificed my life and those of all the brave men around me to save your honor and to maintain your independence from the degrading yoke which those ruthless invaders had come to impose and render perpetual." [8]

Beauregard's amiable vanity is, however, much more obvious than in the mere habit of luxuriant proclamations. It shows in little things. Pierre Gustave Toutant Beauregard! How large and high-sounding! But vulgar war-office officials quickly make it, *Peter*. Fancy! *Peter!* In a very few months G. T. Beauregard is all that is left and Peter is no more heard of.

Then there is delightful commendation of the general by the general. Bull Run was a brilliant victory, no doubt, but others might have been left to mention it. The retreat from Corinth could not have been conducted better. So the retreater assures us, and he ought to know. He will make Charleston as famous for defense as Sarragossa. The defense, when made, is unsurpassed in the world's history, and it causes in the North discouragement as black as followed the triumph of the first Manassas.

Among many fascinating passages in this connection two are perhaps especially significant. "Notwithstanding my additional experience in the command of armies and departments, I feel less confidence in myself than I did two years ago, for I know that if I succeed, I only increase the irritation of certain persons against me, and if I fail, their satisfaction and ire. Without intending to flatter myself, I feel like Samson shorn of his locks." [9] And imagine either Lee, or Jackson, or Johnston writing the following letter to a lady friend, with its delicious mixture of naïveté, self-confidence, and also genuine modesty: "I then had suddenly on the spur of the moment to change my whole plan of battle, with troops which had never yet fought and could scarcely manœuvre. My heart for a moment failed me! I felt as though all was lost, and I wished I had fallen in the battle of the 18th; but I soon rallied, and I then internally pledged my life that I would that day conquer or die. Immediately everything appeared again clear and hopeful, though the worst was yet to come." [10]

After the war Beauregard adopted a curious, ingenious, and not altogether happy method of self-laudation. He had his life written by Colonel Roman who could say things that not even his commander could say himself. The device is not, of course, new. Badeau's "Grant" comes dangerously near the same category. And the old

Chancellor Sully, three centuries ago, sat by and heard his secretary chant his master's astonishing glory to his face. But the Roman-Beauregard partnership takes incontestably the lead of all of them. In an introductory paragraph the general guarantees all his biographer's statements — except those complimentary. The exception might really have been dispensed with.

As one brief specimen of the way the method works take an extract from a letter addressed to the commander-in-chief in regard to Shiloh. "An order was sent quickly along the lines, informing the men that you should ride in front of them and that no cheering should be indulged in. You passed in front of the lines, and never was an order so reluctantly obeyed as was this order, 'No cheering, men!' which had to be repeated at every breath, and enforced by continuous gesture. General Johnston's prestige was great, but the hearts of the soldiers were with you, and your presence awakened an enthusiasm and confidence magical in its effect." [11]

Pages and pages of this sort of thing, with the vivid image of the subject of it smiling and nodding his modest approval, produce the most singular impression on the reader's nerves.

In much the same way, Beauregard's own little book on the first battle of Bull Run is written throughout in the third person, perhaps with the genuine intention of being more modest, but with the practical result of being much less so.

It is to be noted, what indeed we should expect, that this perpetual, complacent vanity was accompanied by little if any sense of humor. No man who caught glimpses, even momentarily, of himself and his achievements under the aspect of eternity could ever have regarded his achievements or himself with such smug satisfaction. Stuart was vain, too; but more in the sense of a full-blooded self-consciousness. He liked to be heard, to be seen, to make the world ring with his mellow voice. But it was a laughing voice and as ready to mock at Stuart as at any one. Beauregard, as a member of his staff writes me,[12] rarely jested with officers or soldiers. The gleam of a jest in his correspondence is also rare enough. "I have written and telegraphed on the subject until my hand is hoarse."[13] And Cooke never saw a smile upon his face from their first meeting until some months later, after the battle of Manassas, though the biographer gives other instances of laughter in the following years. Cooke's comment on the general's smile is worth recording: "His laugh was peculiar; the eyes sparkled, the firm muscles slowly moved, and the white teeth came out with a quite startling effect under the heavy black moustache."[14] The laughter of a martialist, you see, grudging and of necessity, not Stuart's perpetual, joyous bubbling all over.

In one aspect Beauregard's vanity is harmless and amusing; but it had its more serious side in that it made him jealous, sensitive, suspicious, and so contributed a large chapter to the pitiful history of recrimination and fault-finding which makes the years after the war so depressing to read about. Mrs. Chesnut's apt and passionate exclamation on the subject is suitable to many, North and South, besides Beauregard. "Another outburst from Jordan. Beauregard is not properly seconded. *Hêlas!* To think that any mortal general (even though he had sprung up in a month or so from captain of artillery to general) could be so puffed up with vanity, so blinded by any false idea of his own consequence as to write, to intimate that any man, or men, would sacrifice their country, injure themselves, ruin their families, to spite the aforesaid general."[15] No doubt, personal animosity makes men do strange things, without looking to consequences so far as Mrs. Chesnut could do in cold blood. But oh, if some of these really great, really noble, really extraordinary men could for once have dropped their vast ingenuity of self-justification and said simply, "I was wrong, I made a mistake, I am sorry!" Lee did it. And his example shines like a star in a dark night.

Meantime, we must take human nature as it is. Beauregard's was attractive, in some ways really charming; but it had its kinks and quirks and oddities.

He could not get along with Davis. Neither could many others. Estimating himself as highly as Beauregard did, it was natural that he should attribute any apparent slight or neglect on Davis's part to pique and jealousy. Possibly there may have been something of these feelings in the President's attitude. Beauregard at one time allowed himself to be talked of as a presidential candidate and made the movement rather more prominent by ostentatious modesty. It was natural that Davis should not like this. But I think his treatment of his subordinate was based chiefly on lack of confidence in the subordinate's ability, and on a feeling that the work could be done quite as well by men who were more thoroughly in sympathy with the Government.

At any rate, the relations between the two were unpleasant, with evident fault on both sides. Davis, as always where he disliked, made himself extremely disagreeable. Sometimes he patronizes, as when Beauregard complains of a rebuke from Benjamin: "Now, my dear sir, let me entreat you to dismiss this small matter from your mind. In the hostile masses before you, you have a subject more worthy of your contemplation."[16] Sometimes the president takes a sharper tone, as on the same topic: "You surely did not intend to inform me that your army or yourself are outside the limits of the law."[17] If the general proposes a plan, it is disregarded. If he asks for more men, he is told that he should do more with what he has. If he retreats, he has done it too soon, or too late, or unskillfully. If he absents himself for a little time on account of illness, his departure is taken advantage of to put another in his place.

No doubt these things were trying. But they were partly brought about by Beauregard's own desire to be prominent and they were allowed to breed a counter-spirit of animosity quite as discreditable as the president's. The subordinate said very harsh things of his superior. He speaks of the Government's policy in comparison with his own as "the passive defensive of an intellect timid of risk and not at home in war, and the active defensive reaching for success through enterprise and boldness." [18] He assumes, rightly or wrongly, a bitter jealousy on the part of the president and all connected with him. "Kemper quickly obtained for me some two hundred good wagons, to which number I had limited him so as not to arouse again the jealousy of the President's staff." [19] He does not hesitate to say, through his biographer, that the president's neglect of the general's advice had fatal consequence: "The President of the Confederacy, by thus persisting in these three lamentable errors, lost the South her independence." [20] And one little phrase, addressed to the general by a favorite staff officer, is perhaps most significant of all: "As soon as you feel rested I hope you will report for duty and orders to the War Department. I hope that you will be able to do so soon, and thus force your arch-enemy to show his hand decisively at an early day if he dare do it." [21] *Arch-enemy!* It would have been better if Grant or Lincoln had been the arch enemy and not the head of the country all were trying to save.

If Beauregard's hurt vanity had set him at odds with Davis only, there would have been less to complain of.

So many were at odds with Davis! But the circle included more than the president. To establish the record of what the general might have done, it was necessary to cast slurs upon Benjamin, — here not wholly undeserved, — upon Ewell, upon Bragg, upon A. S. Johnston, even upon Lee, who might easily have saved the Confederacy, if he would have done as Beauregard wished him to.

But the most unfortunate of all these contentions was that between Beauregard and Joseph E. Johnston about the first battle of Bull Run. There were undue susceptibilities on both sides. Obviously there was misunderstanding on both sides, which a frank, generous, straightforward spirit of self-sacrifice might easily have removed. Beauregard thought he had won the victory. Johnston thought he had won it. Johnston's tone in the controversy is unamiable and unconciliating. But Beauregard's is far more so. "General Johnston came to Manassas beset with the idea that our united force would not be able to cope with the Federal army, and that we should be beaten — a catastrophe in which he was not anxious to figure on the pages of history as the leading and responsible actor." [22]

Alas, that generous and high-minded men can be betrayed by their passions into such language as this. And Beauregard has altogether too much of it in his little book on the battle of Manassas, published — let us hope by accident — when Johnston was on his deathbed and unable to reply.

In the midst of a great deal of vague and unwarranted attribution of motive the Louisiana soldier does, indeed, make one good point, though it is something in the nature of a boomerang. If Bull Run had been a defeat, he says, does any one suppose that General Johnston would have been so eager to claim the command? We all know he would not. But, then, neither would Beauregard.

And both of them, in slapping back and forth at each other, assume that they have no personal motive, but only desire to establish the truth of history. Oh, the truth of history! How many crimes have been committed in that name! Surely the truth of history is of infinitely less importance than brotherly love. At any rate, it would be far better if history should confuse the leadership of a battle and be able to record that heroic souls lived free from petty carping and ungenerous complaint. It will, indeed, be urged that precisely the truth of history is leading me to unveil these weaknesses. But, at least, it is the truth of history, and not sore pride masking in an odious disguise.

It should, however, be said that during the actual course of the war Beauregard does not seem to have allowed himself to be greatly affected by prejudice or irritability. Later, under the influence of disappointment and criticism and flatterers, his vanity, his dreams of what might have been, grew into an obsession, and made him say things that should never have been said. But while he was actually fighting for the Confederacy, he, for the most part, bore slights and unkindnesses in a charitable and Christian spirit. Thus, he declares himself ready to serve when and where he may be required to do so: "I know not yet to what point I shall be ordered. . . . However, '*L'homme propose et Dieu dispose*'; hence, I shall go with alacrity wherever I am ordered." [23] Instead of scolding Seddon, as most generals were too prone to do, Beauregard recognized the immense difficulties. "In conclusion I can but express my thanks to the Honorable Secretary of War for his good intentions to assist us here. I feel convinced that, so far as he is concerned, we can rely upon him." [24] And again: "I can well understand the perplexities of Mr. Seddon's position." [25] While the following touch is so noble as to outweigh many bitter words and harsh judgments [italics mine]: "Why will not those in authority do promptly what should be done? *This reflection I apply also to myself.*" [26]

The truth is, the man was a genuine patriot, however his patriotism may have been mixed with earthly strain, as in all of us. To be sure, the story of his conduct during the few days of his superintendency at West Point, as General Schaff tells it, is not exactly pretty. When Southern cadets consulted him as to the proper course to pursue, the answer was: "Watch me, and when I jump, you jump. What's the use of jumping too soon?" [27] But those months were a time when decisions were difficult. The best of men, in such a crisis, need to be judged sympathetically, if not leniently. Once enlisted in the war,

Beauregard's thought was really first and foremost for his country.

Words are perhaps hardly sufficient evidence of this; yet some of his words have an energy and a genuineness which it is difficult to resist. "I have not time, if I were so disposed, to favor friends or persecute enemies. My soul and body are in this contest, which is one of life and death to a nation of which I, my family, and friends form a part. I believe and hope that my love of country is unsullied by personal considerations." [28]

Words were by no means all, however. In the general's own narrative of his first meeting with A. S. Johnston note how instinctive pleasure in taking part in a "scene" is mingled with really noble and patriotic feeling. "When General Johnston first met me at Corinth, he proposed, after our staff had retired, to turn over the command of the united forces to me; but I positively declined, on his account and that of the 'cause,' telling him that I had come to assist, but not to supersede him, and offering to give him all the assistance in my power. He then concluded to remain in command. It was one of the most affecting scenes of my life." [29]

There are other incidents about which there was no scene and no display whatever. Thus, after Bragg had been put in his commander's place, Beauregard writes to the War Department, offering to submit his plan of campaign, which he believed meant victory, for Bragg's use.[30] Again, Jordan wrote begging his chief to refuse the command of Charleston as an indignity. Yet when it was offered him, he answered: "I have no preference to express. Will go wherever ordered. Do for the best." [31] Surely it was the response of a noble and finely tempered spirit.

As regards purely military qualities Beauregard was in many ways interesting. He was a fighter, there can be no question of that; had martial instincts that were French, if nothing else was, the *furia francese*, in its native purity. How characteristic are the trifling anecdotes of his youth. When he was a boy of nine, a grown man teased him past bearing. The child seized a stick and flew at his tormentor with such stormy violence that he was obliged to retreat to a shed and remain there till higher powers released him.[32] Again, the boy was walking solemnly into church to his first communion. He heard a drum outside, forgot everything, and ran from the very altar.[33]

As a mature soldier, he had perfect calmness and control in strain and exposure. Defeat could not alter him. He took his measures and gave his orders with promptness and lucidity. When the right moment came, he could rush to lead a charge and sweep every man along with him. In critical dispatches he could drop all his rodomontade and rhetoric. Does not this one, to Van Dorn asking for arms, ring with the crystal sonority of Napoleon's? "I regret I have none; could not remove all I took, but we will take more. Come on!" [34]

As a commander, he always had a grip on his men and could make them do what he wanted. His discipline was founded on sympathy and a thorough understanding of a subordinate's position. At Drewry's Bluff he thought Whiting had failed him utterly and said so in his report, yet in such a way as to keep Whiting's affection and devotion. Those things are the test of a true leader. How simple and charmingly characteristic is the general's own account of a bit of disciplinary work: "By the by, I discharged a few days ago my mounted orderly, the famous Aaron Jones, for neglect of duty, but could not resist his appeal, which was, 'General, I enlisted purposely to be with you, and I would rather die under you than live under any other general.' I scolded him and let him off."[35] He believed that, in a volunteer army, at any rate, more was to be obtained by encouragement and inspiration than by severity. Therefore he urged promotions, honors, and rewards, so far as lay in his power, and he employed a system of himself distributing badges of bravery which made a scene no doubt as grateful to the commander as to the commanded.

Yet he could be absolutely unyielding, if circumstances required it. When a battle was imminent, a soldier begged leave to visit his dying mother. "I can grant no leave." "Only ten days, general." "I will not give you ten hours."[36] That was all there was to it. And where will you find a more terse, vigorous, and scathing accusation of a subordinate than this letter about Ripley, who, it may be remarked, was as rebellious with Lee as he was with Beauregard: "Brigadier-General Ripley is active, energetic, intelligent, ambitious, cunning, and fault-finding. He complains of every commanding officer he has served under, and has quarreled (or had difficulty) with almost every one of his immediately subordinate commanders since his promotion to his present rank in 1861. He obeys orders only so far as they suit his purpose, provided, by disobeying them, he does not incur the risk of a court martial, which, however, he does not much fear, trusting to his intelligence and ability to get clear of the consequences thereof."[37]

As to Beauregard's personal relations with officers and soldiers witnesses differ somewhat. J. E. Cooke says that he had the French habit of mingling freely with the soldiers, chatting with them, and lighting his cigar at their camp-fires.[38] Others describe his manner as distant, though courteous and kindly, and his aide, Major Cooke, writes me that the general was too reserved to have carelessly familiar intercourse with those about him. There was nothing of Stuart's light jest and cordial laughter to make the men feel that their commander was as human as themselves.

Yet Beauregard's popularity was immense. That he should be worshiped in Louisiana was natural, and who would not forgive the Louisianian's remark: "Lee? Lee? Yes, I 've heard Beauregard speak well of Lee." The universal enthusiasm that hailed the victor of Sumter and Bull Run perhaps waned a little, as the war went on; but many continued to the end to cherish the feelings of an admiring civilian who says: "The country looks hopefully—oh! how hopefully—to you in this hour of its deepest trials."[39] When Beauregard went to Charleston, Governor Pickens wrote: "I am rejoiced to see you here again, as there is no general who could have been selected to whom South Carolina could have looked with more confidence for her defense than to yourself."[40] While the testimony of a military man is equally impressive: "Floyd does understand this country and knows how to defend it. Above all, the country believes in him and desires him to be entrusted with its defense. . . . Joe Johnston or Beauregard could alone command the same confidence or more."[41]

With the soldiers everywhere there was even more devotion than with civilians. Beauregard seems to have had the magnetic quality which is hard to seize or to define, but which inspires men to do anything. Pollard quotes the strong assertion that up to the very last days the Army of Northern Virginia would have greeted Beauregard's presence among them with "shouts of joy and demonstrations of wild affection which no other living man could elicit."[42]

The staff officers were devotedly attached to their commander and preferred remaining with him to all other assignments, although the disfavor of the Government made promotion unlikely. It is worth observing that with many of the generals who were in some ways subject to criticism, — Johnston, Beauregard, Longstreet, — those who knew them best thought most of them. Fault-finding might come from outside. But the officers who lived in intimate contact with their chiefs, and should have seen all the faults there were, are usually enthusiastic in devotion and reverence. Do we need better testimony that, in spite of faults, the chiefs were men of heroic stamp and of genuine greatness?

That Beauregard was a general who studied, thought, reflected is not disputable. He read widely on the campaigns of great commanders, Napoleon especially, and the military maxims printed at the end of the little volume on Manassas must be of profit to professional men.

Indeed, it is in this field of brains, of the intellectual side of military matters, that we come across the general's most curious and most interesting characteristic — French, possibly; at any rate, to some degree — his extraordinary activity and fertility of invention and imagination. Not D'Artagnan was more ready with a sudden device or a long-laid scheme for helping a friend or outwitting an enemy. The time which others spent in drilling, or social relaxation, or kindly sleep, was consecrated by Beauregard to devising plans of all kinds worked out in minute detail with adaptation to all possible contingencies.

Naturally, this planning dealt in the main with the grand strategy of the general's own campaigns. Yet he had plenty of imagination to spare for minor matters or those not concerning him. Thus, he propounded to Fremantle at the beginning of the war a scheme for the speedy ending of it,[43] and was only too ready to impart similar schemes to the Government at any time. He was quite prepared to undertake the business of Congress, when the pressure of his own affairs was not too great: "If I can find time before the assembling of Congress again, I may submit the details of these plans for your consideration as a legislator." On the other hand, when a minor expedition is entrusted to a subordinate, the commander throws his imagination as vividly into the detail of it as if he were writing a novel: "About dark on the first calm night (the sooner the better) I would rendezvous all my boats at the mouth of the creek in rear of Cummings Point, Morris Island. Then I would await the proper time of the night, which should not be too early nor too late, in order to take advantage of the present condition of the moon; I would then coast quietly along the beach of Morris Island to a point nearest the enemy's present position, where General Ripley shall station a picket to communicate with you and show proper lights immediately after your attack to guide the return of your boats."[44] Lee would simply have picked out the right man for the job and told him to go and do it. And note that with Beauregard it is not so much a disposition to interfere in the execution of orders as a tendency to outrun in thought the desired course of an artistic conception.

But on actual strategy the man's imagination was inexhaustible. To appreciate its golden and beneficent luxuriance I must summarize briefly the lines it followed. To begin with, in Mexico, a mere captain, he is said to have devised the plan that took the city. Before Bull Run he was urgent with schemes for himself and Johnston, which Lee rejected. Then he made a plan for the battle, which Johnston rejected. Perhaps I cannot better illustrate the sparkling eagerness with which these schemes were conceived than by quoting part of a letter written to Johnston shortly before the battle. Ardor bubbles out of the man like champagne. "We will probably have, in a few days, about forty thousand men to operate with. This force would enable us to destroy the forces of Generals Scott and McDowell in my front. Then we would go back with as many men as necessary to attack and disperse General Patterson's army, before he could know positively what had become of you. We could then proceed to General McClellan's theatre of war and treat him likewise, after which we could pass over into Maryland to operate in rear of Washington. I think this whole campaign could be completed brilliantly in from fifteen to twenty-five days. Oh, that we had but one good head to conduct all our operations!"[45] Now, whose head do you think he meant?

Early in 1862 Beauregard was sent West. Immediately he proposed an elaborate design to Albert Sidney Johnston. Rejected again. All the sojourn in the West was divided between theoretical advance and practical retreat, most skillfully conducted. When Bragg was given the command, his predecessor employed his days of invalid leisure in evolving dazzling outlines of grand strategy, which, as I have said, he was generous enough to offer to the War Department. Here they are, in brief. "You ask what should be done to end this exhausting war [May, 1863]. We must take the offensive, as you suggest; not by abandoning all other points, however, but by a proper selection of the point of attack — the Yankees themselves tell us where. I see by the papers of this morning that Vallandigham is being sent into Bragg's lines. Hooker is disposed of for the next six months at least. Well, let Lee act on the defensive, and send to Bragg 30,000 men for him to take the offensive with at once; let him (or whoever is put in his place) [Beauregard?] destroy or capture (as it is done in Europe) Rosecrans' army; then march into Kentucky, raise 30,000 more men there and in Tennessee; then get into Ohio, and call upon the friends of Vallandigham to rise for his defense and support; then call upon Indiana, Illinois, and Missouri to throw off the yoke of the accursed Yankee nation; then upon the whole Northwest to join in the movement, form a Confederacy of their own, and join us by a treaty of alliance offensive and defensive. What would then become of the North East? How long would it take us to bring it back to its senses? As I have once written you, 'Battles without diplomacy will never end this war.' History is there to support my assertion." [46]

The strenuous and magnificent defense of Charleston left less leisure for brilliant meditation. Yet even during that time the general's brain was far from idle. Then, in the spring of 1864, he went to Petersburg and immediately it became obvious to him that Lee, though a good-enough fighter, knew nothing about the science of war. There was an infallible plan — Beauregard saw it at once — by which Grant could be crushed, Richmond saved, and the Confederacy established. Unfortunately Davis was jealous, and Lee — well, perhaps Lee was busy, and it all came to nothing.

Even when the last guns were firing, at the beginning of March, 1865, this indefatigable dreamer writes to Johnston proposing action by which the tables may be turned: "We could then confidently attack Sherman, expecting to destroy his army. . . . We could then attack Grant with superior forces and expect to defeat him signally." Or, by another alternative, "We could give immediate battle to Sherman, which could be done with almost certainly decisive success." [47]

And what about the value of all these plans? No quality can be of more importance to a really great commander than imagination. We all know what Napoleon's imagination was, magnificently inventive, ceaselessly working. We all know what was achieved by the imagination of Jackson. Beauregard is right in general, when, crying out against Johnston's conservatism, he exclaims: "The history of war is full of buried feasibilities that might have been brilliant realities, if it were not for this 'I dare not' waiting upon 'I would.'" [48]

Only, when a man's imagination overflows with these "feasibilities" for four years and not one of them becomes a "brilliant reality" even once, we grow a little suspicious. In spite of his own ill-health, in spite of the Government's hostility, Beauregard surely had opportunities. Yet no one of his splendid dreams of strategy during the war ever even approached fulfillment. Sumter fell into his arms. Bull Run was won by character, not by genius. At Shiloh he failed to harvest any fruits of Johnston's victory. Some believe he threw them away. At Drewry's Bluff he himself admits that — naturally through the fault of others—his full plans were not carried out. By the very irony of fortune, his greatest glory is in a defense which required no aggressive imagination at all. He listens with beatific contentment to his inspired biographer's assertion that Jackson and Beauregard were the two great strategic geniuses of the war. Alas, he would have been far less contented with the quiet characterization of his own countryman, Grasset: "An ardent heart, a fine-looking soldier, a mediocre strategist, an able engineer." [49] And Lee's gentle comment in a particular instance is equally conclusive: "General Lee spoke in terms of compliment and kindness to General Beauregard; thought the plan well conceived and might be brilliant in its results if we should meet with no disaster in the details, and if the time for its execution had arrived." [50]

Again, imagination so highly developed has its positive dangers. It distracts a man from reality. "Driveling on possibilities," writes Davis to Beauregard himself.[51] Again and again the phrase occurs to me, in spite of its unreasonable savageness. "Driveling on possibilities."

And plans so elaborately developed hamper, because they can never be exactly carried out, and the breaking of one link disorders the whole. If your plan does not work in all its complications, what are you to do? This befell Beauregard at Bull Run, as he himself admits. It befell again at Shiloh. It would have befallen elsewhere.

Also, if you are apt at imagining plans for yourself, you imagine them for your enemy. This was a weakness of Beauregard's. He would have withdrawn before Shiloh because he conceived that Grant would do what Beauregard might have done in his place. And the same thing occurred frequently.

Yet Beauregard's confidence in these schemes of his is inexhaustible and he is able to communicate it to his admirers. He does at times admit the bare possibility of accident. "There still remains, of course, the hazard of accidents in execution, and the apprehension of the enemy's movements upsetting your own." [52] But, for the most part, his plans are absolutely certain of success; they cannot fail, if adopted, to shatter the enemy and free the Confederacy forever and forever. If Lee will do as he says, in the spring of 1864, he will stake his professional reputation that Grant will be crushed and Richmond delivered. Apparently there are to-day people who think that because he was confident, therefore he was right.

In short, even during the war, this "driveling on possibilities" approached a mania. But after the war the results of it were, indeed, deplorable. For the man was by nature kindly, self-sacrificing, patriotic. But his dreams had become realities to him to such an extent that those who had followed their own judgment instead of his grew to seem public enemies, traitors, who had sacrificed a great cause to a personal spite.

A careful study of many of these great soldiers—Johnston, Longstreet, Beauregard, and Northern generals also—leads one to feel that much of the pitiable *post-bellum* discussion, quarreling, and controversy was simply an outlet for nervous wear and tear, a brooding over what might have been—coming to seem what ought to have been—as a consolation for defeat, humiliation, and failure. Beauregard's case is the most curious of these. He lived in an atmosphere of dreams unrealized, of marvelous things that General Beauregard would have done, if only the thoughtless world would have stood by admiring and watched him do them. It was, after a fashion, a useful anodyne for hopes ruined and a great cause lost. Yet it seems to me that I should prefer the laureled grave of Stuart or the last heroic sacrifice of Sidney Johnston.

V

Judah P. Benjamin

CHRONOLOGY

Born in St. Thomas, West Indies, August 6, 1811.
Entered Yale College, 1825.
Admitted to Louisiana Bar, December 16, 1832.
Married Natalie St. Martin, 1832.
United States Senate, 1852.
Bade farewell to Senate, February 4, 1861.
Attorney-General of Confederacy, February, 1861.
Secretary of War, September, 1861.
Secretary of State, March, 1862.
Admitted to bar in England, June, 1866.
Publication of *Benjamin on Sales*, 1868.
Became Queen's Counsel, 1872.
Retired, 1883.
Died in Paris, May 6, 1884.

JUDAH P. BENJAMIN

V

JUDAH P. BENJAMIN

BENJAMIN was a Jew. He was born a British subject. He made a brilliant reputation at the Louisiana Bar and was offered a seat in the Supreme Court of the United States.[1] He became United States Senator. When his State seceded, he went with it, and filled three cabinet positions under the Confederacy. He fell with the immense collapse of that dream fabric. Then, at the age of fifty-four, he set himself to build up a new fortune and a new glory; and he died one of the most successful and respected barristers in London. Such a career seems to offer piquant matter for portraiture. Let us see if it does.

Characteristic of the man at the very threshold is his attitude about such portraiture. He will not have it, if he can help it, will not aid in it, destroys all letters and papers that may contribute to it. "I have never kept a diary, or retained a copy of a letter written by me. . . . I have read so many American biographies which reflected only the passions and prejudices of their writers, that I do not want to leave behind me letters and documents to be used in such a work about myself."[2] And he is said to have quoted early advice given him to the effect that the secret of human happiness was the destruction of writing.[3] On this principle he acted and by so doing certainly made my task more difficult. Indeed, it would have been impossible, except for the researches of Professor Pierce Butler, whose excellent biography must form the basis of all future writing about the Jewish lawyer and statesman.

But if Benjamin's view of biography and its materials is characteristic in its secretiveness, it is also characteristic in its limitation and inadequacy. I take him to have been an honest man. Now an honest man has nothing to gain by destroying records. Talleyrand spent hours of his retirement in burning paper after paper. John Quincy Adams spent hours of both active life and retirement in noting every detail of his existence for posterity. Has he not gained by it? Is there a line of his that does not emphasize his honesty, his dignity, his human worth? Do we not love Pepys far better for his minute confessions, even if he loses a little of his bewigged respectability? No, Benjamin's endeavors to conceal himself remind me a good deal of the ostrich which rests satisfied when it has left perfectly obvious the least intelligent part of it.

The truth is, destruction of records hampers only the honest investigator. The partisan and the scandal-monger remain wholly indifferent. Professor Butler's earnest efforts have accomplished everything possible, in the scarcity of materials, to clear the subject of his biography; but Benjamin's popular reputation will probably remain what it was at the end of the war. That is, both North and South will regard him with dislike approaching to contempt. "The ability of Benjamin was undoubted," says Mr. Rhodes, expressing the mildest Northern view; "but he was by many considered untrustworthy."[4] And the same authority sees nothing in the secretary's career incompatible with complicity in the raid on St. Albans and the attempted burning of New York. A few Southern amenities may also be cited. "The oleaginous Mr. Benjamin," Wise calls him; "his keg-like form and over-deferential manner suggestive of a prosperous shop-keeper."[5] "The hated Jew," says Dodd, "whom the President had retained at his council table, despite the protests of the Southern people and press."[6] And Foote sums him up choicely as "Judas Iscariot Benjamin."[7]

It is our affair, from the mass of anecdote and recollection and especially from such scanty evidence as the gentleman himself could not avoid leaving us, to find out how far this attitude is justified.

To begin, then, with Benjamin's professional life; for he was first and last a lawyer, only by avocation a statesman. And to-day he is probably best, certainly most favorably, known as the author of the exhaustive work entitled "Benjamin on Sales." It is universally recognized that as a pleader in court he had few superiors. His power of direct, lucid statement was admirable, and no one knew better how to present every remote possibility of argument on either side of a case.[8] Even his admirers confess that he sometimes imposed on himself in this way. His enemies maintain that he was not imposed on at all, but argued for the side that paid him, with serene indifference to the right and wrong of it.[9] And they conclude that in politics he was equally indifferent. They forget, however, that the lawyer's second nature does not always drive out the first. Cicero pleaded for many a client whom he despised. Nevertheless, he was a passionate lover of Rome.

As to Benjamin's oratory opinions differ. In England more stress was laid on his matter than on his manner. But in America friends and enemies alike seem to agree that he had unusual gifts. On this point mere printed speeches are not sufficient for a judgment. They lack the gesture, the expression, the fire, cunningly simulated or real. But, so far as such printed testimony goes, I fail to find the basis for the extravagant praise of Benjamin's biographers. His eloquence is neither better nor worse than that of a dozen of his contemporaries, a clever knack of turning large phrases on subjects that breed rhetoric in the very naming of them. His farewell speech in the Senate is lofty and impressive. Who could have failed to be so on such an occasion? He can pass a noble compliment like that to Judge Taney: "He will leave behind him in the scanty heritage that shall be left for his family the noblest evidence that he died, as he had lived, a being honorable to the earth from which he sprang and worthy of the heaven to which he aspired."[10] And a few minutes later he can fall into screaming melodrama: "Accursed, thrice accursed is that fell spirit of party which desecrates the noblest sentiments of the human heart, and which, in the accomplishment of its unholy purposes, hesitates at no violence of assault on all which is held sacred by the wise and good. . . . Mr. President, in olden times a viper gnawed a file." [11]

In both the graces and the defects of Benjamin's oratory it is interesting to note the riches of a well-stored mind. He was a reader all his life, a lover of Shakespeare and the great poets, quoted them and filled his thoughts with them; and this, too, although he was self-educated and had to fight hard for book hours, perhaps all the sweeter when thus purchased.

The strongest feature of Benjamin's speaking is a singular frankness and directness. Now and then he comes out with an abrupt sentence that must have struck the Senate like cold water. "I did not think I could be provoked to say another word on this subject, of which I am heartily sick." [12] "If the object [of a certain bill] is to provide for friends and dependents, let us say so openly." [13] "For you cannot say two words on this floor on any subject whatever that Kansas is not thrust into your ears." [14]

If the test of professional ability is success, Benjamin has been surpassed by few. His income, for America of the fifties, was very large, and when, an old man, he rebuilt his fortunes in London, it climbed again from nothing to seventy or eighty thousand dollars a year. I can find no evidence whatever that these earnings were based upon improper or dubious practice. Just as Professor Butler has succeeded in showing that the stories about the brief sojourn at Yale were purely scandalous, so, I think he has made it clear that Benjamin's connection with various financial schemes before the war, while perhaps indiscreet, was in no way dishonest. And certainly his professional standing in Louisiana was totally different from that of a man like Benjamin F. Butler in Massachusetts.

Moreover, no one can read the universal testimony to his position at the English Bar without believing him to have been a high-minded gentleman. Blaine's contention that the English admired Benjamin because they hated the North must indeed be allowed some weight at the beginning of his career. But no man could have gained increasingly for fifteen years the esteem and personal affection of the first lawyers in London, if he had not deserved it. "The success of Benjamin at the English Bar is without parallel in professional annals," says a good authority,[15] and attributes the fact that it excited no jealousy to "the simplicity of his manners, his entire freedom from assumption, and his kindness of heart."[16] Lord Coleridge called him "the common honor of both Bars, of England and of America";[17] and Sir Henry James, speaking at the farewell dinner given Benjamin on his retirement, says: "The honor of the English Bar was as much cherished and represented by him as by any man who has ever adorned it, and we all feel that if our profession has afforded him hospitality, he has repaid it, amply repaid it, not only by the reputation which his learning has brought to us, but by that which is far more important, the honor his conduct has gained for us." [18] Few men can show a higher testimonial to character than that.

Now let us turn to the political aspects of this varied career. The Senate reports in the "Congressional Globe" during the later fifties show how constant and how many-sided was Benjamin's activity. What has struck me, especially in some of the large semi-private interests that he espoused, is that he failed. He should not have failed. He may have been a great lawyer. To be a great man, he failed too often.

On public questions he invariably took the extreme Southern view; but it is characteristic that he did this without exciting animosity. No senator seems to have been more popular on both sides of the house, and his adversaries regarded him with respect, sometimes even with affection.

When the Confederate Government was organized, Benjamin was first made attorney-general. From this position he quickly passed to that of secretary of war. Here again he was a failure. He had no special knowledge, and this made him obnoxious to soldiers. Even his extraordinary quickness and business instinct were hardly equal to learning a new profession in the complicated conditions then prevailing. Charges of laxity and of corruption amounting to treason are brought against him, I think wholly without foundation. But he struck one rock after another and was finally wrecked by the unfortunate affair of Roanoke Island. Wise charged that the secretary ordered him to remain in an impossible position, refused him powder, and so led up to the disaster. Benjamin remained silent at the time, but afterwards explained that there was no powder, and that he willingly submitted to public censure rather than reveal the deficiency. This is assuredly to his credit. Congress censured him, however, and a resolution was offered, though tabled, "that it is the deliberate judgment of this House that the Hon. Judah P. Benjamin, as secretary of war, has not the confidence of the people of the Confederate States, nor of the Army, to such an extent as to meet the exigencies of the present crisis." [19]

Davis, thereupon, to show his confidence in his favorite, transferred him to the still higher post of secretary of state. It is said that Benjamin here served his chief in innumerable ways, drafting public documents, suggesting and advising on lines quite outside the technical limits of his office. The best known of these activities are in regard to the Hampton Roads Peace Commission and the attempt to make military use of the negroes and even to emancipate them for the sake of securing foreign support. In these attempts also Benjamin failed, or what slight measure of success there was went to the credit of others.

In the State Department proper he devoted all his energy for three years to securing foreign recognition — and failed again, where perhaps no one could have succeeded. A side issue in this departmental work has thrown more serious discredit on his reputation than any other charge that can be plausibly brought against him. Acting generally under Davis, he authorized and instructed the agents in Canada who were to attack the Northern States from the rear, that is, who not only fostered discontent and insurrection, but carried out the raid on St. Albans and attempted to burn New York with its thousands of innocent women and children. There is no evidence that Benjamin planned these undertakings. But we know that he received and read his agent's, Thompson's, account of them, and we do not know that he ever expressed any disapproval. Looked at now, in cold blood, they seem without excuse. We can only remind ourselves that passion has strange pleas, and that the whole South believed the North to be capable of worse deeds than any Thompson contemplated, nay, to have done them.

In this matter of the Canadian attempts Mr. Rhodes is very careful to distinguish Davis from his secretary and to express disbelief that the president could have been capable of such infamy, while implying that his subordinate might perfectly well have been so. I hardly think Benjamin's character deserves this sharp distinction. In any case, I have been most interested to find one of the very greatest of Virginia's statesmen and philanthropists explicitly advocating just such an attempt as that made to fire New York. "She [England]," writes Thomas Jefferson in 1812, "may burn New York, indeed, by her ships and Congreve rockets, in which case we must burn the city of London by hired incendiaries, of which her starving manufacturers will furnish abundance." [20]

In all these manifold schemes of Benjamin I look in vain, so far as the records go, for evidence of large, far-reaching, creative statesmanship. Again and again I ask myself what Cavour would have thought, have devised, have done in that position. For it is sufficiently manifest that a man of Cavour's type was what the Confederacy needed—and did not get. Yet would any man of high statesmanlike genius and close practical grasp have attempted to solve the impossible problem of reconciling the loose theory of state rights and the fiercely centralized government required to cope with the overwhelming force of the United States?

At any rate, Benjamin was no Cavour. His biographer does indeed point out that he had something of the dreamy side of his race, as shown in the unpractical conceptions of his early business effort. But dreamers do not make statesmen, usually quite the contrary. And Benjamin's practical statesmanship was, I think, rather of the makeshift order. It is very rare that in his diplomatic correspondence we find any reference to the cloudy future of the Confederacy, and the only instance in which he amplified on the subject, predicting that "North America is on the eve of being divided into a number of independent Governments, with rival, if not conflicting, interests," [21] is distinctly in the nature of a dream.

A dream also, the dim vision of a Jewish prophet, and clung to with a Jewish prophet's obstinacy, is his ever-recurring hope of European recognition, which should free the South and end the war. Here, again, it seems to me that Cavour would either have put the thing through or early seen its hopelessness. Even Benjamin's own foreign agent declares that failure should have been foreseen and accepted at a very early stage. [22] But Benjamin would not foresee, would not accept. Up to the very last months he believed that recognition must come, that Europe could not be so foolish as to neglect its own interest. And long after the war he told Russell, in London, that "though I have done with politics, thank God! I consider your government made a frightful mistake which you may have occasion to rue hereafter." [23]

Of a similar character, though even more general in the South and less persistent in Benjamin, was the delusion as to the supremacy of cotton.

If, then, Benjamin was not a statesman of a high order or of large and commanding ideas, how was it that he so long held such a prominent place in the Confederate Government? The answer is simple and two good reasons furnish more than the solution of the difficulty.

In the first place, Benjamin was an admirable man of

business, and those who have had the privilege of meeting a good many business men know how rare an admirable man of business is. He was a worker. While he loved ease and luxury, he was capable of enormous labor, did not shirk long hours or cumbrous documents, went right at a job and finished it. He would remain at his desk, when necessary, from eight o'clock one morning till one or two the next. He would work Sundays and holidays. And he did this without fatigue, complaint, or murmur, always cheerfully and easily, and as if he enjoyed it.

Mere industry does not go far, however, or not the whole way. Benjamin had what is worth far more than industry, system. When he went into the War Office, he was no soldier and could not please soldiers. But he was an administrator, and if he had stuck to that phase, I imagine he would have been useful. He began right away to bring order out of hopeless confusion, organized, systematized, docketed. "Having had charge of the War Department but a few days," he writes, "my first effort was to master our situation, to understand thoroughly what we had and in what our deficiencies consisted, but I have been completely foiled at all points by the absence of systematic returns."[24] And again, "Without them [returns] we cannot, of course, administer the service; can make no calculations, no combinations, can provide in advance with no approximation to certainty, and cannot know how to supply deficiencies."[25] A systematizer of this order was a useful creature in Richmond during those four years.

But another quality, even more valuable than business habits, sustained Benjamin in his office: he knew how to handle men. He watched character perpetually, studied the motives of others, their wants, their weaknesses, knew how to adapt himself to them. "No shade of emotion in another escaped Mr. Benjamin's penetration," writes the keen-sighted Mrs. Davis, whose warm admiration of her husband's adviser is one of his best credentials. "He seemed to have a kind of electric sympathy with every mind with which he came into contact, and very often surprised his friends by alluding to something they had not expressed nor desired him to interpret." [26]

How useful this quality was in dealing with Davis can only be appreciated by those who have studied carefully the peculiarities of that noble but complicated personage. A patriotic idealist in purpose, he wished to save his country, but he wished to save it in his own way. From his subordinates he desired labor, quick comprehension, a hearty support of all his plans and methods. Advice he did not desire, and those who gave it had to give it with tact and extreme delicacy. Here was exactly the chance for Judah P. Benjamin. Advice he did not especially care to give, but no man could divine Davis's wishes with finer sympathy, no man could carry out his plans with more intelligent coöperation and at the same time with heartier self-effacement. The patient skill with which the result was accomplished is well indicated by Mrs. Davis when she says: "It was to me a curious spectacle; the steady approximation to a thorough friendliness of the President and his war minister. It was a very gradual *rapprochement*, but all the more solid for that reason."[27] J. B. Jones, who disliked and distrusted his Jewish superior, analyzes the relation between president and secretary with much less approval. "Mr. B. unquestionably will have great influence with the President, for he has studied his character most carefully. He will be familiar not only with his 'likes,' but especially with his 'dislikes.'"[28] And when the diarist hears that the president is about to be baptized and confirmed, he takes comfort because "it may place a gulf between him and the descendant of those who crucified the Saviour."[29] If we accept Benjamin's own words, however, and I think we may, we shall conclude that his devotion to Davis was founded, at any rate in part, on a sincere esteem and admiration. Writing to the London "Times," after the war, he says: "For the four years during which I have been one of his most privileged advisers, the recipient of his confidence and sharer to the best of my ability in his labors and responsibilities, I have learned to know him better perhaps than he is known by any other living man. Neither in private conversation nor in Cabinet council have I ever heard him utter one unworthy thought, one ungenerous sentiment."[30]

No one, then, could long retain Davis's confidence without an abundant supply of tact and sympathy. Probably the two men who made most use of these qualities in their dealings with the President were Lee and Benjamin. But a most instructive difference strikes us here. Lee's tact sprang spontaneously from natural human kindness. He treated his inferiors exactly as he treated his sole superior and was as courteous and sympathetic to the humblest soldier as to the president of the Confederacy. With Benjamin it is wholly otherwise. He was at the War Office for just six months. In that time I will not say he quarreled with everybody under him, but he alienated everybody, and quarreled with so many that his stay there is but a record of harsh words and recrimination. One brief telegram to McCulloch will abundantly illustrate the cause of this state of things: "I cannot understand why you withdrew your troops instead of pursuing the enemy when his leaders were quarreling and his army separated into parts under different commanders. Send an explanation." [31]

This sort of dispatch, from a lawyer who had never seen a skirmish to generals of old experience and solid training, was not likely to breed good feeling, much less to restore it. It did not. Benjamin had trouble with Wise, trouble with Beauregard, trouble repeatedly with J. E. Johnston, and drove Jackson to a resignation which, if it had been accepted, might have changed the course of the war. This is surely a pretty record for six months.

And observe that in many instances the secretary appears to have been right and wise. This only emphasizes the misfortune of his getting into such difficulty. The suavity, the graceful tact, which served him so well with Davis, seem to have deserted him in dealing with those over whom he had control. Or rather, it is said that the very suavity produced double exasperation when it was used merely to glove an arbitrary display of authority. "When I do not agree with Benjamin, I will not let him talk to me," said Slidell, who was his friend; "he irritates me so by his debonnair ways." [32]

And now, with the qualities of Benjamin's public career clearly suggested, let us turn for a moment to his private life and see how that helps to illuminate the other.

To begin with his social interests, involving, as they do, what we have just been discussing. As with Davis, so with all equals, in daily intercourse his manner was full of courtesy, some even say, charm. To be sure, Wise calls him "oleaginous"; but Alfriend, who knew him well, goes to the other extreme: "I have never known a man socially more fascinating than Judah P. Benjamin. He was in his attainments a veritable Admiral [*sic*] Crichton, and I think, excepting G. P. R. James, the most brilliant, fascinating conversationalist I have ever known." [33] One is tempted to blend these two views in Charles Lamb's pleasant characterization of the singer Braham: "He was a rare composition of the Jew, the gentleman, and the angel; yet all these elements mixed up so kindly in him, that you could not tell which preponderated." [34]

Less prejudiced judges than those above quoted render a verdict which is still decidedly favorable. In his earlier career in the United States Senate Benjamin is said to have been generally popular, and to have endeavored always to foster social relations; and Sumner, his bitterest opponent, bore testimony to his kindness of manner and conformity to the proprieties of debate.[35] W. H. Russell speaks of his "brisk, lively, agreeable manner" and calls him "the most open, frank, and cordial of the Confederates whom I have yet met." [36] Thomas F. Bayard, surely a connoisseur, says that Benjamin's "manner was most attractive—gentle, sympathetic, and absolutely unaffected," and that "he certainly shone in social life as a refined, genial, charming companion." [37] And the testimony of his English friends is equally decided. "A charming companion," writes Sir Frederick Pollock, "an accomplished brother lawyer, and a true friend, one I could not easily replace." [38]

In many of these social sketches of Benjamin there is a curious insistence on his smile, which seems to have been as perennial as Malvolio's, if a little more natural. "The perpetual smile that basked on his Jewish lips," [39] says the acrid Pollard. And Jones, in his "Diary," recurs to it almost as a third-rate playwright does to a character tag, so much so that on one occasion he notes Mr. Benjamin's appearance without his smile as of inauspicious omen. "Upon his lip there seems to bask an eternal smile; but if it be studied, it is not a smile — yet it bears no unpleasant aspect." [40]

The implication in some descriptions that the smile and the courtesy were only on the surface is, I think, clearly unjust. Benjamin was not, perhaps, a philanthropist; but there is record of many kindly deeds of his, none the less genuine for not being trumpeted. He once lost sixty thousand dollars by indorsing a note for a friend.[41] Although never especially enthusiastic for his religion, he was ready to give help to a fellow Hebrew who wanted it, and it is said that old and needy Confederates in London did not apply to him for aid in vain.

Also, the smile was for himself, as well as for others. That is, it represented an attitude towards life. Through many ups and downs and odd turns and freaks of Fortune, Benjamin was never discouraged, never depressed. I do not think this meant in him any great strain of heroic fortitude. The smile shows that. It was an easy-going egotism, which neither touched nor was touched deeply, a serene, healthy well-being, which let the blows of adversity strike and glance off, which turned trifles into great pleasures and very great evils into trifles. When work was needed, he worked with all the strength that was in him. When he failed and fell, instead of being crushed, he jumped up, smiled, brushed off his clothes, and worked again. Where will you find a finer instance of recovery after utter disaster than this man's rise in old age from nothing to fortune in a new country and an untried sphere? Even in his formal and official correspondence you catch little glimpses of the easy, devil-may-care fashion in which he took responsibilities that would have crushed others. Thus, he ends a long letter of difficulty and trouble to his predecessor in the War Office: "What a bed of roses you have bequeathed me!"[42] Or he writes to Sidney Johnston — of all men: "In Mississippi and Tennessee your unlucky offer to receive unarmed men for twelve months has played the deuce with our camps."[43] Fancy Lee or Davis writing that!

For a man armed with a smile of this kind religion is a superfluity and it appears that Benjamin had none. He practically dropped his own and never had the interest to pick up any other. He did, indeed, — unless he has been confused with Disraeli, — tell a sneerer at Judaism that his ancestors were receiving the law from Deity on Mount Sinai when the sneerer's were herding swine in the forests of Saxony;[44] but this was to make a point for the gallery, just as his burial in Paris with Catholic rites was *pour plaire aux dames*, unless it was wholly the ladies' doing. His religion would not have been worth alluding to but for the delightful anecdote of Daniel Webster's assuring him and Maury, the scientist, that they were all three Unitarians together. Benjamin denied this, and invited Webster to dine with him to prove it. They dined and argued, but Benjamin would not be convinced, though he did not know enough about the Bible to hold his ground.[45] Oh, to have been present at that dinner! What conversation — and what wine and cigars!

As this discussion may imply, and as abundant evidence proves, Benjamin, for all his smiles and all his optimism, was neither cold nor always perfect in command of his temper. "He was like fire and tow," says Mrs. Davis, perhaps exaggerating in view of an incident to be shortly mentioned, "and sensitive about his dignity." [46] I do not imagine this went very deep, but at any rate the Southern sun had touched the surface with a singular vivacity and petulance. Even in age and in London fogs the temper would fly out. As when, before the solemn dignity of the House of Lords, Benjamin was arguing a case and heard the Lord Chancellor mutter "Nonsense"; the barrister stopped, gathered up his papers, and abruptly departed. So high was his standing at that time that the Chancellor felt obliged to make things right by an apology.

Even more entertaining is the earlier spat between Benjamin and Davis. Senatorial tempers were high-strained in Washington in the fifties and men sometimes fell foul of friends as well as foes. The slap-dash, boyish interchange of curt phrases, even as staled in the cold storage of the "Congressional Globe," must have rejoiced Seward and Sumner. Its straight-from-the-shoulder quality, coming from such reverend sages, recalls the immortal dialogue which Dr. Johnson reports as occurring between himself and Adam Smith. "What did Smith say, sir?" *Dr. Johnson:* "He said I was a liar." "And what did you say?" "I said he was a" — never mind what. Benjamin's language was more senatorial, but not too much so. "The Senator is mistaken and has no right to state any such thing. His manner is not agreeable at all." *Davis:* "If the Senator happens to find it disagreeable, I hope he will keep it to himself." *Benjamin:* "When directed to me, I will not keep it to myself, I will repel it *instanter*." *Davis:* "You have got it, sir." [47]

And pistols for two, of course. But kind friends prevented the future Secretary of State from shooting at his President. More seriously instructive and profitable is the contrast between the explanations offered by the two men in the Senate. Davis's is in his best vein, nobly characteristic, as thoroughly frank as it is manly and dignified. Benjamin's is well enough, but cautious, as if he were afraid of his position and anxious not to say a word too much.[48]

The keen sensibility, whether superficial or not, which appears in these incidents, characterized Benjamin in other ways besides temper. He liked excitement. It was the excitement of public contest that made for him, I think, the charm of his profession. After the war he was offered an excellent opening in Parisian finance, but he preferred to fight his way up in the English courts. And there is a remarkable sentence in his speech at the farewell dinner, when he mentions having been ordered to avoid the excitement of active practice: "I need hardly tell an audience like this that to tell me or any person of a nature like mine to abstain from all possible excitement is to tell him to cease the active exercise of the profession; for without the ardor of forensic contest what is the profession worth?" [49]

He liked excitement in the form of games also; liked billiards and whist. Russell even records as Washington scandal that he lost the major part of his very large income at cards.[50] His biographer denies this, but in rather mild fashion, asserting that he was "not a rabid gambler," [51] and Benjamin himself seems rather less concerned at the accusation than at Russell's ingratitude in making it.[52]

On graver points of morals I find no trace of any charge against Benjamin whatever. But, in spite of his immense capacity for work, he was generally known as a lover of ease and good living. This, assuredly no vice in itself, came almost to appear like one in the last hungry months of the Confederacy. Very characteristic of the man, more so, perhaps, than she meant it, is Mrs. Davis's little sketch: "He used to say that with bread made of Crenshaw's flour, spread with paste made from English walnuts from an immense tree in our grounds, and a glass of McHenry sherry, of which we had a scanty store, 'a man's patriotism became rampant.'" [53] Alfriend, also, gives us a significant touch: "Mr. Benjamin loved a good dinner, a good glass of wine, and revelled in the delights of fine Havana cigars. Indeed, even when Richmond was in a state of siege he was never without them." [54] Right beside this I do not think it cruel to put his own letter to soldiers who were starving on half rations and to whom a crust was luxury [italics mine]. "Hardship and exposure will undoubtedly be suffered by our troops, but this is war, and *we* cannot hope to conquer our liberties or secure our rights by ease and comfort." [55]

On this very point of good eating, however, we must at the same time note the man's kindliness and gentle heart. What he liked he thought others would like and was glad to get it for them, if he could. Thus Mrs. Davis records that at a very good dinner Benjamin seemed ill at ease and confessed that he was thinking how much his brother-in-law, left alone at home, would enjoy some of the delicacies; whereupon he received a share to take with him and went away contented.

Undeniably, in the matter of relatives Benjamin appears at his best, and his affection and thought for them — thoroughly racial attributes — are pleasant to read about. With his French Catholic wife he did not indeed wholly agree. There was no formal separation or quarrel. But for the greater part of the time, she lived in Paris and her husband in America. Benjamin's biographer attributes this largely to faults of her disposition. Perhaps he is right. But I would give a good deal for Mrs. Benjamin's view of her husband. So far as I know, only one recorded sentence of her writing twinkles in the memory of men. But that one is a jewel. It paints the woman; it paints the Southern and Creole class, and much that is Northern and human also; it suggests wide possibilities of domestic infelicity; and it shows charmingly that Benjamin had found the superlative in an art in which he could furnish a good comparative himself. He writes to his wife urging economy, and she writes back: "Do not speak to me of economy; it is so fatiguing."[56] Miss Austen might have invented the phrase, she could not have bettered it.

But Benjamin afforded rather a singularity in matrimonial affairs by apparently caring much more about his wife's relatives than he did about her. And to those connected with him by blood, his daughter, sisters, nieces, and nephews, he was deeply and devotedly attached. His few extant letters to them form very attractive reading and show a man as lovable as he was clever. They are full of a light and graceful playfulness, gossiping of trivial things in just the way that love appreciates.

Yet how infinite are the shades and diversities of character! For all this graceful playfulness in his private letters, for all his reported wit in conversation, I do not find that Benjamin had much of that complicated emotion which we call humor. Is it that he does not view life from a large enough angle? In this regard how striking is the difference between him and Lincoln! When the Lord

Chancellor said, "Nonsense," Lincoln would not have stalked out. He would have told a story and the Lord Chancellor would have wished to do the stalking. When Davis said a sharp thing, Lincoln would have said a gentle one, and got the best of it. Read in the "Congressional Globe" the debate on secession and see how Baker of Oregon simply demolishes Benjamin, not by argument, but by pure Lincolnian quizzing, which Benjamin cannot meet because he cannot understand it.

Benjamin smiled perpetually, Lincoln, I imagine, rarely. But how much more Lincoln's smile meant! Benjamin's cheerful countenance gave no weight at all to the tragedies of existence.

And now, I think, we are in a position to consider what was Benjamin's real attitude towards the Confederacy. First, was he an able, selfish, scheming, unscrupulous adventurer, who played the game simply for his own personal ambition and aggrandizement, a sort of Talleyrand? This may be excluded at once. It would be difficult to imagine Talleyrand writing confidentially, as Benjamin did in regard to the release of Brownlow: "Better that any, the most dangerous enemy, however criminal, should escape, than that the honor and good faith of the Government should be impugned or even suspected."[57] If there were no other evidence that the secretary did not belong to the type above indicated, little more would be needed than his own clearly genuine comparison of Gladstone and Disraeli, all in favor of the former, who, indeed, is said to have been his idol.[58] Gilmore's brief description is vital on this point: "There is something, after all, in moral power. Mr. Benjamin does not possess it, nor is he a great man. He has a keen, shrewd, ready intellect, but not the stamina to originate, or even to execute, any great good or great wickedness." [59]

But again, some who recognize Benjamin's honesty assert that he took up the Confederate cause as a mere law case, utterly indifferent to the wrong or right, or to any personal issue, giving it his best service as long as he could, then turning cheerfully to something else. Here also I think there is error. The man's whole heart was in the work and he felt for it as deeply as he could feel. Passage after passage in his public and private writings shows indisputably the partisan hatred and the devoted enthusiasm of the loyal citizen. "I entertain no doubt whatever that hundreds of thousands of people at the North would be frantic with fiendish delight if informed of the universal massacre of the Southern people, including women and children, in one night." [60] "No people have poured out their blood more freely in defence of their liberty and independence, nor have endured sacrifices with greater cheerfulness than have the men and women of these Confederate States. They accepted the issue which was forced on them by an arrogant and domineering race, vengeful, grasping, and ambitious. They have asked nothing, fought for nothing, but for the right of self-government, for independence."[61] "How it makes one's breast swell with emotion to witness the calm, heroic, unconquerable determination to be free that fills the breast of all ages, sexes, and conditions."[62]

Like many other Southerners, Benjamin rather melodramatically declared that he would never be taken alive. He never was. Like many others, he declared that he would never, never, submit. Lee, Johnston, Davis, Stephens submitted; Benjamin never. His Jewish obstinacy would not be overcome.

No, it is utterly unjust to deny that his patriotism was genuine or that he gave his very best sincerely and in his way unselfishly to what he felt to be his country. Only with him nothing went deep. When the struggle was over, it was over. Some measure of his sunny cheerfulness must be credited to self-control. Most of it was temperament. Lee, too, made no complaint; but the tragedy of his people was written perpetually on his face. Benjamin's face would not take impressions of that nature. Not one regret for a lost cause or a vanished country is to be found in his few personal letters that have come down to us. "I am contented and cheerful under all reverses," he writes. And, though this particular phrase was used to cheer his anxious family, it is intimately characteristic of his permanent attitude.

The truth is, he was a man placed in a position too large for him, and he rattles about in it. The crises of history always exhibit such misfits, in lamentable number. But with Benjamin the impression prevails that he was of remarkable ability, an adventurer of genius but of little character. This view was strong upon me when I began to study him. Now I am forced to the opposite conclusion, that his character was respectable, if not unexceptionable, but his ability mediocre. Davis, while meaning only to be complimentary, damned the ability with the faintest possible praise, to perfection: "Mr. Benjamin, of Louisiana, had a very high reputation as a lawyer, and my acquaintance with him in the Senate had impressed me with the lucidity of his intellect, his systematic habits, and capacity for labor." [63]

In short, he was an average, honorable, and, in politics, rather ineffectual gentleman. Perhaps he would have preferred a different verdict. If so, he should not have destroyed those papers.

VI

Alexander H. Stephens

CHRONOLOGY

Born in Wilkes County, Georgia, February 11, 1812.
Franklin College, Athens, Georgia, 1828.
Country school teacher, 1833.
Admitted to the bar, 1834.
Member of State Legislature, 1836.
Member of Congress, 1843.
Retired, 1859.
Vice-President of Confederacy, February 9, 1861.
Took part in Hampton Roads Conference, February 3, 1865.
Arrested, May 11, 1865.
Imprisoned in Fort Warren, Boston Harbor, till October 12, 1865.
Member of Congress, 1873.
Governor of Georgia, 1882.
Died March 4, 1883.

ALEXANDER H. STEPHENS

VI

ALEXANDER H. STEPHENS

HUMAN nature is full of contradictions, which give it much of its charm. But the character and career of Alexander H. Stephens seem to involve contradictions beyond the share of most of us.

In physique he was abnormally frail, delicate, and sensitive, nervous sometimes to the point of hysteria; yet he had the spirit of a gamecock, was ready for a duel when honor required it, walked right up and struck a far bigger man who had insulted him and who nearly murdered him in consequence. Perhaps with some braggadocio, but with more truth, he said of himself: "I am afraid of nothing on earth, or above the earth, or under the earth, but to do wrong." [1]

He was studious by nature, longed for quiet, and solitude, and meditation. Yet he lived in a perpetual whirl, either drawn by a thousand activities abroad, or beset by a throng of visitors at home. "I supposed when I got this room I should be by myself, . . . but I do nothing the livelong day but jabber with each transient interloper who may be disposed to give me a call." [2]

He was probably one of the most logical, clear-headed, determined defenders of slavery and of the thorough subordination of black to white. Yet few men have been more sensitively humane, more tenderly sympathetic with suffering in either white or black. The negroes loved him, and on one occasion after the war three thousand freedmen gathered on his lawn and serenaded him with passionate admiration and devotion.

No man was more bitterly opposed to secession and to the war than he was. No Southerner made a harder or more nearly successful fight to prevent the withdrawal of his State. Yet when Georgia went, he not only went with her, but became the vice-president of the Confederacy. He himself puts this contrast vividly in his diary, written while a prisoner at Fort Warren, in 1865. "How strange it seems to me that I should thus suffer, I who did everything in my power to prevent [the war]. . . . On the fourth of September, 1848, I was near losing my life for resenting the charge of being a traitor to the South, and now I am here, a prisoner under charge, I suppose, of being a traitor to the Union. In all, I have done nothing but what I thought was right." [3]

Nor is the list of Stephens's contradictions yet summed up — not nearly. The second officer of the Confederacy and a devoted champion of its cause, he was persistently opposed to the conduct of the Government from beginning to end. He opposed Davis radically as to the finances and as to cotton, he opposed conscription, he opposed martial law, he considered that the president's whole course was dictated either by gross misjudgment or by a belief in the necessity of dictatorial power. And here we have, I think, a rather piquant attitude for a man who held the next to the highest place in a new-born nation fighting for life and death.

These considerations make the vice-president, if not the greatest, certainly the most curious and interesting, figure in the lightning-lit panorama of Confederate history.

In analyzing Stephens's career, the question of health, negatively important for most leaders of men, becomes enormously positive. From his birth in 1812 to his death in 1883, his life seems to have been a long disease, forever on the verge of terminating fatally. It may be that the rough experiences of pioneer farming in his childhood — the corn-dropping, the sheep-tending, exposure, hardship — injured him permanently, or saved him, who knows? So with the long, desperate battle for an education and a profession, in solitude and poverty. The battle may have weakened, may have toughened, perhaps both.

At any rate, we rarely hear of him, except suffering. All the descriptions of him emphasize some phase of physical weakness and inadequacy. His own account at twenty-one sets the note: "My weight is ninety-four pounds, my height sixty-seven inches, my waist twenty-seven inches in circumference, and my whole appearance that of a youth of seventeen or eighteen. When I left college, two years ago, my net weight was seventy pounds. If I continue in a proportionate increase, I shall reach one hundred pounds in about two years more."[4]

Later portrayals have sometimes an unkindly touch, as the caustic diatribe of the robust Dick Taylor, no doubt in some points slightly justified: "Like other ills, feeble health has its compensations, especially for those who unite restless vanity and ambition to a feminine desire for sympathy. It has been much the habit of Mr. Stephens to date controversial epistles from 'a sick chamber,' as do ladies in a delicate condition. A diplomat of the last century, the Chevalier d'Éon, by usurping the privileges of the opposite sex, inspired grave doubts concerning his own." [5]

But most observers rather seem impressed with the contrast between the man's physical deficiencies and his splendid spiritual strength. At the height of his congressional career in Washington (1855) a keen-sighted journalist noted that, in the stress of great occasions, "the poor, sickly, emaciated frame, which looks as if it must sink under the slightest physical exertion, at once grows instinct with a galvanic vitality which quickens every nerve with the energy of a new life, imparts to every feature a high, intellectual expression, makes the languid eyes glow like living coals, and diffuses a glow of reviving animation over the pallid countenance." [6] Even more striking is another picture taken in the same place in 1872, after war and imprisonment had done their worst. "An immense cloak, a high hat, and peering somewhere out of the middle a thin, pale, sad face. How anything so small and sick and sorrowful could get here all the way from Georgia is a wonder. If he were laid out in his coffin, he need n't look any different, only that the fire would have gone out in the burning eyes. Set as they are in the wax-white face, they seem to burn and blaze. That he is here at all to offer the counsels of moderation and patriotism proves how invincible is the soul that dwells in this sunken frame. He took the modified oath in his chair, and his friends picked him up and carried him off in it as if he were a feather." [7]

How far this fiery energy of the soul was responsible for the weary failure of the body, who shall say? But never was there man in mind and spirit more heartily and vividly and incessantly and at every point alive than Alexander H. Stephens. From childhood he fought his way in the world, fought for education, fought for success as a lawyer, fought for political distinction. He liked fighting. "I was made to figure in a storm, excited by continual collisions. Discussion and argument are my delight; and a place of life and business therefore is my proper element. . . . I long to be where I shall have an argument daily." [8]

In age and in prison the fire, indeed, might burn a little low. "Personal ambition had no part in anything I have done." [9] But in the early days the man panted to get upward, to do something, to be something. "I believe I shall never be worth anything, and the thought is death to my soul. I am too boyish, childish, unmanful, trifling, simple in my manners and address." [10] When he had become something — not enough — never enough — the record of work he did is, for an invalid, quite inexplicable; or rather, it fully explains the invalidism. "I rise and breakfast at eight; then commence with my mail. Frequently I do not get half through that before I am bored almost to death with calls on business of all sorts; then to the Committee at ten; then to the House at twelve; then to dinner at four; then calls before I leave the table till twelve at night. Then I take up and get through my unfinished reading of letters and newspapers of the morning; and then at one o'clock get to bed. I now have about one hundred letters before me unanswered." [11]

This petulance, this vivacity, this mad energy of living in a frame half dead remind one constantly of Voltaire, who, with his little, weak, and shattered body, went on for fifty years, making enemies and smashing them, puncturing social rottenness with his fierce wit, blasting others' great lies and telling petty lies of his own, sometimes pitiable, sometimes malignant, often fascinating, but always, always splendidly alive. Stephens made few enemies, told no lies, was neither pitiable nor malignant; but he was splendidly alive until the coffin-lid put out the torch that seemed to have exhausted its fuel long before.

But though Voltaire had plenty of physical ills, I find no evidence that he suffered from melancholy or mental depression. Stephens did. The jar of over-tense nerves mingles curiously with his eager bursts of ambition and aspiration: "My feelings and hopes seem ever to be vibrating between assurance and despondency. My soul is bent upon success in my profession, and when indulging in brightest anticipations, the most trivial circumstance is frequently sufficient to damp my whole ardor and drive me to despair." [12]

This tendency to depression was not merely the reaction from disappointed hopes or dreams unrealized. It was a constitutional melancholy, which, not only in youth, but even in middle life, seems to have eaten into the man's very soul. The words in which he describes it most definitely have a strange, poignant bitterness that wrings the heart: "Sometimes I have thought that of all men I was most miserable; that I was especially doomed to misfortune, to melancholy, to grief. . . . The misery, the deep agony of spirit I have suffered, no mortal knows, nor ever will. . . . The torture of body is severe; I have had my share of that. . . . But all these are slight when compared with the pangs of an offended or wounded spirit. The heart alone knoweth its own sorrow. I have borne it these many years. I have borne it all my life." [13]

To his beloved brother Linton he endeavors to describe his spiritual malady. "It is the secret of my life. I have never told it to any one." [14] But his speech, usually so lucid, is incoherent, stumbling, and obscure. It appears that his physical deficiencies wounded him, as they did

Byron; he shrank and withered under the jeers and mocking looks of those who could not see his soul. Then the stung soul rebounded and strove with every ounce of will to make the mockers love him by doing good to them in strange new ways of overwhelming potency. But the explanation is neither clear nor wholly sufficient, sounds manufactured to fit facts beyond the vision of even the explainer. All we can say is that we get dim glimpses of a spiritual hell.

What is supremely interesting about Stephens is that he neither accepts this condition of things nor submits to it. Such a wretched frame for such a fierce vitality might easily have made another Leopardi, veiling all the light of heaven in black pessimism, cursing man and nature and God with cold irony for the vile mistake of his creation. Stephens fights his ills, makes head against them, never lets himself be really prostrated by physical torture or mental agony. Worsted for the moment, he forever reëmerges, with some new refuge, some new comfort, some new device of cure.

One day he tries Burton's "Anatomy of Melancholy," finds it excellent on homœopathic principles, and recommends it to his brother, though Burton himself is inclined to advise all melancholy persons to shun his majestic folio.

More serious than such bookishness is the clear determination to overcome mental misery by effort of will. "I have in my life," he says, "been one of the most miserable beings that walked the earth. . . . Without enjoyment, without pleasure, without hope, and without sympathy with the world." [15] But the unfailing remedy, for those who will but try it, is the absolute control of thought. "Never let the mind dwell upon anything disagreeable — turn it to something else." "Great and heroic effort was necessary at first and for a long time." But "with a proper discipline of oneself in this way, ever keeping the passions in perfect subjection, contentment and happiness are attainable by all." [16] I do not read that he ever attained them, but others may by following his precepts. He fought for them, at any rate.

Stoical self-control was not his only refuge. He had one higher — God. In his youth he declined to be educated for the ministry and I do not think he was ever consistently satisfied as to speculative religion. But he seems to have had a keen and mighty sense of the divine in spiritual things and in his hours of agony he seeks solace there and finds it. He devotes a portion of every day to communion with God in prayer and gets from it comfort in his anguish, light in the valley of dark shadows, and the growth of a kindlier, sweeter temper towards his fellow-men.[17] In old age, in sickness, in solitude, in prison, he sums up thus the mighty help that God has been to him: "That the Lord is a strong hold in the day of trouble I know. But for his sustaining grace, I should have been crushed in body and soul long ere this." [18]

Nevertheless, with a temperament so introspective, brooding, and sensitive, it is doubtful whether even religious contemplation would have saved Stephens from melancholy and morbidness. It might have lifted him above the pessimism and misanthropy of Leopardi only to land him in the deeper spiritual wretchedness of Amiel. Contemplation, even divine, is not always sufficient to save such a temperament from ruining itself.

A better, surer remedy, at least a needed balance-wheel, is action, constant contact with the busy, outward, stupid hurry of the world. Stephens knew this and had the courage and the energy to force himself out of himself. He may have possessed "a charm against loneliness," as his brother writes; but he knew that in loneliness lay his danger and he kept as much as possible in the bright current of turbulent humanity, even when all his inclinations bade him fly from it. "It seems to me that but for an effort that no other mortal upon earth would make, I should sink into profound indifference to all things connected with men and their affairs. But with that effort that I daily exert, to the persons about me I appear, I have no doubt, to be one of the most cheerful and happy men upon earth." [19]

As a result of this he had people near him always. His hospitality was notorious even in the hospitable South. Though he was far from wealthy, his mansion, Liberty Hall, was open to all men at all times. Rich and poor, high and low, ignorant and learned, gathered there, and feasted at the owner's spiritual table as well as at the material. "Distinguished visitors from everywhere sought the sage's dwelling; so did hungry tramps, black and white." [20]

Like many persons of melancholy temperament, he was rich in delightful social qualities, made his guests feel thoroughly at home, studied their needs and ministered to them. And that specially frequent concomitant of melancholy, a dainty and sometimes a boisterous sense of humor, he had in a very high degree. His letters and his diary abound with good stories. What a quaint comic invention is the imaginary Finkle, through whom at irregular intervals he narrates his autobiography. His prison life at Fort Warren appears to him to be full of humorous matter. When he is not weeping over it, he is laughing at it. One of the best specimens of his dry wit, though more bitter than is usual with him, is the comment with which he closes some rather severe remarks on Davis. "It is certainly not my object to detract from Mr. Davis, but the truth is that as a statesman he was not colossal. . . . After the Government was organized at Montgomery, it was reported that he said it was 'now a question of brains.' I thought the remark a good one." [21]

These social qualities — cheerfulness, kindliness, sympathy — won friends for Stephens everywhere. In college, though poor, he was generally beloved and gathered all the young men around him. During his political life in Washington it was the same. The venerable John Quincy Adams saluted him with verses more notable for feeling than for genius. Members of all parties treated him with affection and respect. When he gave up his congressional seat in 1859, he received the unusual honor of a dinner tendered by a list of members of both houses of Congress without party distinction, headed by the Speaker of the House and the Vice-President. "I like Stephens," wrote an opponent. "With all his bad politics he is a generous-hearted fellow and of brilliant genius." [22]

This universal popularity was by no means confined to men of Stephens's own rank in life, but was perhaps even greater among the common people. "Thank God for little Alex," shouted crowds assembled on his first appearance after being wounded by a political adversary. And the negroes, especially those in his own service, were as enthusiastic and devoted as the whites.

It will be evident that qualities like these seemed to pave the straight way to political success. In a certain sense Stephens had such success in large measure. Why that success was limited will become clearer as we go on. But in the tactful management of men for a political purpose he had few superiors. And his art was largely sincerity. He made it manifest that he himself acted only from a profound and well-reasoned conviction; that he would throw over his party and even his constituents in a moment, if his conviction was against them; and the remnant of honesty which is latent in all men, politicians as well as others, responded to such straightforward uprightness. History records few finer things than Stephens's manly stand against the rush of secession in his State. Protesting in the face of angry thousands, he almost swept the current back. And what is perhaps most impressive of all, he so far retained the confidence and affection of his opponents that they elected him a chief officer of their government when they had established it.

The same qualities that made Stephens acceptable in general social and political circles made him deeply beloved in the more intimate relations of life. He never married. Yet children were very dear to him and he was keenly susceptible to the charm of women's society. Twice at least he was in love. In the first case poverty as well as ill-health obliged him to control his passion. On the second occasion, he was already in Congress and well-to-do in the world. The match was suitable and the lady, it seems, not unwilling. But he would not ask her to marry so frail a bit of humanity. "A woman's due," he thought, "was a husband on whom she could lean and not an invalid whom she must nurse." [23] It was, perhaps, a mistake, for both him and her. At any rate, it added to his bitterness of spirit. Once again one is reminded of Leopardi.

In every way Stephens was a man to whom affection meant much. He had the deepest love for home, for Georgia, her hills, and streams, and forests. His outcry for her from his Northern prison is poignant in its pathos:

"Let my days be brought to an end in my own native land! Let my last breath be of my own native air! My native land, my country, the only one that is country to me, is Georgia. The winds that sweep over her hills are my native air. There, I wish to live, and there to die."[24] His home farm may be barren, may be simple. It has neither luxury nor splendor. But to him it is everything. When a young man, just beginning life, with boundless ambition, a good opening and large salary were offered him away from home. But he unhesitatingly preferred to practice in his native town, though earning only a few hundred dollars a year.[25] And in old age and exile, as he turned generally to Georgia, so he longed most of all for the remembered haunts of youth and happiness. "That old homestead and that quiet lot, Liberty Hall, in Crawfordsville, sterile and desolate as they may seem to others, are bound to me by associations tender as heartstrings and strong as hooks of steel."[26]

These local affections sometimes take the place of human ties, and there are men — men especially — who, if they can live where they will, care not with whom they live. It was not so with Stephens. His love for his friends was as deep as his love for home. Among the great number of these none was nearer than Robert Toombs, and the marked contrast between the two men makes their intimate relation singularly charming. Stephens was little and frail; Toombs huge and solid. Stephens was a thinker; Toombs a liver. Toombs conquered men; Stephens charmed them. Very often the two took different sides and opposed each other energetically. Yet at the same time they praised, admired, and loved each other, and were rarely estranged, even for a brief interval. In the midst of the secession fury there was a certain coldness; but after Stephens's great anti-secession speech Toombs led the cheering for the beloved enemy, though he remarked to a friend who complimented him on it, "I always try to behave myself at a funeral." [27]

The best of Stephens's affection, however, went to his family. His mother died when he was very young, but his love for his father's memory has a depth and tenderness which is quite irresistible. Surely few sons could write, in old age, a tribute so impressive and so complete as the following: "Never was human anguish greater than that which I felt upon the death of my father. He was the object of my love, my admiration, my reverence. It seemed to me impossible that I could live without him; and the whole world for me was filled with the blackness of despair. . . . Whenever I was about to do something that I had never done before, the first thought that occurred to me was, what would my father think of this? . . . The principles and precepts he taught me have been my guiding-star through life." [28]

Even deeper and more absorbing was Stephens's love for his young half-brother, Linton, whom he educated, trained, and advised through boyhood and young manhood, and who afterward became his closest confidant.

To Linton he poured out all his hopes and sorrows and desires both public and private. Linton himself was a man of great ability, deservedly prominent in Georgia politics. He was also a man of singular charm, as fully appears from Waddell's excellent life of him. To have been looked up to and worshiped by such a man is not the least of Stephens's claims upon our interest, and the elder brother returned the devotion of the younger with all the passion of a heart keenly sensitive and not distracted from its sole object by either wife or child. The perpetual recurrence of Linton's name in his brother's letters and diary almost recalls Madame de Sévigné's unlimited adoration of her daughter. "Oh, if I had Linton with me now, how full would be my joy notwithstanding I am a prisoner! How light is my burden compared with what it has been! The full dawn of day is certainly upon me! May the sun of my deliverance soon arise! Oh, may Linton soon come!"[29]

The affection which could not satiate itself with humanity overflowed further in a notable tenderness for animals, especially for dogs. Stephens had always one or more of these to tend, to confide in, or to frolic with. When absent from home, he writes of them with a solicitude which is sometimes amusing, but more often pathetic. Over the blindness of one of them, Rio, he sorrows as over the affliction of a friend. He walks with Rio to guide the dog's steps and he buries him with a touch as characteristic in its simple vanity as in its profound emotion: "The world will never see another Rio. And few dogs ever had, or ever will have, such a master. Over his grave I shed a tear, as I did over him frequently as I saw nature failing." [30]

Perhaps it is possible to overdo this matter of sympathy with animals. It seems to some of us that the universal pity of the nineteenth century rather tended to increase the aggregate of sentient woe than to diminish it. When Uncle Toby spares the pestilent fly, we love him for it, especially as he was not aware of the huge maleficence with which later investigation was to load that domestic parasite. But when Stephens mourns over the necessary destruction of prison bedbugs, he seems to push altruism to the edge of the ludicrous — and over. "I have often felt sorry for what I have to do to these bloodsuckers. Most willingly would I turn them loose and let them go away, if they would go and stay, but this they will not do. Between them and me, therefore, there is 'an irrepressible conflict.' Either I or they must be extinguished." [31]

In the more important field of pity for human suffering and of attempts to relieve the wretched and to assist the struggling and downtrodden, we can have nothing but admiration for Stephens's persistent endeavor. He does, indeed, as with regard to Rio above, indulge in very frank statement of his own merit in this kind: "While I have been here I have with free will and of my own accord labored, I think, more for the benefit of others than

I have for myself, which is more than many mortals I ever knew could say for themselves."[32] But the merits require no such emphasis. They are great and indisputable. Probably few persons of his means have done more for others than Stephens did. He was constantly educating young men, so that all those of promise in his home town appealed to him and many from outside. During the war he was devoted in his attendance upon prisons and hospitals, visiting them often with fruit and flowers, which, I think, was inventing a charming function for that generally useless functionary, a vice-president. "Whenever I see a head at an iron grate, my heart is interested,"[33] he wrote, before he had passed four months behind an iron grate himself. It may be noted that one of the points in which he differed from the Government was his belief that prisoners of war should be set free, since the Confederacy was not able to provide for them properly. If sometimes, with men as with animals, his heart outran his head, who will blame him? It is worth while to be fooled occasionally by vice and idleness, worth while to be "like a ship otherwise stanch but eaten up by barnacles that he cannot dislodge" for the sake of winning the slave's simple eulogy: "He is kind to folks that nobody else will be kind to. Mars Alex is kinder to dogs than mos' folks is to folks."[34]

It is to be observed here, further, that Stephens's charity went much back of the hand. Oftentimes the fingers spread widely when the heart is tight shut, and some who are ready to give to a beggar are less ready to forgive an enemy. In spite of momentary outbursts and conflicts Stephens cherished no grudges and hated no one. The quick petulance of his nervous temperament sometimes leads him to express himself violently in his private letters. But the tone of his controversial book on the war is throughout tolerant with a tolerance which I find in few besides Lincoln and Lee. Indeed, it is interesting that one of Lincoln's last efforts at conciliation before the great struggle should have been his well-known correspondence with Stephens, in which both men appear so much to advantage.

This tolerance is still more marked in dealing with friends than with foes. Coming fresh from the reading of so many volumes of reminiscences that were harsh and bitter, filled with striving to justify the author at the expense of all those who had fought side by side with him, I was especially impressed with the gentleness and courtesy of Stephens's book. He disagrees with many. He condemns none. Even of Davis, whose policy he thought absolutely wrong, he has no unkind or cruel personal criticism. They met as friends, he says, and they parted as such. "I doubt not that all — the President, the Cabinet, and Congress — did the best they could from their own conviction of what was best to be done at the time." [35] It does not seem a great admission; yet how few are ready to make it.

The root of this kindly and universal tolerance is to be

found in a cardinal principle of Stephens's nature, which it is now time to take up and investigate. The man was essentially an intellectualist, and guided his life, far more than most men do, by systematic reasoning. I have already made it quite clear that this does not mean that he was cold or insensible. Most certainly he was not. Neither does it mean that he had the calm, dispassionate, scientific spirit of the nineteenth century, which observes all facts curiously without special eagerness to relate them to preconceived theories. Stephens was a deductive thinker of an older type. He reasoned from accepted generalizations to very positive conclusions. And even in this line his thinking was neither profound nor original. In his letters he is perpetually turning over rather glaring commonplaces, and the comparison of his diary with that of Amiel, which I have already suggested, will show at once that the Southern statesman had very little power of going to the bottom of things.

Nevertheless, in a tumult of passions, and preconceptions, and prejudices, he strove mightily to clear his mind of cant, to get at the conclusions of calm reason as to the terrible questions put before him, and then to act on those conclusions singly, honestly, unflinchingly, with absolute disregard of party, or tradition, or convention. In a time when the still voice of thought was well-nigh drowned in the furious outcry of politicians and fanatics, surely this quality must receive a high degree of commendation.

It was this which made him so patient with those who differed from him, this which made him so genuinely humble and modest. He reasoned to his conclusions and acted on them. But others had their own conclusions and must act on them. Oddly enough this very intellectual tendency which made him modest made him vain; as we have exactly the same tendencies exhibited in Cicero, as confirmed an intellectualist as ever lived, and placed in times and situations quite similar to Stephens's. To a man like Cicero it is equally natural to admit that his opponent may be right and to feel that his opponent and everybody else should recognize the simple fact of Cicero's own power and achievement. In Stephens the vanity is, of course, in no way so colossal as Cicero's, though at times it finds an expression curiously like that of the Roman orator: "I made a speech on Wednesday in Sparta. I produced I was told a powerful effect. Many said it was the greatest speech I ever made. This I say to you though but to few would I so express myself"; [36] which reminds one of Professor Phillips's characterization, "A chronic magnifier of his own importance." [37] But the allowance for possible error in his reasoning is as large and fine in Stephens as ever in any man. "It may be that if the course which I thought would or could then save it [the Confederate Government], or would or could have saved it at any time, had been adopted, it would have come as far short of success as the one which was pursued; and it may be, that the one which was taken on that occasion, as well as on all the other occasions on which I did not agree, was the very best that could have been taken." [38] How refreshing that is in all the jar and clash of positive assertions and violent opinions and dogmatic assurance of a world of might-have-beens. One should read also the admirable letter in which Stephens discusses the possibilities, if the whole burden of the Government, in the event of Davis's death, should fall upon his own shoulders.[39] The clear appreciation of the abstract end to be attained is no finer than the full recognition of the immense difficulties and his own unfitness to encounter them.

Yet if Stephens was modest where he admitted the possibility of error, and anxious for confirmation when he mistrusted his own judgment — "I did not wish to be coarser in my language than the occasion required. Was I enough so or not? Was I too short or not?" [40] — he was rocklike when he had deduced his conclusions, knew his ground, and felt that he was right. "I cannot be mistaken — I never was deceived a second time by any man," [41] he writes as to human character; and an interruption during his celebrated answer to Campbell, of Ohio, brought out one of those tremendous sentences in which a man strips his whole soul bare all at once. "You are wrong in that," interjects Campbell. "No, sir," replies Stephens. "I am never wrong upon a matter I have given as close attention to as I have given to this." So a god might answer.[42]

And he would stand by these intellectual conclusions to the issue of life or death. Huge Judge Cone had called Stephens a traitor. Stephens retorted with the lie and threatened to slap the judge's face. They met. The judge demanded a withdrawal. Stephens refused and struck. There was an instant collision. Cone pulled out a knife and slashed his opponent again and again, got him down, and cried, "Retract, or I 'll cut your damned throat." "Never!" said Stephens; "cut if you like." He caught the descending knife-blade in his bare hand, which was cut to pieces, and he went to the hospital, when his adversary was dragged off, with eighteen knife-thrusts in his body and arms. The man simply could not say he was wrong when he knew he was right. It is like the legend of Galileo, who succumbed to the gentle persuasions of the Church and yet whispered, "*E pur si muove*."

It is most interesting to follow out this intellectual tendency in the different phases of Stephens's life. To begin with, he was a man of system and exactness. Manifold and varied as his occupations were, he yet, where possible, arranged his time according to a schedule and gave certain hours to certain pursuits. Moreover, he had a fine memory for minute details and was always strong in dealing with figures and statistics. Art and the artistic side of literature seem to have had little attraction for him. His reading, which was both careful and extensive, was mainly in history and in lines of practical thinking and morals. So with the natural world. He had, as already noted, a profound, instinctive love for the surroundings that meant home. Beyond this, he was chiefly interested in minute observation of the weather and took just pride in having been the means of publishing the reports of the weather bureau which have since become of such immense value to the country.

As regards religion, I have already pointed out its significance to Stephens on the emotional side of his nature. He always retained a respect for the literal interpretation of the Bible, which was perhaps rather inconsistent with advanced thought, even in his day. Yet in some quarters he had the reputation of an atheist, and it is evident from his diary that he had a strong disposition to subject religious views to the strict intellectual test which he applied to other matters. It seems odd at first, yet it is really characteristic, that with this tendency he should have combined a strong tincture of superstition. His diary contains numerous discussions of good and ill luck, and he takes an undeniable interest in seeing the new moon over the right shoulder. "If there is anything in signs, I shall certainly have good luck this moon."[43]

In his own profession of the law Stephens's fine intellectual sincerity stands out fully and well proves that success requires neither dishonesty nor shuffling. "What business do you follow, Alex?" said his uncle to him in the early days. "I am a lawyer." After a solemn silence, the uncle spoke again. "Alex, don't you have to tell lies?"[44] Alex did not have to tell lies. Hear what he says, reviewing his career in old age: "No advocate should ever assert as matter of fact in his client's case what he knows is not such; any code of morals justifying him in this does not deserve the name."[45] And again, more personally: "My rule from the time I was admitted to the bar was: first, to investigate a case submitted to me, to inquire into the facts and the law applicable to it; then, if I did not believe the party entitled to success before the court, I told him so and declined to appear or prosecute the case."[46] Stephens believed that the object of law was justice and that the lawyer's high function was to reconcile differences and remedy evils. He detested prejudice of party, or locality, or class, or station. This feeling he carried so far that it sometimes itself became prejudice and led him into a singular tirade against what is surely a most worthy and respectable portion of the community. "If I am ever to be tried for anything, may Heaven deliver me from a jury of preachers! . . . Their most striking defect is a want of that charity which they, above all men, should not only preach but practise." And he speaks further of "The usual bloodthirsty propensity" of "that calling."[47] Stephens's religion was different enough from Voltaire's. Yet here one would think Voltaire was speaking.

It was in politics, however, that Stephens's natural characteristics came to their fullest fruition. As a speaker he was much praised and was effective and successful. "All lungs and brains," one admirer said of him.[48] But to me the most impressive eulogy is Lincoln's. Think of winning these words from such a source: "I just take up my pen to say that Mr. Stephens, of Georgia, a little, slim, pale-faced, consumptive man, has just concluded the very best speech of an hour's length I ever heard. My old withered dry eyes are full of tears yet." [49]

Nevertheless, Stephens mistrusted oratory, as one who knew its dangerous power.[50] When he had conviction with him, he could give it all the graces of persuasive eloquence. But conviction was essential. Without it the rest was but as a tinkling cymbal. Where conviction led him he would go, no matter what friend deserted him or what party disclaimed him. He even carried his anti-partisan feeling so far as to hope that the presidential election of 1852 might fall into the House of Representatives. "It would be a decided step towards putting an end to these party conventions and irresponsible bodies of men who now virtually make choice of our chief magistrate to the entire subversion of the theory of the Constitution." [51] He argued for the abolition of his own seat in Congress. He told the South that their agitators had done more than anything else to bring on the war.[52] He fought secession with all his might. "If they [the secession leaders] without cause destroy the present Government, the best government in the world," he wrote, "what hope would I have that they would not bring untold hardships upon the people in their efforts to give us one of their own modeling?"[53] At the same time he was an ardent advocate of slavery, believing — with Lee — that slavery presented the most satisfactory solution of the difficult relation between whites and blacks and that it was the duty of the superior race to protect and care for the inferior. On behalf of his State he resented the usurping attitude of the Richmond Government. Yet when the state governor began to act as the president had acted, Stephens was just as hot in opposition.

All these things he did in perfect good temper and kindliness and he could not understand why his opponents would not take it so. He was only acting from his convictions. He supposed they were acting from theirs. Why should they be angry with him? Yet they were, and too many of his compatriots sympathized with the caustic remark of General Taylor, "Mr. Stephens, with all the impartiality of an equity judge, marked many of the virtues of the Government north of the Potomac and all the vices of that on his own side of the river."[54]

First, last, and always the compass of Stephens's political life was his belief in human liberty, as expressed in the compact between sovereign States known as the Constitution. Admirably characteristic is the account of his youthful interview with President Jackson. Stephens expressed some doubt as to the action of the troops against the Indians, in view of state jurisdiction. "Jurisdiction, by the Eternal! When the United States Mail is robbed and citizens murdered!"[55] shouted the president. But Stephens was ready to be murdered himself rather than give up a principle. Why should not others be? I really believe he would have preferred being torn to pieces by a mob to having that mob repressed by troops illegally. This is fine, but is perhaps carrying intellectualism rather far.

So after the war. He was ready to accept the result and to work loyally for the future. But he could not give up the principle—never. And he wrote his immense, two-volume book—dialogued, thoroughly Platonic, thoroughly intellectual, in which, as in Plato, men of straw are set up to be bowled over by masterly dialectic—a learned book, an awe-inspiring book, as dead as a volume of eighteenth-century sermons.

In short, he was an idealist, an ideologue, Napoleon would have said, who would have introduced reason into this chaos of unreason, this curious and fascinating inferno, which we call life. Because life would not heed him he resented it, but in the gentlest and most affectionate fashion, returning good for evil in every way he knew.

In the political world, where he figured most, he seems to have been pitifully ineffectual. We saw in the case of Benjamin that the lack of deep and heartfelt convictions, a shallow opportunism, prevented the man from making any distinguished mark on the history of his time.

Curiously enough, with Stephens the same result followed from an exactly opposite cause, and the excess of conviction most nobly nullified a prominent and notable career. But I feel sure that posterity will adjust the difference and that Stephens will grow more and more in our history as a figure of commanding purity, sincerity, distinction, and patriotism.

ROBERT TOOMBS

VII

Robert Toombs

CHRONOLOGY

Born in Wilkes County, Georgia, July 2, 1810.
Entered Franklin College, Athens, Georgia, 1824.
Admitted to the bar, 1830.
Married Julia DuBose, 1830.
Entered State Legislature, 1837.
Entered Congress, 1844.
Supported Compromise of 1850.
Entered U.S. Senate, 1853.
Pro-slavery speech in Tremont Temple, January 24, 1856.
Confederate Secretary of State, February 27, 1861.
Resigned, July 24, 1861.
Brigadier-General, 1861–62.
Resigned, March 4, 1863.
Active in framing of Georgia Constitution, 1877.
Died, December 15, 1885.

VII

ROBERT TOOMBS

"HE is the most remarkable man in many respects that the South has ever produced and it is doubtful if the records of a lordlier life than his can be found in the history of our Republic. He has never moved as other men, never worked by ordinary standards. He has been kingly in all his ways, lavish in his opinions, disdaining all expediency or deliberation, and moving to his ambitions with a princely assumption that has never been gainsaid by the people, and seldom by circumstances." [1]

This paragraph, printed in a Georgia paper at the time of Toombs's death, for all its extravagance of statement and eulogy, strikes a good note for beginning the study of him. There was something lordly in the man, something commanding; and it is a matter of the greatest interest to see why his achievements did not correspond to his apparent gifts.

All agree that his physique was most impressive. Constant riding and other vigorous exercise kept him in excellent condition up to advanced years, though the assertions of some of his biographers as to his unfailing health are contradicted by many passages in his letters. Mrs. Davis's admirable portrait of him should be borne in mind. "Mr. Toombs was over six feet tall, with broad shoulders; his fine head set well on his shoulders, and was covered with long, glossy black hair, which, when speaking, he managed to toss about so as to recall the memory of Danton. His coloring was good, and his teeth brilliantly white, but his mouth was somewhat pendulous and subtracted from the rest of the strong face. His eyes were magnificent, dark and flashing, and they had a certain lawless way of ranging about that was indicative of his character. His hands were beautiful and kept like those of a fashionable woman." [2]

These physical qualities must be taken into account in considering Toombs's speaking, and it was as a speaker that he most impressed his contemporaries. Though his enunciation was too thick and harsh, Stephens considered him to be one of the greatest stump orators of any age or country.[3] All the vigor, all the violence, all the fiery ardor and eager enthusiasm of that passionate temperament were poured into his words. He spoke to convince, if possible; if not, to overwhelm. Energy, frankness, directness were the qualities of his oratory. His great admirer, Colonel Reed, does not believe that he corrected his speeches, does not believe that he could correct them. "Of all speakers and orators I ever knew or heard of, he has used the file the least." [4]

For the man was essentially a fighter and would yield to no one. His college life, in the late twenties, was in the main a record of unruly pranks, ending in a hasty request for honorable dismissal before some exceptional enormity became known to the authorities.

A little later he earned the title of captain by serving under General Scott in the Creek War.

The chief fighting of Toombs's early life, however, was done at the bar. He threw himself into the study of law with the passion which he showed in everything. At first he did not succeed in practice. Perhaps clients distrusted his too combative qualities. But his energy, enthusiasm, and splendid gift of speech soon overcame this coldness, and wealth began to pour in upon him in a steady stream. He not only had "a passion for the contest of the court-house," but he was willing to prepare himself for it by determined labor. He would bear down opposition by the rush and vehemence of his oratory; but, if necessary, he could also analyze a complicated question, financial or other, in its minutest details. No one was more voluble where speech seemed indicated; yet when circumstances required brevity, he could eliminate every superfluous word. In one instance his adversary had exhausted the court, the jury, and the subject. Toombs simply rose and said: "May it please your Honor, Seizin, Marriage, Death, Dower," sat down, and won his case.[5]

Few lawyers of that day kept out of politics. None was less likely to keep out of them than Toombs. He early began to devote his thought and his tongue to what he considered the welfare of his country, and he continued to do so, in one way or another, almost until his death. But to a temperament like Toombs's the natural course of politics was usually opposition. Heaven knows, there is enough to fight in the world, if a man wants fighting. And Toombs did. When he saw a rascal's head, he hit it, and few even determined optimists will deny that he might be kept busy. I cannot vouch for the following comment on him; but if not true, it is well invented: "Revolution was the one instinct of his nature, absolute as that of sex in other men. 'Do you mean revolution?' a gentleman once asked of him in my presence. 'Revolution, yes; always, and ever, and from the first, revolution. Revolutionary times,' he added, 'there are, and there will be no good times but revolutionary times.'"[6] And almost equally significant in the same line are his own undisputed words, written when he was looking for a refuge after all the tempests of the Civil War: "I now think best of Mexico. It has many advantages for the people who seek to establish themselves of the better classes. I do not care for its disorders. That perhaps is not unfavorable to 'novi homines.'"[7] And this was a broken man of nearly sixty!

Thus, both as representative and senator, Toombs's voice was apt to be heard loud in the negative. Curiously enough, he and Stephens were always intimate friends and their course was usually the same, but from somewhat different reasons. Stephens's cool intellect saw the doubts, the modifications, to any popular course of action. If his clear vision led him away from his friends, he left them, but he left them with reluctance. Toombs, too, had his intellectual convictions, often admirably sane, and broad, and far-reaching; but he had no reluctance about following them anywhere.

To begin with, he hated the party system. "A nursery of faction,"[8] he called it. It was not recognized by the Constitution. Why should he recognize it?

Acting on this principle, he fought friends as well as foes. If the common cry was war, this panoplied herald of good tidings could raise his trumpet voice for peace. Why should we fight England over a boundary? He was for peace — for honorable peace. "It is the mother of all the hopes and virtues of mankind."[9] Why should we annex Texas and plunder Mexico? Greed, greed, all greed. "A people who go to war without just and sufficient cause, with no other motive than pride and the love of glory, are enemies to the human race and deserve the execration of all mankind. What, then, must be the judgment of a war for plunder?"[10]

With domestic matters there was the same strenuous ardor. Congress itself was not to be respected, if not respectable. He speaks of "members of the two Houses of Congress who come here three months in one year and eight months in another — which is about three times too long in my judgment." Public improvements and public facilities which tended to abridge the rights of the individual — he would have none of them. The post-office

—a dubious thing, the post-office. "I do not think it right, before God, for me to make another man pay my expenses."[12] Rivers, harbors! What are they compared to corruption? "Instead of leaving the taxes or the money in the pockets of the people, you have spent nine months in endeavoring to squander and in arranging to have more to squander in the next Congress."[13] Railroads! Why, our old Roman virtue will not allow us even to approve of one to benefit our own home town.[14]

Then there are pensions, a pestilent legacy of a heroic struggle. The old soldiers themselves, if they are the men I take them for, will refuse them. Hurt my popularity? What do I care for my popularity? Do you suppose I am here to please myself? I had rather be at home, on my farm, with my wife, my slaves, and my cattle. Another thing, this cry of Americanism, Know-Nothingism. I scorn it to your faces. And you may turn me out, if you like. Are not Catholics as good as Protestants, if they serve God? So he spoke, in the height of the fanatical fury, and openly gave a large subscription to a Catholic church.

Everywhere it was the individual against the mob, high or low, forward or backward. The rich were not to be favored at the expense of the poor. At the same time, let his enemies criticize his own lavish living and see what they would get. "Who would say that he had not earned his money? He had a right to spend it as he chose. Perish such demagogy — such senseless stuff."[15]

And the people cheered him for his candor and audacity.

As for that mysterious phantom, the money power, which broods, like a shadow, over the young twentieth century, this Boanerges of liberty divined, detected, and defied it sixty years ago, in a little different form, but in language which might come from the White House to-day. "I have perceived that this mischief is widespread, this corruption greater, this tendency to the destruction of the country is more dangerous. The tendency to place the whole government under the money power of the nation is greater and greater."[16]

And while many of these protests were uttered in the name of the sacred principle of State Rights, let that principle itself once impose any obnoxious restraint, and its sanctity became as questionable as that of any other. Thus, in opposing certain obstructions to a projected scheme, he cries out: "Public opinion will take them away, even though a sovereign state may stand up for them. Nothing else can reach Pennsylvania in this matter but public opinion, and public opinion will prevail in Pennsylvania as it has done elsewhere."[17] And the public opinion of the world finally prevailed in all the States of the Confederacy, in spite of Toombs and thousands like him, with their inviolable sovereignty.

In all these various causes of opposition there was the same impetuous ardor of argument, the same splendid fury of invective, which, backed by the masterful presence and the thunderous voice, must have gone a long way to produce submission, if not conviction. Listen to the way in which he upbraids the Senate for sloth and hesitancy. "Are we incapable of deciding subjects here? Why, sir, the gravest questions of peace and war and finance and everything concerning a great government, are decided in almost all countries in one sitting. Here, after years of labor, seas of words, boundless, illimitable seas of words, and speeches to enlighten others, we come now to what I trust is a consummation of this difficulty, and we are asked for time because gentlemen do not understand it. I do not think they will ever understand it any better." [18]

But of course all other disputes and battles were trifling and of minor significance compared to the great struggle between slavery and abolition, between North and South. The opportunities given by such a conflict were things of ecstasy to a nature like Toombs's, and he breathed the fiery atmosphere as if it were his native clime. Scene after scene is depicted, in which he stood out alone against a howling mob, bellowing at them what pleased him without regard to what pleased them, and in the end overcoming even hatred by mere force of temperament.

Toombs's power in this regard was divined by Stephens long before the actual crisis came and the latter gives a striking account of sending his friend to New York to face a bitterly hostile audience and of the way in which Toombs, partly by clever ruse, partly by overmastering argument, succeeded in gaining a hearing and more than a hearing.

Then there was the furious contest over the speakership of the House in 1849. Owing to the secession of the Southern Whigs, of whom Toombs was one, no majority vote could be secured and Toombs insisted that the House, not yet formally organized, could take no action in the matter. Members proceeded to take action. Toombs protested. Members shouted him down. He would not be shouted down. "You may cry 'order,' gentlemen, until the heavens fall; you cannot take this place from me."[19] "Confusion increased," says the biographer. "Members called out to encourage Mr. Toombs, and others to put him down. In the midst of this Babel he continued to speak, his black hair thrown back, his face flushed, and his eyes blazing like suns."[20] He continued to speak, and in the end they heard him. It was a disgraceful exhibition, said the Northern papers. However that may be, one cannot help agreeing with Stephens that it was a splendid physical and oratorical achievement.

Even more notable, though the opposition was moral, not physical, was Toombs's defense of slavery in Tremont Temple, Boston, in 1856. The actual audience was decorous enough; but when one thinks of the man and the place, of all he represented and of the passionate anti-slavery spirit boiling about him, the occasion stands out as picturesque, to say the least.

Not less characteristic, in view of all it meant, is the coolness of his testimony concerning the assault made by Brooks upon Charles Sumner. Toombs was charged with having given Brooks the support of his presence, if not more. His answer, not merely to the indignant Senate, but to the angry millions of the insulted North, is startling in its imperturbable insolence. "As for rendering Mr. Sumner any assistance, I did not do it. As to what was said, some gentlemen present condemned it in Mr. Brooks; I stated to him, or to some of my own friends, probably, that I approved it. That is my opinion."[21] And again: "So far as relates to interfering, or giving assistance, he is right. I gave none. I did not put in, and should not on that side."[22]

So we come to the break and the great parting. But before considering Toombs's activity in this, let us look at some of the other elements of his character. For the more I study these prominent men of the Civil War period, and indeed the prominent men of any period, the more I see that their greatness consists largely in a balance of qualities; that is, even when they have one quality in marked excess, it is tempered, restrained, and modified by a striking makeweight of its opposites. Thus, so far, we have seen Toombs as a fighter, riotous, rebellious, exulting in the extravagant and often ill-timed display of violence, almost a sort of political mountebank. Yet he was also something far more than this and something far different.

He had a splendid sense of humor. This, as might be expected, was often rough, noisy, and boisterous, and did him damage; but it had its charm, nevertheless. He enjoyed practical jokes, like a great boy, as when, at Taylor's suggestion, he switched off in the dark a train-load of Governor Brown's pet state troops for a fight in South Carolina.[23] He used a shrewd and savage wit in assailing his political adversaries. "You have heard what the gentleman says about my coming home to practice law. He promises, if elected to Congress, he will not leave his seat. I leave you to judge, fellow-citizens, whether your interests in Washington will be best protected by his continued presence or his occasional absence."[24] Some one urged that an antagonist had made at least one good appointment. "That may be," answered Toombs, "but that was not the reason it was made. Bacon was not accused of selling injustice. He was eternally damned for selling justice."[25]

The same shining vivacity of repartee seems to have been always ready, in private society as in public gatherings. That keen and passionate tongue must indeed have been somewhat dreaded. How bitter is the story of the red-headed man! Toombs was dining with Scott and told of a woman who rushed about in a steamer explosion, crying, "Save the red-headed man, save the red-headed man." The red-headed man was saved, but the woman appeared quite indifferent. "He owes me ten thousand dollars," she explained. "General," said

Toombs, turning to Scott, "the Union owes you ten thousand dollars." [26] These outbursts must have done Toombs more harm than any one else, as the rodomontade about calling the roll of his slaves at Bunker Hill Monument, or the careless remark, "We are the gentlemen of this country," which gave rise to William Whitmore's pamphlet of "The Cavalier Dismounted," or the stuffing of an innocent English peer with monstrous tales of slaveholding obliquity which were afterwards recorded in print to the serious discredit of the narrator.[27]

Yet there is general agreement that Toombs was one of the most brilliant and fascinating of talkers, and Linton Stephens, no bad judge, says: "Toombs, or Tom Thomas, can, and frequently do, speak more witticisms in one night than Rabelais in a lifetime wrote." [28]

The sunniest, the sweetest, the most winning picture of Toombs and his laughter is that admirably given by Mrs. Davis. "During the time of the highest excitement over the compromise measures, when Mr. Toombs was on his feet twenty times a day, he rose at daylight, took French lessons with his daughter, and became a good French scholar so far as reading the language went. He would sit with his hands full of the reporter's notes on his speeches for correction, with 'Le Médecin Malgré Lui' in the other hand, roaring over the play. I said to him, 'I do not see how you can enjoy that so much.' He answered, 'Whatever the Almighty lets his geniuses create, He makes some one to enjoy: these plays take all the soreness out of me.'"[29] Something to love here, is there not?

And if the man liked laughter, he liked sunshine and quiet also, country air, and trees, and flowers. He himself said that "in a very busy and tempestuous life a spacious garden with orchards and vineyards, was to him an unfailing source of recreation and pleasure."[30] He was a practical farmer, too, himself superintended vast plantations and had an army of slaves under his charge. Stephens, an unimpeachable witness, tells us that "his plantation discipline and his treatment of his slaves was on a perfect system of reason, justice, and humanity, looking as much to the welfare of his dependents as to his own pecuniary interests," and that his system and its success were wonderful. He would have as overseers only men of sobriety, good sense, and humanity.[31]

In the personal relations of life, also, Toombs seems to have been full of charm. One vice he had, the taste for alcohol, which in later years overcame him disastrously. But even this, throughout his active life, he could and did control, when necessary, just as he dropped smoking, when he thought it injurious. "I found that smoking was ruining my throat and I quit it."[32] In any case excessive drinking was but a feature of his strong social instinct and his love for the warm contact of his fellowmen. A true Southerner, he was ready to entertain everybody, and protested against the establishment of a hotel in his home town. "If a respectable man comes to town, he can stay at my house. If he is n't respectable, we don't want him here at all."[33] How charming is the phrase, quoted by Reed, with which he made right a momentary awkwardness of unexpected guests at table. "O, I do not object to having more friends than room; it is usually the other way in this world."[34] He was sensitive, emotional, ready to respond to any stimulus of affection or pathos. "In speaking of the death of Mr. Brooks the other day in the Senate, he broke out in weeping and had to stop," writes Stephens.[35] The warmth and whole-heartedness of his friendship show in his words about Crittenden: "The very prince of good fellows. I know not his superior on all the earth, in all those qualities of head and heart which we must love and respect";[36] and Gabriel Toombs's passionate outburst reflects something of the feeling of those who had intimate personal relations with his brother: "While I am entirely independent of my brother in the sense the world calls independent, no mortal perhaps was ever more dependent upon another for happiness, than I am upon him."[37] These vital, abounding natures win a devotion which paler souls can never know.

Toombs's religious experience seems to have been rather elementary, but sincere. It was amusingly mixed with the impetuosity which characterized him in everything. When his wife was dying, he had some talks on serious subjects with the family doctor, who was anxious to put him in the right way. "Why, doctor, I am a prayerful man. I read the Bible and the Prayer Book every day." "Then why not be baptized, General?" "Baptize me, doctor," was the prompt reply.[38]

Especially attractive is Toombs's affection for his wife and the tenderness apparent in the few published fragments of his letters to her. She was a woman well worth his attachment and the perfect marital fidelity, emphasized by all his biographers, is distinctly noticeable in a man of such a vigorous and impetuous temperament, beset at all times by so many temptations. The frankness, sincerity, and genuine humility of his nature show well in a passage written to Mrs. Toombs, after their daughter's death: "God bless you! Pray for me, that I may be a better man in the next year than in all the old ones before in my time."[39] And equally attractive is the following expression of gratitude after twenty years of marriage: "I know for whatever success in life I may have had, whatever evil I may have avoided, or whatever good I may have done, I am indebted to the beautiful, pure-hearted, true, little girl, who on the 18th of November, 1830, came trustingly to my arms, the sweetest and dearest of wives."[40]

Toombs's excellent balancing traits were by no means confined to domestic and social life. We have seen something of his headlong fury; but this was constantly tempered by shrewdness, by foresight, by restraint and moderation, when these qualities were clearly called for by circumstances. We have already heard Stephens testifying that his friend was an admirable man of business. Adversaries even asserted that "he loaned like a prince and collected like a Shylock." [41] Certain it is that he had a remarkable grasp of finance, could unravel a complicated web of figures with precision and rapidity, and seize and clarify the essential features of the most bewildering business tangle. His letter to the Augusta "Constitution" (August 12, 1863) is one of the clearest and ablest criticisms of the unfortunate Confederate financial policy.[42]

In his profession I have before referred to his immense labor in getting at the facts. He was, indeed, quick to grasp essential points, but he did not neglect supplementing them by details that were essential also. "In reading the report of a case, or an author on any subject, he at once seizes upon the real ideas, gleaning the vital part from the general verbiage by a process rapid as intuition," says Stephens.[43] And when the material was thus once prepared it was presented to the court, with vigor and passion, indeed, but also with method and thoughtful intelligence. "As a lawyer, I have never seen his equal before judge and jury," adds the same excellent authority.[44]

And in law he was as honest as he was able. "An able lawyer and an honest man," writes Mr. Rhodes; "though harsh and intolerant in expression, he was frank in purpose." [45] Good stories are told, illustrating his absolute probity and determination to keep his hands clean.

"Yes, you can recover in this suit," he said once to a client, "but you ought not to do so. This is a case in which law and justice are on opposite sides." And on the client's insisting, Toombs remarked, "Then you must hire some one else to assist you in your damned rascality."[46] Again, a lawyer asked him what fee should be charged in a certain case. "Well," said Toombs, "I should have charged a thousand dollars; but you ought to have five thousand, for you did a great many things I could not have done."[47] And to the end of his life he boasted that he had never had a dirty shilling in his pocket.

Even in politics we find these curious contradictions of moderation and sagacity, often of marked conservatism, mingling with the ardor of Toombs's general temperament. It was said of him that he was "violent in speech but safe in counsel," and many things prove that it was often so, though careful study of his general correspondence and of his whole career makes it evident that the violence went deeper than speech. It would be an entire mistake to set him down as a fanatic. According to his own definition, "a fanatic is one of strong feelings and weak points."[48] About him there was nothing weak, neither points nor feelings. A fanatic is apt to be a mild man worked by an idea into fury. Toombs worked fury into the mildest ideas. Yet, when he willed, he could be sedate and reasonable. To one who has been startled by the vehemence of some particular outburst, the full reading of many of his speeches is a revelation of dignity, sobriety, and common sense. In numerous instances the course he recommended and urged and followed was the course of moderation and fairness. And what finer warning could be held out before a radical party than his conservative reminder: "Truth is often strangled in the house and by the hands of its own friends by a struggle for that which is impossible to-day but which may easily be accomplished to-morrow." [49]

Acting in this spirit, he supported Clay and Webster in the Compromise measures of 1850, making himself extremely obnoxious to the Southern fire-eaters by doing so. And I think the importance of this conduct of the moderate Whigs cannot be too much insisted upon. They roused the wrath of violent partisans in all sections, and Webster, at least, earned the hatred and contempt of a large number of his constituents. Yet it would be easy to maintain that the patriotic action of that group of Whig leaders in 1850 saved the Union, not only then, but forever. They delayed the conflict for ten years, and during those ten years the North had time to accumulate the resources which, even so, were barely sufficient to enable it to overcome.

Again in the great Kansas struggle, Toombs's voice was given for moderation and prudence. "Senator Toombs introduced a bill which, in fairness to the free-state settlers, went far beyond the measure that earlier in the season had been drawn by Douglas," says Mr.

Rhodes.[50] And elsewhere, "When Toombs said he was willing to take the will of the people [of Kansas] in a proper and just manner and abide by the result, he was sincere. An old Whig, he had the Whig love of the Union." [51]

Still another curious case of Toombs's moderation is the Boston speech above referred to. In going straight into the centre of the hostile country and speaking on the subject of bitterest contention, slavery, he was indulging all his native instincts of combativeness. But once there, the speech he made was a model of simple, honest, reasonable statement of the very best that could be said for his fellows and himself. No more persuasive, more manly, more human argument for negro servitude was ever uttered than Toombs presented in the headquarters of abolition on the platform of Tremont Temple in 1856.

And so, when we come to the last great crisis of all, we find Toombs, the revolutionist, the hothead, the fire-eater, not doing his best at every opportunity to foment sedition and urge an outbreak, but keeping his temper, counseling moderation, anxious, to the very end, to cling to the old ties, if it were possible. "The temper of the North," he writes at one time, "is good, and with kindness and patronage skilfully adjusted, I think we can work out of our present troubles, preserve the Union, and disappoint bad men and traitors." [52] It is true, he had his moments of forgetfulness. "Toombs has just delivered a speech of the most abusive and inflammatory character of Judge Douglas. He spoke like a madman and acted like a fanatic," writes Stephens.[53] Yet, during much of the time, his counsel was for restraint, deliberation, and endurance as long as endurance was possible. With calm foresight he deprecated any contemptuous assertion that the people of either section of the Union would be found cowardly when the crisis came: "Sir, if there shall ever be civil war in this country, when honest men shall set about cutting each other's throats, those who are least to be depended on in a fight will be the people who set them at it." [54] So late as December, 1860, he earned the ill will of the violent party in his own State by opposing immediate secession. He thought that definite action should be fixed for March 4, yet even as to this he adds the admirable words: "I certainly would yield that point to correct and honest men who were with me in principle, but who were more hopeful of redress from the aggressors than I am, especially if any such active measures should be taken by the wrongdoers as promised to give us redress in the Union." [55] It is only when he has been forced to abandon all hope that he commits himself in final and characteristically decisive language: "I will tell you, upon the faith of a true man, that all further looking to the North for security for your constitutional rights ought to be abandoned. . . . Secession by the 4th day of March next should be thundered from the ballot-box by the unanimous voice of Georgia on the 2d day of January next." [56]

The same spirit of provident foresight followed Toombs even into the inception of the Confederate policy, when all the hotheads were clamoring for fire and steel. During the discussion in the cabinet over attacking Sumter, he spoke vehemently and decidedly in opposition: "Mr. President, at this time, it is suicide, murder, and will lose us every friend at the North. You will wantonly strike a hornet's nest which extends from mountains to ocean, and legions, now quiet, will swarm out and sting us to death. It is unnecessary; it puts us in the wrong; it is fatal." [57]

We might, then, suppose that this arch-rebel, with brains tempering his rebellion, who had been so prominent all through the long political contest, would have stood out among the foremost when rebellion took organized shape. It is most curious and instructive to see how, after all, the dominant instincts of his nature prevented this from coming to pass. At first his name was mentioned for president of the Confederacy and he was thought of by many very seriously as a candidate. How far he himself sought the office may be questioned. In earlier life he declared, "I have an unaffected repugnance to official station and my interests harmonize with my inclination in this respect. Politics with me is but an episode in life, not its business." [58] While, under the Confederacy, writing, with entire frankness, to his wife, he disclaims all ambition: "I want nothing but the defeat of the public enemy and to retire with you for the balance of my life in peace and quiet in any decent corner of a free country." [59] But such disclaimers do not count for much.

Stephens, who liked Toombs and disliked Davis, but who was not usually much blinded by his feelings, would have preferred to see the former at the head of the Government. "Thrift follows him, unthrift Davis. Had Toombs been made President — that he was not, was only an accident — it is my conviction that the whole scheme of action, nay, the results would have been changed. . . . The object sought would have been one less objectionable to the North. It would, after two years of war, have been gained by a special treaty because it was strictly constitutional. But Davis, Davis — I know not why he was elected president of the Confederacy, except that he never succeeded in anything he undertook." [60]

In spite of Stephens's weighty authority, I cannot imagine Toombs succeeding at the head of a great government. Impetuous tempers are, indeed, sometimes sobered by responsibility; yet is it possible that one so utterly untrained to obey should ever have been able to command? The president of the Confederacy required a tact in dealing with difficult situations and difficult characters, a tolerance of opinion contrary to his own, a breadth of human understanding and sympathy, such as were hardly to be found in Lee and Washington, and such as are certainly not indicated in Toombs. Those who are inclined to Stephens's view should consider well the little scene depicted by the diarist, Jones, as occurring in the War Office at Montgomery, when the Confederacy was hardly born. Toombs was holding forth to members of the cabinet — in a public office, mind you, before the gaping clerks. "He was most emphatic in the advocacy of his policy, and bold almost to rashness in his denunciation of the mainly defensive idea. He was opposed to all delays as fraught with danger. . . . He was for making the war as terrible as possible from the beginning. It was to be no child's play. . . . He denounced with bitterness the neglect of the authorities in Virginia. The enemy should not have been permitted to cross the Potomac. . . . Virginia alone could have raised and thrown across the Potomac 25,000 men, and driven the Yankees beyond the Susquehanna. But she, to avoid responsibility, had been telegraphing Davis to come to the rescue; and if he (Toombs) had been in Davis's place, he would have taken the responsibility."[61] This is the tongue which, Stephens thinks, could have saved the Confederacy!

Well, he did not become president, at any rate, and it is to be noted that he characteristically gave his hearty support to the election of Davis. What then? Davis, who realized how mighty a power the man had been, was ready to offer him a place in the cabinet, the most honorable, if not the most important, and Toombs became secretary of state. He held the position about five months. His biographer implies that having put everything in the best possible shape, he sought a more active life. This is not the general view. Some maintain that he had not the system or the practical gifts for managing so great an office and they cite his sarcastic remark that he carried the records of the State Department under his hat. They misjudge him. We have already seen that he was master of all the details of handling a great plantation and that in these he could be systematic enough. Such of his state papers and dispatches as have been printed are admirable in their vigor, brevity, and point.

The true explanation of his failure is supplied by Mrs. Chesnut, in her usual terse and vivid fashion: "Incompatibility of temper. Mr. T. rides too high a horse; that is, for so despotic a person as Jeff Davis."[62] And Toombs himself indicates the same condition of things in a letter to his wife referring to a later suggestion that he should be secretary of war, a position, by the way, for which Stephens considered him peculiarly qualified: "I thought I had been very explicit on that point. I would not be Mr. Davis's chief clerk. His Secretary of War can never be anything else. . . . So far as I am concerned, Mr. Davis will never give me a chance for personal distinction. He thinks I pant for it, poor fool."[63] As a practical illustration of Toombs's respect for government and empowered authority nothing could be more delightful than his public dispatch to a quite properly qualified committee which required him to give up some part of his cotton-planting and substitute the production of food-supply. Toombs does not believe in this policy and therefore answers: "I refuse a single hand. My property, as long as I live, shall never be subject to the orders of those cowardly miscreants, the Committee of Public Safety of Randolph County, Georgia, and Eufaula. You may rob me in my absence, but you cannot intimidate me." [64]

There remained the army. It is true that few civilian generals on either side greatly distinguished themselves. Yet it seems as if Toombs's fighting temper might have come to the front, if any one's could. Did it? A friend who knew him well said of him: "He had one ambition, and that to the highest office within the Confederacy. That could not be gratified. He had another, to be Commander-in-Chief of the armies. That could not be gratified. He had no more." [65] As to the ambitions, who shall say? The fact is that the disappointed statesman plunged into a military career with headlong energy and that he came out of it pretty much as he had come out of the political. Why?

Certain excellent military qualities he undoubtedly had. He was brave, rashly, extravagantly brave. He had the gift of inspiring others with his own bravery. History will not forget his magnificent defense of the bridge at Antietam. Lee's praise of any man is the most enduring badge of glory, and Lee said: "General Toombs's small command repulsed five different assaults made by greatly superior forces, and maintained its position with distinguished gallantry." [66]

Also, Toombs was beloved by the men of his brigade and took excellent care of them. He looked out for their health and comfort in every possible way. "Whether against Johnston, Longstreet, or Hill, the First Brigade, First Division, was sure of a fearless champion in the person of its commander," says the ardent biographer.[67]

The biographer seems to overlook the somewhat extraordinary sound of commending an officer with so much enthusiasm for his bellicose attitude against his own superiors. But here, as everywhere, we meet in Toombs the same old defect. He was a splendid individual fighter; but he could not learn that fighting, like everything else, to be fruitful and efficient, requires, first of all, subordination. He could not learn discipline.

Thus, one of his sick soldiers was refused hospital on account of some technicality. Toombs was told that the rules were fixed by General Johnston. He rode right up to the general's tent and spoke out in his emphatic fashion. "You have been too rash," protested his own surgeon; "you will be arrested."[68] Johnston did not arrest him, because he liked him and was generous himself. But another commander would have done so.

Again, Toombs lost no opportunity of holding forth, even to his men, on the proper conduct of the war. If he disapproved of the action of his superiors, he did not hesitate to say so, and often without very thorough knowledge of what his superiors were aiming at. He hated West Point because it meant discipline and training. Thus he writes of Joseph E. Johnston: "I never knew as incompetent [an] executive officer. As he has been to West Point, tho, I suppose he knows everything about it."[69] And again: "Johnston is a poor devil, small, arbitrary, and inefficient. Like Walker, he undertakes to do everything from a mere fondness for power and does nothing well. He harasses and obstructs but cannot govern the army."[70] Toombs hated Davis, because Davis supported West Point. "Davis and his janissaries [the regular army] conspire for the destruction of all who will not bend to them, and avail themselves of the public danger to aid them in their selfish and infamous schemes."[71] When the general rejoined his regiment after arrest, he is said to have cried out, "Go it, boys! I am with you again. Jeff Davis can make a general, but it takes God Almighty to make a soldier."[72] Comment is needless.

Nor did he hesitate at direct disobedience when it suited him. The attack at Golding's farm, during the Seven Days' battles, made against Lee's explicit orders, is hardly in point, because Toombs claimed to have instructions from his immediate superior. But in the campaign of Second Bull Run Toombs's brigade was ordered by Longstreet to guard a certain ford. Longstreet's delicious, patronizing account of the affair should be read in full[73] and compared with Toombs's considerably differing version.[74] But from both it is evident that Toombs withdrew the picket without orders, and, however excellent his motives, it was quite natural that Longstreet should put him under arrest, which he did.

Moreover, ready as Toombs was to criticize others, he had no notion of being criticized himself. D. H. Hill, not noted for his soft tongue, rode up in the middle of an action, and not understanding the circumstances, blamed Toombs for the conduct of his troops. "You are always crying out, fight, fight," said Hill, in substance; "why don't you fight?" Toombs resented this bitterly and would have insisted on a duel if Hill would have met him.[75]

It is hardly necessary to follow Toombs the soldier any further. Many fine things are told of him, notably his whole-hearted submission when taken back to duty after the arrest by Longstreet.[76] Longstreet liked him, as, indeed, did every one, and said of him admiringly that he needed only discipline to make him a great general. Perhaps he needed some other things; but discipline was the crying need of his whole life, and it is pathetic to see such exceptional gifts falling, falling by rapid stages from the candidacy for president to a petty and insignificant position in the Georgia militia. Mrs. Chesnut sums up his career and the whole tone of his correspondence under the Confederacy with splendid vividness, if perhaps a little too vividly: "Toombs is ready for another revolution and curses freely every Confederate from the President to a horseboy. He thinks there is a conspiracy against him in the army. Why? Heavens and earth! Why?"[77]

The Confederacy falls and Toombs falls with it, what distance he has left to fall. In his own opinion, at any rate, the North was thirsting for his blood, and the melodramatic incidents of his escape from capture must have afforded him infinite pleasure; flights, disguises, concealments, thrilling hints of treachery, also the protection of lovely and intellectual young women. He was "a Chesterfield with ladies," says his biographer. "The general would walk to and fro along the shaded walks and pour forth, in his matchless way, the secret history of the ruin of the Confederate hopes."[78] How I should like to have heard him!

And now comes the last curiosity in this extraordinary career. Before the war, in times of organized society, the man had stood forth a splendid rebel. Then, when rebellion became the fashion and had spread to everybody about him, he sank into complete insignificance. Comparative peace was restored, comparative organization; and immediately, as a rebel and a fighter, he came once more to the front. After he returned from his long exile in Europe, he struck in at once with vehement battle against all the sins and errors of carpetbag reconstruction. Heaven knows it was a fine opportunity! How he must have luxuriated in the tempest of epithets which he hurled against the dominant party that was over-riding him and his fellows: "Its tyranny, its corruption, its treachery to the Caucasian race, its patronage of vice, of fraud, of crime and criminals." [79] What hearty wealth of honest egotism rings in his cry of disgust at the things that were going on about him: "I am sorry I have got so much sense. I see into the tricks of these public men too quickly. When God Almighty moves me from the earth, he will take away a heap of experience. I expect when a man gets to be seventy he ought to go, for he knows too much for other people's convenience." [80] But the best thing in the later correspondence, as illustrating the value of a man's comment on his own character, is the following [italics mine]: "I had hoped to be there myself, but the arbitration in the Whitfield case is protracted by Hill and his villains with the hope of annoying me out, but you know I generally take a through ticket. *The thing is unbearable except by a man of my philosophy.*" [81]

In this last phase, again, as so frequently before, we should note the makeweight of sound common sense and real constructive intelligence. No one's brain was more helpful than Toombs's in framing the new constitution of Georgia. And in opposing things in general, he opposed some particular things for which wise men can never commend him too much. He opposed the popular election of judges, and when told that it worked well where it had been tried, answered, with the classical colloquialism he loved to use: "It is easy to take the road to hell, but few people ever return from it." [82] He opposed the too hasty allotment of privileges and powers to railroads and corporations. His words would find many to-day to echo them, few to improve them. "What do I see before me? The grave. What beyond that? Starving millions of our posterity, that I have robbed by my action here, in giving them over to the keeping of these corporations. The right to control these railroads belongs to the State, to the people, and as long as I represent the people, I will not relinquish it, so help me God!" [83]

A fighter, you see, so long as breath was in him, a rampant individualist, a champion of all the wordy ideals of the eighteenth century, the embodiment of passionate will, which would not be over-persuaded or over-ridden, or broken down. Although he nominally accepted Christianity and even declared on his deathbed that he "had not a resentment. I would not pang a heart," [84] yet he remained proud, haughty, self-confident to the very end. "Yes, I know I am fast passing away. Life's fitful fever will soon be over. I would not blot out a single act of my life." [85] The United States Government had conquered him, subdued him, constrained him. It governed Georgia and he was a Georgian. But he never forgave. "Pardon?" he said, when they asked him to sue for amnesty; "Pardon for what? I have not pardoned you all yet." [86] And he declared that he would die as he had lived, "an unpardoned, unreconstructed, unrepentant rebel." [87]

Together with not a few other of the admirable qualities of Milton's Satan, he had in a high degree the one quality which we respect most in that heroic, if somewhat unregenerate, type of Promethean rebellion, —

> " The courage never to submit or yield,
> And what is else not to be overcome."

VIII

Raphael Semmes

CHRONOLOGY

Born Charles County, Maryland, September 27, 1809.
Midshipman, United States Navy, 1826.
Admitted to the bar, 1834.
Lieutenant, 1837.
Married, 1837, Annie E. Spencer, of Cincinnati.
Both land and sea service in Mexican War.
Commander, 1855.
Secretary Lighthouse Board, 1858–61.
Commanded Sumter, 1861.
Commanded Alabama from August, 1862, to June, 1864.
Defeated by Winslow in the Kearsarge, June 19, 1864.
Confederate Rear Admiral, 1864.
Surrenders with Johnston, May 1, 1865.
Arrested, 1865, but released under amnesty.
Law and journalism till death, August 30, 1877.

RAPHAEL SEMMES

VIII

RAPHAEL SEMMES

IT is not likely that the romance of the one hundred and thirty volumes of Civil War Records will ever be written; yet the diligent searcher of those records finds many picturesque points to relieve his tedious hours. For instance, there is the matter of proper names. The novelist who invented "Philip St. George Cocke" as a military hero would be laughed at for excess of fancy. Yet the Confederates rejoiced in such a general, who was killed early and is said to have been a good fighter. At any rate, he wrote up to his name in almost unbelievable fashion. He is not to be confused with his feebler Union duplicate — I mean feebler as regards nomenclature — Philip St. George Cooke.

Then there is Captain Coward, a brave and able soldier, who has served his state efficiently both during the war and since. Still with that name would you not have chosen to be a preacher, or a plumber, or to follow any respectable profession of peace, rather than to inflict such a military *lucus e non lucendo* on a mocking world? And the parents of this unfortunate, when they had the whole alphabet to choose from, preferred to smite their offspring with the initial "A.," perhaps hoping, affectionately but mistakenly, that Alexander, or Ajax, or Achilles, would suffice to overcome the patronymic blight.

All which is but a prelude to the introduction of Raphael Semmes. Is not the name a jewel in itself? In Latin countries Raphael may be a fairly common appellation; but we Saxons are usually familiar with only three instances of it, two artists and an archangel. Elements of both these characters appear in the subject before us, but I think the artist predominated and the other irresistibly suggests Lamb's description of Coleridge, "an archangel — a little damaged."

Really, for a pirate, could anything be finer than "Raphael Semmes"? And it is always as a pirate that I shuddered at the commander of the Alabama in my boyhood dreams. I thought of him as a joyous freebooter, a Kidd, or a Red Rover, or a Cleveland, skimming the blue main like a bird of prey, eager to plunder and destroy, young, vigorous, splendidly bloodthirsty, gay in lace and gold, perhaps with the long locks, which, Plutarch assures us, make lovers more lovely and pirates more terrible. I cherished this vision even while I knew only vaguely of a certain Semmes. When better knowledge added "Raphael," my dream became complete.

Now it must go with the other dreams of boyhood; for better knowledge still assures me that the man was not a pirate at all. I have his own word for this — or words, some hundred and fifty thousand of them. I have also most touching and impressive narratives of his crew, who were of so sympathetic a disposition that they were moved by their first captive's tears to the point of collecting a purse for him.[1] I do not understand that they continued this habit; but to the very end I have no doubt the hard plight of an orphan would have worked upon their feelings as volcanically as upon the pirates of Gilbert and Sullivan.

Perhaps more convincing than such somewhat *ex parte* evidence, and, indeed, conclusive, are the calm statements of Union authorities. Through the war "pirates" was the universal cry of the Northern Government and press. But Professor Soley, as competent as any one to give an opinion, declares that, "Neither the privateers, like the Petrel and the Savannah, nor the commissioned cruisers, like the Alabama and the Florida, were guilty of any practices which, as against their enemies, were contrary to the laws of war."[2] While Robert A. Bolles, legal adviser of the Navy Department, writing in the "Atlantic Monthly," shortly after the war, to explain why Semmes was not prosecuted, asserts that he was "entitled to all of the customary cheats, falsehoods, snares, decoys, false pretences, and swindles of civilized and Christian warfare," and that "the records of the United States Navy Department effectually silence all right to complain of Semmes for having imitated our example in obedience to orders from the Secretary of the Confederate Navy."[3]

It is impossible to imagine anything more satisfactory

than this, coming from such a source, and the talk of "pirates" seems to be forever disposed of. Nevertheless, there is one authority on the other side, of such weight and significance that I cannot altogether pass him by. This authority — American — is, indeed, speaking of privateers in the Mexican War; but the methods and practices animadverted upon are so closely akin to those of the Alabama that that vessel could hardly have escaped being included in the condemnation, in spite of her claim to be a duly authorized Confederate cruiser.

Our authority, then, speaks thus of the composition of crews. "It is necessary that at least a majority of the officers and crew of each vessel should be citizens; not citizens made *ad hoc*, in fraud of the law, but *bona fide* citizens; and any vessel which might have attempted to cruise under a letter of marque and reprisal, without this essential requisite, would have become, from that moment, a pirate."[4]

Again, this writer expresses himself in the severest terms as to commerce-destroying generally. "Indeed, there is a growing disposition among civilized nations, to put an end to this disreputable mode of warfare under any circumstances. It had its origin in remote and barbarous ages, and has for its object rather the plunder of the bandit than honorable warfare. . . . From the nature of the material of which the crews of these vessels are composed — the adventurous and desperate of all nations — the shortness of their cruises, and the demoralizing pursuit in which they are engaged, it is next to impossible that any discipline can be established or maintained among them. In short, they are little better than licensed pirates; and it behooves all civilized nations, and especially nations who, like ourselves, are extensively engaged in foreign commerce, to suppress the practice altogether." [5]

By this time, I imagine that the indignant Southern reader is inquiring what twopenny authority I am thus setting up against the best legal judgment of the North itself. I answer, with hilarious satisfaction, no less an authority than Captain Raphael Semmes, who, in discussing the question generally with regard to Mexico, had little forethought of himself as a commissioned officer of the Confederate States.

No doubt he would have had a luxury of excuses and explanations, many of them reasonable. Still, I think we have here a delightful illustration of the difference between abstract theories and concrete applications, and if Seward and Welles could have got hold of this passage, they would have hailed it with infinite glee, as indeed the utterance of a Daniel come to judgment.

Pirate or not, the career of the Sumter, and far more that of the Alabama, have a flavor of desperate adventure about them, which does not lack fascination for lovers of romance. "Engaged in acts somewhat suggesting the pranks of the buccaneers," is the modest comment of Second Lieutenant Sinclair, and the facts amply bear him out. The Alabama was built by stealth in England, sailed from Liverpool under the British flag, and was commissioned practically on the high seas. Her crew were largely ruffians, sharked up from the worst corners of British seaports, requiring at all times a watchful eye and a heavy hand. The voyage was everywhere, now in Atlantic fog, now in Indian sunshine, battles with tropic storms, owl-flittings in murky twilight. Sometimes there would come a few days' repose in dubiously neutral ports. The captain would slip on shore for a touch of firm land, the sound of a woman's voice, perhaps a long ride over snowy mountains or through strange forests. On his return he would find half his crew drunk, the United States consul stirring up all sorts of trouble, and an order to depart at once, half-coaled and half-provisioned. Or, as at Cape Town, among the friendly English, he would be nearly suffocated with intrusive popularity.

Then it was up anchor and away, long months at sea, incessant watchfulness. But the monotony was broken almost daily by fierce swoops upon Northern merchantmen, which were stopped, examined, seized, their crews taken aboard the Alabama, the vessels themselves— since there were no Confederate ports to send them to— usually burned with all their cargo, serving sometimes as a decoy to lure yet other victims within the reach of the greedy aggressor. Any passengers on board the prizes were treated as were the crews, detained on the Alabama only until some convenient means was found of getting rid of them. Now and then among these were ladies, who at first regarded their captors with exaggerated fears. But the young officers managed to overcome this in most cases and the lieutenant who boarded one large steamer returned with his coat quite bare of buttons which had been cut off for mementoes. Assuredly this was playing the pranks of the buccaneers with a certain gayety.

The sordid side of such work is obvious enough. For a commissioned war-vessel to sail about the world, doing no fighting, but simply capturing and destroying unarmed merchantmen, seems in itself neither very useful, very creditable, nor very amusing. As to the usefulness, however, the Alabama's depredations probably did as much as anything to develop the peace spirit among the merchants of the North, and Semmes was no doubt right in thinking that he seriously diminished the pressure of the blockade by drawing so much attention to himself. And he is further right in asserting, as to discredit, that what damage he did to property and injury to persons is not to be named with the damage and injury done by Sherman without one whit more military excuse.

As to amusement, that is, excitement, the course of the Alabama supplied enough of it. Not to speak of winds and storms, to which she was incessantly exposed in her practically unbroken cruise of two years, there was the ever-present necessity of avoiding the Union men-of-war, a fleet of which were on the lookout, flying close upon her traces in every quarter of the globe. With the Northern press and the suffering merchants everywhere calling for redoubled vigilance and an immense reward of glory awaiting the destroyer of the dreaded destroyer, every Union officer was most keenly alert. For instance, it is interesting to find Admiral Mahan, as a young midshipman, begging the Navy Department to give him a ship that he may pursue Semmes, then in command of his first vessel, the Sumter: "Suppose it fails, what is lost? A useless ship, a midshipman, and a hundred men. If it succeeds, apart from the importance of the capture, look at the prestige such an affair would give the service."[6]

To evade hostility like this meant excitement enough. Yet for three years, in his two ships, Semmes did it, fighting only once with an inferior vessel, the Hatteras, which he sank. When at last, on the 19th of June, 1864, in the English Channel, he met the Kearsarge on nearly equal terms, it was by his own choice, not by compulsion, and on the whole, his ship made a good and creditable ending, though Professor Soley is no doubt right in thinking that the defeat was owing rather to inferior training and marksmanship on the Alabama than to the chain protection of the Union vessel of which the Confederates made so much.

But what we are seeking is a closer knowledge of Semmes himself. To accord with his firefly craft and with "pranks resembling those of the buccaneers" you no doubt imagine a gay young adventurer, handsome, gold-laced, laughing, swearing, singing, in short, the romantic freebooter of my dreams above mentioned.

The real Semmes was nothing of the sort. To begin with, at the outbreak of the war he was an elderly man. Born in 1809, he took his early training in the United States Navy, then returned to civil life and practiced law, then went into the Mexican War, and served all through it with credit and distinction, disappearing afterward in the routine of government service.

Seen as others saw him in 1860, he was anything but a gallant adventurer. He was not handsome, he was not winning, he was not magnetic. In fact, he gave rather the impression of a grave and reverend professional man than of a dashing captain, and some of his prisoners at first sight mistook him for a parson, an illusion quickly dispelled by a habit of marine phraseology which would not have been pleasing to Lee or Jackson. "Lean, sallow, and nervous, much less like a mariner than a sea-lawyer," says Rideing of him, after the war.[7] He was cold, quiet, and reserved, talked little with his officers, depended little on their advice, but made his own decisions and took all the responsibility for them. When the approach of the great final conflict aroused him sufficiently to make him ask Lieutenant Sinclair how he thought it would turn out, the lieutenant was quite overcome: "I was surprised that he should care to have my opinion, or that of any one else; for he rarely addressed any of us off duty, and never asked the advice or opinion of his subordinates on weighty matters." [8]

I do not know what better testimony to respectability, sanity, and conservatism could be had than that of Alexander H. Stephens, and Stephens speaks of Semmes as follows: "For some years before secession he was at the head of the Lighthouse Board in Washington. He resigned as soon as Alabama seceded, though he agreed with me thoroughly in my position on that question, as his letters to me show. He was a Douglas man, and you need not therefore be surprised when I tell you that I considered him a very sensible, intelligent, and gallant man. I aided him in getting an honorable position in our navy, and in getting him afloat as soon as possible, which he greatly desired." [9]

Fortunately, however, we are not obliged to depend on any external testimony. We have plenty of writing of the man's own which throws wide light upon his soul. He kept a careful log-book of both his cruises. This was used as a basis for the book written about him, called, "Log of the Sumter and Alabama," and again, by himself, in his huge "Memoir of Service Afloat during the War Between the States." But the original, as printed in the "Official Records," is far more valuable than the later studied and literary narratives.

To begin with, one cannot help being impressed with his fine intelligence. He had a mind constantly working, and trained to work with ease, assurance, and dispatch. This is perhaps most striking in his immense legal ingenuity. His position brought him daily into contact with the nicest and most puzzling international questions, both of law and morals, from the disposition of his prizes to the disposition of himself, when he surrendered his vessel, let her sink under his feet, and after he was picked out of the water by the English yacht, Deerhound, betook himself to England and safety, instead of to the Kearsarge and a Northern prison. On all these points he is inexhaustible in legal lore, fertile in persuasive argument, and most apt and energetic in making every possible suggestion tell.

Nor would I intimate that in all this abundant discussion he is not sincere, or any less so than the average lawyer. He is, indeed, quick to take advantage of every quibble. But the long legal cases in regard to many of his captures recorded in his log-book — that is, mainly for his own eye — seem to me to indicate a mind much open to conscientious scruples and a feeling that his elaborate argument must convince himself as well as others.

More attractive evidence of Semmes's intellectual power than that furnished by his legal pyrotechnics is his early book about the Mexican War. This is as intelligent a narrative of travel as can readily be found. There is not only the wide-open eye of the sympathetic observer; but the comments on the social life of the people, on their industries, their manners, their morals, their government, and their religion, are sober, fruitful, and suggestive, and may be read to-day with perhaps even more profit than fifty years ago.

Still, a pirate might be intelligent. Let us take other aspects of Semmes's character. How did he treat his prisoners, of whom, first and last, there must have been hundreds? His own account and that of his officers is, of course, highly favorable. He admits that at first, as a measure of retaliation for Union treatment of captured "pirates," he was unnecessarily rigid in the use of irons; but in the main he asserts that captives were made as comfortable as circumstances permitted and he insists especially that at no time was there any pillaging of private personal property. "We may as well state here," writes Lieutenant Sinclair, "that all our prisoners were housed on deck from necessity, the berth-deck being crowded by our own men. But we made them as comfortable as we could under the circumstances, spread awnings and tarpaulins over them in stormy weather, and in every way possible provided for their comfort. They were allowed full rations (less the spirit part) and their own cooks had the range of the galley in preparing their food to their taste. Indeed, when it is considered that our men had watch to keep and they none, they were better off for comfort than ourselves."[10] This, of course, refers only to the men. When women were brought on board, they were given the officers' own staterooms.

Both Semmes and his lieutenants take great pride in the humane treatment of those on board the large steamship, Ariel. When the ship was taken, the plan was to burn her and land the prisoners at Kingston. There was fever in Kingston, however; so, rather than expose so many persons to danger of infection, the vessel was allowed to go on her way under bond. Semmes's remark on this in his log (not in his published narrative) savors delightfully of the charity of Glossin in "Guy Mannering." "It would have been inhuman to put ashore, even if permitted (and I greatly doubted on this point), so large a number of persons, many of whom were women and children, to become victims, perhaps, to the pestilence." [11]

And what do the prisoners themselves say about it? Naturally their view was somewhat different. Complaints appear of rough usage, chiefly of the employment of irons, which was at times manifestly necessary, where the number of captives was so large. "The manner of the master of the steamer was overbearing and insolent in the extreme," writes one victim; "and it was at the great risk of the personal safety, if not of the life, of the deponent, that he so strenuously insisted upon his ship and cargo being released." [12] But in general there is a remarkable — all the more so because grudging — agreement that things were conducted peaceably and civilly and that no personal violence was used in any case. Here again the testimony of Bolles, who had made a thorough and hostile investigation, is conclusive. "In no one single solitary instance was there furnished a particle of proof that 'the pirate Semmes,' as many of my correspondents called him, had ever maltreated his captives, or subjected them to needless and unavoidable deprivation."[13]

It may be suggested that this line of conduct was dictated rather by policy than by kindness of heart. What, then, was Semmes's treatment of his crew? On this point, also, the testimony is conflicting. I have said that they were necessarily a rough lot. Semmes puts it more strongly: "The fact is, I have a precious set of rascals on board — faithless in the matter of abiding by their contracts, liars, thieves, and drunkards."[14] To have managed such a company, in sole authority, for two years, over the vast solitudes of ocean, is in itself strong testimony to executive ability and force of character. It is evident that stern and constant severity was needed and Semmes employed it, as he himself admits. I do not find any proof that the severity was excessive. In cases of open and extreme disorder punishment was awarded by formal court martial, and not suddenly, nor in anger. The harshest instance seems to have been that of the captured deserter Forrest,[15] who, after being several times "spread-eagled" in strenuous fashion, was put ashore in irons on a desert coast, the crew, without the knowledge of the captain, subscribing a purse which they hoped would enable him to get off, as it did. But the officers agree that Forrest's rascality stood out, even in that choice collection.

It is as to the result of this severity in discipline that there is a most interesting disagreement of witnesses. Semmes himself declares that it accomplished its object. "Many of my fellows, no doubt, thought they were shipping in a sort of privateer, where they would have a jolly good time and plenty of license. They have been wofully disappointed, for I have jerked them down with a strong hand, and now have a well-disciplined ship of war."[16] His officers confirm his statement energetically. Lieutenant Sinclair writes: "No better proof of the judicial methods of discipline outlined by Semmes could be submitted, than that under them, though engaged in acts somewhat suggesting the pranks of the buccaneers, our crew were as well held in hand as though serving on an English man-of-war in times of perfect peace, and at the same time in a state of perfect contentment."[17]

With this beatific vision it is really amusing to compare the assertions of some of the prisoners on the Alabama, who inspected conditions with a curious, though perhaps a somewhat malignant eye. "All the men forward are English and Irish," says one observer, "no Americans. The officers are Southerners, and, with the exception of the captain and first lieutenant, seem ignorant of their duties. The discipline on board was not very good, though the men seemed to be good seamen. They were over an hour setting the two topgallant sails. The men appeared to be dissatisfied."[18] And if it be urged that this was in September, 1862, before conditions were comfortably adjusted, we can turn to a still more severe account given by a reliable witness, in November, 1863, when the Alabama had run more than half of her troubled course. "Crew much dissatisfied, no prize money, no liberty, and see no prospect of getting any. Discipline very slack, steamer dirty, rigging slovenly. Semmes sometimes punishes, but is afraid to push too hard. . . . Crew do things for which would be shot on board American man-of-war; for instance, saw one of crew strike a master's mate; crew insolent to petty officers; was told by at least two thirds of them that they would desert on the first opportunity. . . . While on board saw drill only once, and that at pivot guns, very badly done; men ill-disciplined and were forced to it; lots of cursing."[19]

In such surroundings it might be vain to look for personal attachment. Perhaps even Jackson or Stuart would have been unable to inspire any. Still, in his book — the passage does not occur in his log — Semmes speaks of both officers and crew with what appears to be real affection. "When men have been drenched and wind-beaten in the same storm, . . . there is a feeling of brotherhood that springs up between them, that it is difficult for a landsman to conceive."[20] His sailors certainly had immense confidence in him, as well they might, and it is said that after the loss of the Alabama, many of them came and begged him to procure another ship. I do not find related of him, however, any incident so touching as that told by his first officer, Lieutenant Kell, — too simple and too human to have been invented, by Kell, at any rate, — of the dying seaman, who, as his superior was leaving the Alabama, then about to sink, "caught my hand and kissed it with such reverence and loyalty — the look, the act, lingers in my memory still." [21] Surely they were not all infernal rascals on board that pirate.

If we look at Semmes, for a moment, in other concerns of life besides the official, we shall find much that is attractive to complete the picture of him.

So far from having anything of the typical pirate's mercurial affections, he seems to have been a man of peculiarly domestic habit, much attached to his wife and to his children. The temporary presence of children and their mothers on the Alabama is referred to in his book with great feeling: "When I would turn over in my cot, in the morning, for another nap, in that dim consciousness which precedes awakening, I would listen, in dreamy mood, to the sweet voices over my head, . . . and giving free wing to fancy, I would be clasping again the absent dear ones to my heart." [22] Less literary, and therefore even more convincing, are the little touches of tenderness interspersed among the scientific observations and political discussion of the log-book. "The governor sent me off a fine turkey, and some fruit, and his lady a bouquet of roses. The roses were very sweet, and made me homesick for a while."[23] Again, "I am quite homesick this quiet Sunday morning. I am two long, long years and more absent from my family, and there are no signs of an abatement of the war."[24]

The same sensibility that shows in this home feeling manifests itself in other ways. Semmes was not only a wide reader in his profession and in lines connected with it, but he loved literature proper, read much poetry and quotes it often. He was singularly sensitive to beauty in any form.

Above all, his diary reads almost like that of a naturalist—Darwin or Bates—in its singularly close, intelligent, and affectionate observation of nature. Roving all over the tropic world of land and water, at a time when such study was less common than now, he kept his eyes open for both exceptional and ordinary natural phenomena. He had the keenest interest in the working of tides, storms, and currents, and not only records minutely all the empirical detail of such matters, but goes into elaborate discussion of the causes of them, illustrating with plans and diagrams which quaintly diversify the cargo-lists of Yankee schooners and the recital of attempts to blarney pompous officials of Portugal and Spain.

Nor is the appreciation of the charm of nature less than the sense of its scientific interest. Every opportunity of landing is seized as giving the tired sea-wanderer a chance to satisfy his love of the soil, and he paints delightful pictures of tropic scenes and things and people. Here again the more elaborate specimens are to be found in the books, especially in the earlier one on Mexico; but I prefer the piquant freshness of little touches jotted down, under the immediate impression, in the diary of the day. How graceful, for instance, is this description of Fernando de Noronha: "The island in the season at which we visited it was a gem of picturesque beauty, exceedingly broken and diversified with dells and rocks and small streams, etc. It was the middle of the rainy season. The little mountain paths as we returned became little brooks, that hummed and purled on their rapid course." [25] Or this, again, of Martinique: "In the afternoon strolled on the heights in the rear of the town, and was charmed with the picturesque scenery on every hand. The little valleys and nooks in which nestle the country houses are perfect pictures, and the abrupt and broken country presents delightful changes at every turn." [26] While the following passage adds a personal note which is as attractive as it is evidently sincere: "Visited the Savannah [Fort St. Louis] to hear the music, which is given every Sunday evening. It was a gay and beautiful scene, the moon, the shade trees, the statue of Josephine, the throng of well-dressed men and women, the large band and the fine music, the ripple of the sea, and last, though not least, the katydids, so fraught with memories of home, dear home!" [27]

And if Semmes was emotional and sensitive, he was also conscientious, high-principled, and genuinely religious. *Aide-toi et Dieu t'aidera*, "God helps those who help themselves," was the delightful motto of the Alabama, and past question her commander trusted in God as well as in his own right arm. He inherited the Catholic faith and persisted in it with evidently sincere as well as intelligent devotion. His argument, in his book on Mexico, for the value to humanity of a liturgical service is as clear and cogent as his criticism of the excessive influence of an ignorant clergy in Mexican life. The touches of personal religion in his diary are absolutely free from pretentiousness and are very winning in their simplicity. Sometimes, indeed, there is a naïve mixture of his worldly occupations with his spiritual zeal: "I have thus spent a busy day, without having time even to read a chapter in the Bible, and all for nothing — one Dutchman and two Englishmen."[28] But elsewhere the fervent outpouring of pious ejaculation is quite unmingled with any taint of sordid cares. "My life has been one of great vicissitude, but not of calamity or great suffering, and I have reason to be thankful to a kind Providence for the many favors I have received. I have enjoyed life to a reasonable extent, and I trust I shall have fortitude to meet with Christian calmness any fate that may be in store for me, and to undergo the great change, which awaits us all, with composure and a firm reliance upon the justice and goodness of God."[29] I think you must be asking now, with some astonishment, where is that pirate?

The practical Christian virtues, too, seem to be present, in desire at least, as well as Christian aspiration. Some of Semmes's reported utterances might make one think he lacked patience. He thinks so himself: "I am not discouraged, but I have had an excellent opportunity to practice the Christian virtue of patience, which virtue, I think, I am a little deficient in."[30] Humility, also, he endeavors to cultivate, when winds and seas tempt an angry criticism of the order of nature. "One of the most temper-trying of the *contretemps* of a seaman's life is, when your position is such as to render your latitude very important to you, to have a squall come up, just before it is time to look out for the sun, and to rain and obscure everything until it is a very [few] minutes too late for you, and then to have the sun shine out brightly, as if in mockery of your baffled desire. Such was the case to-day, this being the second day that we are without an observation for latitude. But I endeavor to profit by these trials, as they teach me a lesson of humility. What is man, that the sun should shine for him? And then, in our stupidity, we fail to see things in their true light; all the occurrences of nature, being in obedience to wise laws, must of course, be the best."[31]

With the insight into Semmes's inner life and private character thus acquired we are better able to appreciate the really lofty motives that animated him in his public service. His perfect courage, his entire determination and persistence in effort, are beyond dispute. Read the accounts of the calmness and self-sacrifice with which, in spite of a painful wound, he managed every detail of his last combat. The only aspersion upon him here is that he did not give himself up as a prisoner after being rescued by the Deerhound. It is possible that Lee or Albert Sidney Johnston would have done this; but I do not believe there were many officers in either the Union or the Confederate service who would have strained honor to a point so quixotically fine.

And back of the persistence in effort was an equally indisputable patriotism. Whether we agree with Semmes or not, we must recognize that he believed as heartily in the cause he was fighting for as did Davis or Lee. Thoughts like the following, confided to the intimate privacy of his diary, are incontestable evidence of sincerity as well as of devotion: "My dear family I consign with confidence to God's care, and our beloved country I feel certain He will protect and preserve, and in due time raise up to peace, independence, and prosperity. Our struggle must be just and holy in His sight, and as He governs the world by inexorable laws of right and wrong, the wicked and cruel people who are seeking our destruction cannot fail to be beaten back and destroyed. But it may be His pleasure to scourge us severely for our past sins and unworthiness, and to admit us to His favor again, only when we shall have been purified."[32]

Nor was this patriotism of Semmes much tempered by personal ambition or by any stimulus of excitement or adventure. As to ambition, however, it may be interesting to compare Semmes's letter to Howell Cobb, suggesting that it would be well for the Confederacy to have only a small regular navy and to give resigning United States naval officers rank equivalent to what they formerly held.[33] But the captain of the Alabama was well over fifty, and at that age personal comfort means more than plaudits and laurels. It is really most curious to see the supposedly triumphant and exultant pirate sighing over the tediousness and weariness of his lot and eager to give "a thousand leagues of sea for one acre of barren ground." "Perhaps this constant, stormy tumbling about at sea is the reason why we seamen are so calm and quiet on shore. We come to hate all sorts of commotion, whether physical or moral."[34] And again, even more vividly and pointedly: "Barometer gradually falling. Ship rolling and pitching in the sea and all things dreary looking and uncomfortable. I am supremely disgusted with the sea and all its belongings. The fact is, I am past the age when man ought to be subjected to the hardships and discomforts of the sea. Seagoing is one of those constant strifes which none but the vigorous, the hardy, and the hopeful — in short, the youthful, or, at most, the middle-aged — should be engaged in. The very roar of the wind through the rigging, with its accompaniments of rolling and tumbling, hard, overcast skies, etc., gives me the blues."[35]

Yet, in spite of age, of gray respectability, of undeniable fine qualities, there is in Semmes a certain strain of the pirate, after all. About many of his utterances there is a violence not only fierce but coarse, a tone of offensive vituperation much more appropriate to Captain Kidd than to a Christian soldier. His own friends recognize this to the extent of apologizing for it. "Semmes's verbal and written utterances," says Sinclair, "manifest a bitterness of feeling towards his foes which is calculated to mislead one respecting his real character. . . . He was uniformly just in his decisions. He respected private property and private feelings. And it was the rule, rather than the exception, that he provided in the best possible way for his prisoners, military and civil; and we have often seen that he gave them boats and whatever their ships afforded of comfort and luxury to get away with. This was not the conduct of a malevolent partisan, but distinctly that of a generous and chivalrous foe. It is by his acts rather than by his utterances that a man like Semmes should be judged. He had a noble and generous soul."[36] Unfortunately our words sometimes go further than our acts, especially when we print them, and it is hard to reconcile all that Semmes wrote with perfect nobility or generosity.

It is true, he had much excuse. He was pursued with scorn and vilification which no one thought of bestowing on Johnston or Lee; yet there was no reason for calling him a common malefactor and enemy of the human race, any more than them. It is true, further, that his tongue often belied his real feeling, as it occasionally showed itself, for instance when, long after the war, he replied "very gently" to Mrs. Kell, who asked him to help reconcile her husband, "He has fifteen years or more longer to live to feel as I do. I am fifteen years his senior. Give him that long to grow reconciled to things as they are."[37] Finally, it is true that the ugly violence of expression does not appear in the earlier Mexican book, which is a model of dignity, sanity, and self-restraint. In short, a nervous, sensitive, high-strung nature was irritated beyond control of itself by the long strain of toil and hardship and exposure. As Semmes himself admirably expresses it, speaking of his own antagonist, Winslow: "I had known, and sailed with him, in the old service, and knew him *then* to be a humane and Christian gentleman. What the war may have made of him, it is impossible to say. It has turned a great deal of the milk of human kindness to gall and wormwood."[38] Certainly Semmes's human kindness had been gravely affected in that fashion, and none of the above explanations will serve to excuse a manner of speech which would have been impossible not only for Lee or Stephens, but even, under any circumstances, for Beauregard, or Johnston, or Longstreet.

Such a charge must be supported by illustrations,

however offensive. But it should be understood that these illustrations are not unique, but merely represent the general tone of Semmes's book, "Memoirs of Service Afloat during the War between the States." Even in the earlier, simpler diary of actual war days, a note is sounded that is far from agreeable. "If the historian perform his duty faithfully, posterity will be amazed at the wickedness and corruption of the Northern and Western people, and will wonder by what process such a depth of infamy was reached in so short a time. The secret lies here: The politicians had become political stockjobbers, and the seekers of wealth had become knaves and swindlers; and into these classes may be divided nearly the whole Yankee population. Such is 'Plymouth Rock' in our day, with its Beechers in the pulpit and its Lincolns in the chair of Washington, its Sumners and Lovejoys in Congress, *et id omne genus* in the contract market."[39]

One expects this sort of abuse from irresponsible agitators, both North and South. One does not expect it from officers and gentlemen. But the language of Semmes's book is far worse. "The pay of the Federal Consul at Maranham, was, I believe, at the time I visited the town, about twelve hundred dollars per annum. As was to be expected, a small man filled the small place. He was quite young, and with commendable Yankee thrift, was exercising, in the consular dwelling, the occupation of a dentist; the 'old flag' flying over his files, false teeth, and spittoons. He probably wrote the despatch, a copy of which had been handed me, in the intervals between the entrance and exit of his customers. It was not wonderful, therefore, that this semi-diplomat, charged with the affairs of the Great Republic, and with the decayed teeth of the young ladies of Maranham, at one and the same time, should be a little confused as to points of international law, and the rules of Lindley Murray." [40]

The man who wrote that had a coarse streak in him somewhere. Stuart liked rhetoric, but he could never have written that. Jackson detested Yankees, but he could never have written that.

And with this vein of detestable facetiousness Semmes mingles an almost equally trying assortment of cheap heroics. He quotes Byron, "Don Juan," and "The Corsair," and "The Island," until you would think Conrad and Lara were his ideals and Jack Bunce, *alias* Altamont, his model.

Such a tribute to the power of the gallery goes far to prepare us for the description furnished by one of Semmes's captives, the master of the Brilliant, a description no doubt exaggerated, but which may not seem so much so now, as when we were fresh from the touching — and absolutely genuine — confessions about home and God. It may be added that this passage furnishes the only explanation I have seen of "Old Beeswax," a name accepted by Semmes himself and frequently referred to by officers and crew. I quote from the New York "Herald" of October 17, 1862: "Captain Hagar says that, however much Semmes may have had the appearance of a gentleman when an officer of the United States Navy, he has entirely changed now. He sports a huge mustache, the ends of which are waxed in a manner to throw that of Victor Emmanuel entirely into the shade, and it is evident that it occupies much of his attention. His steward waxes it every day carefully, and so prominent is it that the sailors of the Alabama call him 'Old Beeswax.' His whole appearance is that of a corsair, and the transformation appears to be complete from Commander Raphael Semmes, U.S.N., to a combination of Lafitte, Kidd, and Gibbs, the three most noted pirates the world has ever known."

So, you see, I can cherish a watery image of my pirate, after all. And if the words attributed to him by his near friend, Maffitt, on the sinking of his ship, are genuine, neither Cleveland nor the Red Rover could have struck an attitude or phrased an exit more effectively. "Raising his sword with affectionate solicitude, he gently placed it on the binnacle, sorrowfully exclaiming, 'Rest thee, excalibur, thy grave is with the Alabama.'"[41]

Excalibur! oh!

IX

The Battle of Gettysburg

IX

THE BATTTLE OF GETTYSBURG

IT was the climax of a struggle that had been inevitable for fifty years; and only now, fifty years later, can we look back calmly and disentangle the complicated motives and passions that led up to it.

In the Revolutionary War Massachusetts and Virginia, New York and Georgia, fought side by side, with equal courage and equal sacrifice. All alike felt that free men must move freely to the full and perfect realization of a great republic in a great new continent.

Then the dividing-line came to be drawn more and more sharply. The North was busy, eager, restless, full of new thoughts and new devices, impatient of tradition and dignity, always looking forward. It lived in cities, amidst the hurry and bustle of cities, the whir of machinery, the smoke of factory chimneys, everywhere the ardor for progress, material and spiritual.

The South was dreamy and quiet; it loved old days and old ways, old stately manners. It dwelt in broad fields, by quiet rivers, handed down possessions and ideas from father to son, and read the books and thought the thoughts of a hundred years before. To a people so living, the sleepy service of the negro slave was in the natural order of things, just as the impatient North believed that nothing was well done that a man did not do for himself.

In the same way the North, with its seven-league boots of progress, stepped right over the old state limits, and forgot them, looking every day more to the Union as the central organ of government, while the South wanted as little governing as possible, and that little done by Virginia, or South Carolina, or Mississippi.

How could they long get on together? Both sides loved their country and American ideals. Both sides produced great men, men of power, men of patriotism, who strove with all their might to reconcile the difference between the opposing forces. As we look back now, it seems as if that could and should have been done. But the chasm was too wide and too deep. The South called the North "shopkeepers," and said the Northern soul was tainted with the sordid greed of gain — and there was some truth in it. The North called the South "slave-drivers," and said that slavery was a relic of barbarism, utterly out of date in free America — and there was truth in this also. Bitter words bred bitter feelings, and bitter feelings bitter words again, until it seemed as if there was nothing but bitterness.

Meanwhile the great West was growing. Which should it belong to, North or South? Whichever won the West would undoubtedly be the controlling power in the nation. The struggle was long and complicated. When at last the North definitely won, politically, with the election of Lincoln, the Southern States had become so estranged from their Northern sisters that they refused to live with them any longer, and that meant war.

Perhaps war was indispensable to show each side the great qualities of the other. For at the beginning each despised the other. The war would be brief enough, said the North, for the South was all bluff and bluster, but when it came to real fighting, would do nothing. The war would be brief enough, said the South, for what could clerks and lawyers and factory hands do against a people who lived on horseback, and were quick with their weapons? So both sides talked in the early days of '61. After four years they were wiser.

At first the South was doubtless better prepared. More clearly than the North, she had seen trouble coming. Her leaders were men of fighting spirit, who took practical military measures at once. The common soldiers, though all a little too ready to be officers, as Stuart said, were in fine training, accustomed to outdoor life, good riders, and much more used to arms than the average Northerner. The heavy, unwieldy bulk of the North got into battle slowly; it could not realize that a life-and-death struggle was at hand. Moreover, the North had to invade and attack, always the more difficult part to play.

The great drama falls as naturally into acts as a Shakespearean tragedy. Act one: alarms, excursions, challenge, and counter-challenge, still some belated attempts at conciliation and reconciliation. Then the guns heard at Sumter wake the dullest from their sleep. There is busy marching to and fro, a death here, a death there, a broken skirmish with uncertain victory. Two armed mobs gather near Washington, rush at each other, sway back and forth like two monsters in blind fury, part, and the routed Unionists hurry in confusion from the field of Bull Run, leaving the South victor in the first great battle.

Act two keeps the South still ahead. In the West, to be sure, one Union man, with slow, steady, iron fist, hammers his way upward, regardless of opposition, indifferent to failure, seeing the end clearly from the beginning. Moreover, the Union navy, with its strangling blockade, played from the first the part that was to prove most significant of all.

But the eastern side of the stage, the more conspicuous side, was for two years full of Southern triumph. Jackson, dashing hither and thither with the speed of Napoleon, drove his bewildered opponents from the Valley. Lee, succeeding Johnston in command of the Army of Northern Virginia, drew Jackson to himself, and compelled the superior forces of McClellan to abandon the Peninsula. Lincoln, seeking a great man in vain, tried the boasting Pope. Lee and Jackson beat him at Bull Run. McClellan was tried again, failed to conquer at Antietam, and was dropped once more. Lincoln turned to Burnside, and Burnside hurled thousands to death against Lee and Jackson on the heights of Fredericksburg. Lincoln turned to Hooker, and Hooker entangled "the finest army on this planet" in the thickets of Chancellorsville, where Lee and Jackson throttled it in a close-drawn net of woven steel.

And act two closed with Southern triumph, so that Lincoln told his God "that we could not stand another Chancellorsville or Fredericksburg." And his God heard him, for in Virginia the South never really triumphed any more.

All this Southern victory came under one man, one of the great soldiers of the world, Robert E. Lee. This man typified all that was best in the South. A member of one of the most distinguished Virginia families, he had the fine qualities of his class, with none of its weaknesses. He had courage without bluster, dignity without arrogance, reserve without haughtiness, tranquillity without sloth. A soldier in all his regal bearing, in every fibre of his body, his character was far larger than is essential to the profession of arms. In the great decisions of life he guided his action by what seemed to him the principles of duty, and by those only. Political animosity long called him, and sometimes still calls him, traitor; but if the word means a man who sells his convictions for a price, it was never less deserved. For three years the South gave him absolute trust, and no people ever trusted more wisely.

As a soldier, Lee was bold to excess. Working with the swift agency of "Stonewall" Jackson, he struck blow after blow, each more aggressive and more audacious than the preceding one, till he came to feel that the shifting and uncertain Union leadership was no match for him anywhere. With Jackson's aid he won the splendid victory of Chancellorsville. Then, although Jackson was gone, Lee thought he could invade the North, destroy Hooker and his demoralized army, and perhaps dictate terms of peace in Washington, or even in Philadelphia or New York. With triumph in his heart and in the hearts of his soldiers, he crossed the Potomac, and marched north to the vicinity of the little town of Gettysburg.

Meanwhile the Union army had again changed commanders, and Hooker had given place to General George G. Meade. Meade was a plain man, a quiet man; seeing him in private life, you would never have taken him for a soldier. He dealt little in the fuss and show of war, little in words, wrote no magniloquent dispatches. The last thing he talked of was himself, and therefore, after the great struggle was over, others got much credit that should have been his.

But he was a thinker; he believed that battles depended more on brains than on sabres; he thought out his strategy to the end, yet was quick also to meet an emergency that disarranged his thinking. Above all, he should be forever honored for the circumstances under which he fought Gettysburg. To take a beaten army from a beaten commander, and at three days' notice fight a battle against troops like Lee's under a general like Lee, was as hard a task as was ever imposed on mortal man in this fighting world. Meade accepted it without a murmur, and saved a nation. Yet some grumble because he did not do more.

So the battle at Gettysburg came. Neither commander meant to fight just there. But the strange chances of war brought on a conflict in a position eminently favorable to the Union army, and correspondingly difficult for the Confederates. Meade's troops held a curved ridge, where he could easily support one part of his line with another. Lee had to spread his forces outside the ridge, and could not be sure of their attacking all at once. Yet, overconfident, he determined to fight, feeling that to withdraw would mean the foiling of all his hopes.

On the last day of June the Union troops entered the town of Gettysburg at the northern end of the ridge above mentioned. On July 1, the Confederates began to attack them there. Neither commander-in-chief was on the field. Reynolds, one of the ablest and one of the noblest of the Northern generals, had charge at first, and would probably have prevented disaster if he had lived. But he was shot early in the fighting.

Doubleday and Howard, who succeeded him, could not control the situation. The Confederates swept on impetuously, and it almost looked as if the experience of

Chancellorsville were to be repeated. But there was no Stonewall Jackson to profit instantly by the enemy's confusion. Hancock, sent forward by Meade to take entire command, succeeded in pulling the troops together; and Ewell, who was at the head of Jackson's corps, did not venture, in the uncertainties of coming darkness, to carry out the discretionary instructions that Lee had given him.

Therefore, when night closed, the Union army still held the strong position on the ridge, and the Confederates had won no real victory. Their success had been such, however, as to convince most of them, including the commander-in-chief, that the next day would set Meade and his troops in full retreat toward Washington.

The next day came, July 2. Meade had established himself firmly on the curve of the ridge; his flanks supported each other. But at the southern end of the ridge, Great Round Top and Little Round Top were, in the morning, unduly exposed. It was here that Lee, relying upon Ewell at the northern end to distract the attention of the enemy, determined to make his main attack.

This attack was to be led by Longstreet, a splendid fighter, but a man too confident in his own opinions, and in this case, perhaps justly, in the opinion that Lee was making a mistake. Longstreet's heart was therefore not wholly in his work, and either from this reason, or from difficulties really insurmountable, he did not begin the assault on the Round Tops until the afternoon, when it was too late.

When he did attack, it was indeed magnificent. Gray and blue fought with equal valor. Perhaps they realized that they were making history, and that the fate of a nation depended on their efforts; or perhaps they fought without any realization except that they were Americans, and that those heights were to be taken or to be held. But, as throughout the whole war, with courage so equal, defense was stronger than attack.

Again and again Longstreet hurled his columns at those rocky slopes, sometimes gaining a foothold in one place, sometimes in another. Each time Sickles, Warren, Humphreys, and the rest threw the aggressors back, and the immense advantage of the curved Union position enabled Meade to sustain weak and threatened points, while Lee's separated flanks could not act in harmony with each other.

Thus, at the end of the second day, the Confederate general had tried both wings of his antagonist, and in spite of temporary shifts of fortune, had found them both invulnerable.

There remained the Union centre, Cemetery Hill, as yet untried. To storm that high point, which could be readily strengthened by troops hurried from either flank, seemed a wild adventure. Events proved that it was a wild adventure. When the general-in-chief assigned the task to Pickett's splendid division, which had all this time been held in reserve, Longstreet, the corps commander, again protested. "There never yet were 15,000 men who could cross that plain and take that hill," he said.

But Lee believed in his troops; believed that they could go anywhere and do anything. He believed that with proper support from other divisions and from artillery, Pickett's 15,000 men could cross that plain and take that hill. And he ordered them to do it.

Friends assert and foes admit that it was one of the great charges of the world. First came the prelude from an orchestra of scores of cannon, the roar of an artillery duel unsurpassed even in the battles of Napoleon. Still the cannon thundered, and still Longstreet delayed to say the word for those 15,000 to march out to death. At last, when ammunition was failing, he gave in.

Forth rode Pickett, with his long locks and his chivalrous bearing. At his back were regiments with the best blood of the South — men ready to die for what they believed as good a cause as any man ever died for. In front of them rose the slopes of Cemetery Hill, crowned by walls and fences, and defended by men whose courage was equal to their own. On swept those splendid lines, winning the admiration of friend and foe alike. Shell hissed over them, shot tore through them, men fell to right and left, ranks thinned, whole regiments wavered; still they pressed on, reached the foot of the hill, swarmed up it, and for a moment mingled in furious conflict with the defenders. Then they rolled back, the few that were left of them, not routed, not flying, but sullenly, slowly, back across the blood-soaked plain, among the heaps of dead. Gettysburg was over. The third act of the drama was finished. The Union was saved.

Yes, saved. Gettysburg, with Vicksburg, completed the climax. The fourth act dragged on through the vicissitudes of Chickamauga and Chattanooga in the West. The repulses of the Wilderness and Cold Harbor gave the Confederacy momentary hope. But the slow, strangling grip of Sherman's host in Georgia at last prepared the way for the fifth and final act, which terminated in the long agony of Petersburg and Appomattox.

Yes, the Union was saved. And to-day the North has no more reason to rejoice at it than the South has. Think what secession and separation would have meant: two nations forever facing each other in arms across the Potomac! A standing army of half a million men on each side would have been needed, in instant readiness for war likely to come at any moment over disputes about territory, disputes about emigration, disputes about commerce; especially disputes about slavery, if, as is probable, the Confederacy had continued to be a great slave empire.

Think what it means for the development of this great continent! Instead of two, or perhaps half a dozen, rival nations straining every effort to outdo one another in military equipment, jealous of one another's glory and prosperity, we are one great nation of brothers, all profiting by one another's progress, all alike proud of one civilization, one Constitution, and one flag.

Think what it means for more than this one continent! Nearly one hundred and fifty years ago our fathers began a great new experiment in democracy — the government of the people, by the people, and for the people. What if, after less than a century of trial, the experiment had failed, and the great, growing, triumphant republic had fallen to pieces, shattered by its own weight, giving evidence to its enemies that the people could not harmonize their discords; that they could not govern and control themselves. For this the old aristocracies of Europe had waited; this they had gloated over in anticipation. Bull Run, Fredericksburg, Chancellorsville filled the French and English conservatives with ecstasy. Gettysburg taught them that the United States were not yet dead, Appomattox that they were still united, and that democracy was still the hope of the world.

As South and North grow nearer and nearer together, the anniversaries of these events must be more and more cherished. All animosity will pass out of them. Meade and Lee, Hancock and Longstreet, Reynolds and Pickett, even more, the common soldiers, North and South both, were all Americans, all ours, ours to praise, ours to be proud of, ours to learn from. The inheritance of their courage, their sacrifice, their loyalty to high ideals is one of which no country can ever have too much. And if the tradition of these great souls brings with it glory, it brings duty with it also. We are not called upon to go out and fight in arms as they did, but there is plenty of fighting left. The danger to a republic from open war is great. The danger from self-indulgence, from pampered living, from the spirit of letting others do things, is even greater. I am ready to believe that at a sudden call of duty our automobiling, dancing, money-getting youth would respond as did those of '61, drop their play, and go out to attack or defend a Cemetery Hill. But I wish we could make them remember that even in common, humdrum, daily life every man has his Gettysburg sooner or later. Let him fight it and win it, so that his little republic — for of such is made the great Republic — shall be forever triumphant and free.

THE END

NOTES

TITLES OF BOOKS MOST FREQUENTLY CITED, SHOWING ABBREVIATIONS USED

Battles and Leaders of the Civil War.	*B. and L.*
BUTLER, PIERCE, *Judah P. Benjamin.*	Butler.
CHESNUT, MARY BOYKIN, *A Diary from Dixie.*	Mrs. Chesnut.
CLEVELAND, HENRY, *Alexander H. Stephens.*	Cleveland.
The Cruise of the Alabama and Sumter. From the private journals and other papers of Commander Raphael Semmes, C.S.N., and other officers.	*Alabama and Sumter.*
The Congressional Globe.	*Globe.*
COOKE, JOHN ESTEN, *The Wearing of the Gray.*	Cooke, *Wearing.*
DAVIS, JEFFERSON, *The Rise and Fall of the Confederate Government.*	Davis, *Rise and Fall.*
DAVIS, VARINA HOWELL, *Jefferson Davis.*	Mrs. Davis.
FREMANTLE, A. J., *Three Months in the Southern States.*	Fremantle.
HUGHES, ROBERT M., *General Johnston.*	Hughes.
JOHNSON, BRADLEY T., *A Memoir of the Life and Public Services of Joseph E. Johnston.*	Johnson.
JOHNSTON, JOSEPH E., *A Narrative of Military Operations.*	Johnston, *Narrative.*
JOHNSTON, R. M., and BROWNE, W. H., *Life of Alexander H. Stephens.*	Johnston and Browne.
JONES, J. B., *A Rebel War Clerk's Diary.*	Jones, *Diary.*
KELL, JOHN MCINTOSH, *Recollections of a Naval Life.*	Kell.
KOHLER, MAX J., *Judah P. Benjamin: Statesman and Jurist,* in *Publications of the American Jewish Society,* no. 12.	Kohler.
LONGSTREET, HELEN D., *Lee and Longstreet at High Tide.*	Mrs. Longstreet.
LONGSTREET, JAMES, *From Manassas to Appomattox.*	Longstreet, *M. to A.*
MCCLELLAN, H. B., *Life and Campaigns of Major General J. E. B. Stuart.*	McClellan.
MAURY, DABNEY H., *Recollections of a Virginian in the Mexican, Indian, and Civil Wars.*	Maury.

Official Records of the Union and Confederate Armies (volumes referred to by serial numbers, Arabic).	*O. R.*
Official Records of the Union and Confederate Navies.	*O. R. N.*
PHILLIPS, ULRICH B., *The Life of Robert Toombs.*	Phillips.
POLLARD, EDWARD A., *The Early Life, Campaigns, and Public Services of Robert E. Lee, with a Record of the Campaigns and Heroic Deeds of his Companions in Arms.*	Pollard, *Lee.*
POLLARD, EDWARD A., *The Life of Jefferson Davis.*	Pollard, *Davis.*
POLLARD, EDWARD A., *The Lost Cause.*	Pollard, *L. C.*
REED, JOHN C., *The Brothers' War.*	Reed.
RHODES, JAMES FORD, *A History of the United States from the Compromise of 1850.*	Rhodes, *U.S.*
RICHARDSON, J. D., *Messages and Papers of the Confederacy.*	Richardson.
ROMAN, ALFRED, *The Military Operations of General Beauregard.*	Roman.
SEMMES, RAPHAEL, *Service Afloat and Ashore during the Mexican War.*	*Mexican War.*
SEMMES, RAPHAEL, *Memoirs of Service Afloat during the War between the States.*	*Service Afloat.*
SINCLAIR, ARTHUR, *Two Years on the Alabama.*	Sinclair.
SOUTHERN HISTORICAL SOCIETY PAPERS.	*S. H. S. P.*
STEPHENS, ALEXANDER H., *Recollections of.*	Stephens, *Diary.*
STEPHENS, ALEXANDER H., *A Constitutional View of the Late War between the States.*	Stephens, *War between the States.*
STOVALL, PLEASANT A., *Robert Toombs.*	Stovall.
TOOMBS, ROBERT; STEPHENS, ALEXANDER H.; and COBB, HOWELL, *The Correspondence of*, edited by ULRICH B. PHILLIPS, in *Annual Report of American Historical Association*, for the year 1911.	*Toombs Correspondence.*
WISE, JOHN S., *The End of an Era.*	Wise.

NOTES

CHAPTER I

1. J. D. Cox, *Military Reminiscences of the Civil War*, vol. II, p. 190.
2. E. P. Alexander, *Military Memoirs of a Confederate*, p. 577
3. *M. to A.*, p. 432.
4. *L. C.*, p. 439.
5. Quoted in Hughes, p. 293.
6. Johnson, p. 304.
7. J. R. Young, *Around the World with General Grant*, vol. I, p. 212.
8. *The Home Letters of General Sherman*, p. 264.
9. J. C. Ropes, *The Story of the Civil War*, vol. II, p. 158.
10. Maury, p. 176.
11. Fremantle, p. 124.
12. Hughes, p. 32.
13. J. W. Jones, *Life and Letters of General Robert E. Lee*, p. 41.
14. Hughes, p. 195.
15. *O. R.*, vol. 14, p. 464.
16. Johnson, p. 99.
17. *O. R.*, vol. 99, p. 1247.
18. Johnson, p. 266.
19. Mrs. Chesnut, p. 249.
20. Mrs. D. Giraud Wright, *A Southern Girl in '61*, p. 155.
21. Johnson, p. 567.
22. *O. R.*, vol. 36, p. 199.
23. *O. R.*, vol. 76, p. 882.
24. *O. R.*, vol. 5, p. 987.
25. *O. R.*, vol. 14, p. 508.
26. *O. R.*, vol. 36, p. 216.
27. *O. R.*, vol. 36, p. 207.
28. *O. R.*, vol. 38, p. 1070.
29. Hughes, p. 86.
30. W. T. Sherman, *Memoirs*, vol. II, p. 141.
31. In Pollard, *Davis*, p. 376.
32. Fremantle, p. 125.
33. *O. R.*, vol. 14, p. 551.
34. *O. R.*, vol. 5, p. 1065.
35. Hughes, p. 85.

36. *O. R.*, vol. 14, p. 499.
37. *O. R.*, vol. 5, p. 1075.
38. *O. R.*, vol. 35, p. 726.
39. *O. R.*, vol. 53, p. 742.
40. *O. R.*, vol. 56, p. 801.
41. Communicated by Captain F. M. Colston, to whom it was related by General S. D. Lee.
42. Hughes, p. 155.
43. *O. R.*, vol. 56, p. 857.
44. *O. R.*, vol. 5, p. 1062.
45. *O. R.*, vol. 58, p. 603.
46. *O. R.*, vol. 58, p. 604.
47. *O. R.*, vol. 59, p. 618.
48. *O. R.*, vol. 35, p. 781.
49. Harvie to Davis, *O. R.*, vol. 53, p. 490.
50. Mrs. D. Giraud Wright, *A Southern Girl in '61*, p. 185.
51. *No Name Magazine*, September, 1890, p. 226.
52. Evansville *Courier*, April 12, 1891.
53. *R. and F.*, vol. I, p. 355.
54. *O. R.*, vol. 99, p. 1308.
55. *B. and L.*, vol. IV, p. 273.
56. Military Historical Society of Massachusetts, *Publications*, vol. I, p. 122.
57. *B. and L.*, vol. II, 209.
58. *B. and L.*, vol. II, p. 203.
59. *B. and L.*, vol. II, p. 205.
60. *Narrative*, p. 54.
61. *Narrative*, p. 229.
62. *Narrative*, p. 269.
63. Conversation with Colonel Allan, in Marshall Papers (MS.).
64. *U.S.*, vol. II, p. 460.
65. Johnson, p. 327.
66. Johnson, p. 329.
67. Johnson, p. 308.
68. *O. R.*, vol. 5, p. 105.
69. Hughes, p. 84.
70. R. Stiles, *Four Years under Marse Robert*, p. 90.
71. J. D. Cox, *Military Reminiscences of the Civil War*, vol. II, p. 53.
72. Fremantle, p. 117.
73. Hughes, p. 306.
74. *The History of the Rebellion* (American ed., 1827), vol. III, p. 1327.
75. *O. R.*, vol. 5, p. 1059.
76. *O. R.*, vol. 35, p. 624.

77. *O. R.*, vol. 5, p. 777.
78. John Esten Cooke, *Life of General Robert E. Lee*, p. 66.
79. *O. R.*, vol. 12, p. 275.
80. *O. R.*, vol. 35, p. 624.
81. R. Stiles, *Four Years under Marse Robert*, p. 90.
82. Mrs. D. Giraud Wright, *A Southern Girl in '61*, p. 240.
83. *Four Years under Marse Robert*, p. 90.
84. Hughes, p. 29.
85. *O. R.*, vol. 58, p. 543.
86. *O. R.*, vol. 38, p. 948.
87. *M. to A.*, p. 100.
88. *O. R.*, vol. 56, p. 878.
89. D. H. Maury, in *S. H. S. P.*, vol. XVIII, p. 179.
90. *O. R.*, vol. 76, p. 891.
91. Mrs. Chesnut, p. 350.
92. Mrs. Pickett, in *Lippincott's Magazine*, vol. LXXIX, p. 55.

CHAPTER II

1. In *S. H. S. P.*, vol. I, p. 100.
2. McClellan, p. 8.
3. R. E. Frayser, in *S. H. S. P.*, vol. XXVI, p. 89.
4. McClellan, p. 29.
5. McClellan, p. 32.
6. Cooke, *Wearing*, p. 39.
7. H. von Borcke, *Memoirs of the Confederate War for Independence*, vol. II, p. 60.
8. John Esten Cooke, *Mohun*, p. 158.
9. McClellan, p. 390.
10. J. Scheibert, *Der Bürgerkrieg in den nordamerikanischen Staaten*, p. 67.
11. *O. R.*, vol. 12, p. 1038.
12. *O. R.*, vol. 28, p. 55.
13. Cooke, *Wearing*, p. 27.
14. *O. R.*, vol. 16, p. 732.
15. McClellan, p. 409.
16. *O. R.*, vol. 16, p. 742.
17. *O. R.*, vol. 108, p. 860.
18. In letter to the author.
19. *O. R.*, vol. 16, p. 726.
20. *O. R.*, vol. 40, p. 789.
21. McClellan, p. 321.
22. *O. R.*, vol. 16, p. 731.
23. *O. R.*, vol. 12, p. 1036.

24. *O. R.*, vol. 28, p. 54.
25. Fremantle, p. 293.
26. J. Scheibert, *Der Bürgerkrieg in den nordamerikanischen Staaten*, p. 59.
27. *O. R.*, vol. 13, p. 514.
28. In Fitzhugh Lee, *General Lee*, p. 337.
29. *O. R.*, vol. 5, p. 177.
30. Longstreet, *M. to A.*, p. 573.
31. J. Scheibert to J. W. Jones, in *S. H. S. P.*, vol. IX, p. 571.
32. John S. Mosby, *Stuart's Cavalry in the Gettysburg Campaign*, p. xix.
33. Letter to McClellan, in McClellan, p. 256.
34. *O. R.*, vol. 5, p. 1063.
35. Cooke, *Wearing*, p. 31.
36. *O. R.*, vol. 40, p. 821.
37. *O. R.*, vol. 13, p. 518.
38. John S. Mosby, *War Reminiscences and Stuart's Cavalry Campaigns*, p. 220.
39. John S. Mosby, *War Reminiscences*, p. 229.
40. Fitzhugh Lee, in *S. H. S. P.*, vol. I, p. 102.
41. John S. Mosby, *War Reminiscences*, p. 228.
42. Cooke, *Wearing*, p. 18.
43. *War Reminiscences*, p. 231.
44. Cooke, *Wearing*, p. 23.
45. John Esten Cooke, *Stonewall Jackson*, p. 51.
46. *O. R.*, vol. 28, p. 54.
47. *O. R.*, vol. 108, p. 594.
48. *S. H. S. P.*, vol. XI, p. 510.
49. In *S. H. S. P.*, vol. I, p. 101.
50. *Wearing*, p. 19.
51. Cooke, *Wearing*, p. 23.
52. H. von Borcke, *Memoirs of the Confederate War for Independence*, vol. I, p. 309.
53. John Esten Cooke, *Stonewall Jackson*, p. 375.
54. J. W. Jones, *Life and Letters of General Robert E. Lee*, p. 391.
55. *O. R.*, vol. 12, p. 1040.
56. *O. R.*, vol. 12, p. 1037.
57. *O. R.*, vol. 48, p. 102.
58. John Esten Cooke, *Stonewall Jackson*, p. 399.
59. H. B. McClellan, in *S. H. S. P.*, vol. VIII, p. 191.
60. Cooke, *Wearing*, p. 25.
61. Cooke, *Wearing*, p. 25.
62. H. von Borcke, *Memoirs*, vol. I, p. 195.
63. Cooke, *Wearing*, p. 200.
64. H. W. Manson, in *The Confederate Veteran*, vol. II, p. 12.

65. H. von Borcke, *Memoirs*, vol. II, p. 16.
66. Cooke, *Wearing*, p. 26.
67. John Esten Cooke, *Mohun*, p. 26.
68. H. von Borcke, *Memoirs*, vol. II, p. 49.
69. Cooke, *Wearing*, p. 29.
70. John Esten Cooke, *Mohun*, p. 26.
71. *O. R.*, vol. 16, p. 737.
72. *O. R.*, vol. 28, p. 54.
73. *O R.*, vol. 44, p. 690.
74. *O. R.*, vol. 40, p. 836.
75. *O. R.*, vol. 40, p. 792.
76. *O. R.*, vol. 16, p. 741.
77. *O. R.*, vol. 16, p. 742.
78. General T. F. Rodenbough, in *Photographic History of the Civil War*, vol. IV, p. 69.

CHAPTER III

1. *O. R.*, vol. 26, p. 903.
2. Fremantle, p. 242.
3. Pollard, *Lee*, p. 420.
4. Fremantle, p. 273.
5. Fremantle, p. 267.
6. Pollard, *Lee*, p. 419.
7. Fremantle, p. 273.
8. *O. R.*, vol. 2, p. 544.
9. Fremantle, p. 261.
10. *O. R.*, vol. 26, p. 926.
11. *O. R.*, vol. 89, p. 1140.
12. *M. to A.*, p. 30.
13. *B. and L.*, vol. II, p. 524.
14. *O. R.*, vol. 110, p. 549.
15. *O. R.*, vol. 110, p. 550.
16. *S. H. S. P.*, vol. v, p. 71 (in article reprinted from the Philadelphia *Times*).
17. *O. R.*, vol. 49, p. 713.
18. Fremantle, p. 246.
19. Quoted by Mrs. Longstreet, p. 83.
20. *B. and L.*, vol. II, p. 390.
21. *B. and L.*, vol. II, p. 663.
22. *B. and L.*, vol. II, p. 663.
23. *B. and L.*, vol. II, p. 665.
24. *B. and L.*, vol. III, p. 246.

25. *S. H. S. P.*, vol. v, p. 60 (in article reprinted from Philadelphia *Times*)
26. *S. H. S. P.*, vol. v, p. 68 (in article reprinted from Philadelphia *Times*).
27. To Lee, *O. R.*, vol. 49, p. 699.
28. Mackall to Johnston, *O. R.*, vol. 53, p. 742.
29. *O. R.*, vol. 110, p. 560.
30. *Ibid.*
31. *M. to A.*, p. 66.
32. *M. to A.*, p. 546.
33. *M. to A.*, p. 547.
34. *O. R.*, vol. 54, p. 502.
35. *O. R.*, vol. 54, p. 498.
36. *O. R.*, vol. 56, p. 756.
37. *O. R.*, vol. 56, p. 757.
38. *O. R.*, vol. 54, p. 468.
39. *O. R.*, vol. 54, p. 500.
40. Jones, *Diary*, vol. II, p. 215.
41. *M. to A.*, p. 507.
42. *O. R.*, vol. 89, p. 1268.
43. *O. R.*, vol. 96, p. 1258.
44. *O. R.*, vol. 96, p. 1289.
45. Mrs. Longstreet, p. 115.
46. Mrs. Longstreet, p. 65.
47. Mrs. Longstreet, p. 83.
48. Mrs. Longstreet, p. 62.
49. Mrs. Longstreet, p. 84.
50. *M. to A.*, p. 384.
51. G. M. Sorrel, *Recollections of a Confederate Staff Officer*, p. 88.
52. *S. H. S. P.*, vol. IV, p. 64.
53. *M. to A.*, p. 375.
54. *S. H. S. P.*, vol. XIV, p. 118.
55. *B. and L.*, vol. II, p. 674.
56. *M. to A.*, p. 65.
57. Mrs. Longstreet, p. 125.
58. *B. and L.*, vol. II, p. 405.
59. *O. R.*, vol. 12, p. 566.
60. *B. and L.*, vol. III, p. 350.
61. *O. R.*, vol. 108, p. 1056.
62. *O. R.*, vol. 108, p. 663.
63. Mrs. Longstreet, p. 118.
64. *Ibid.*
65. Mrs. Longstreet, p. 117.
66. Mrs. Longstreet, p. 116.
67. Lieutenant Owen, in *B. and L.*, vol. III, p. 97.

68. *O. R.*, vol. 110, p. 582.
69. Mrs. Longstreet, p. 224.
70. Fremantle, p. 278.
71. R. Stiles, *Four Years under Marse Robert*, p. 247.
72. *M. to A.*, p. 566.
73. *M. to A.*, p. 638.

CHAPTER IV

1. Samuel Phillips Day, *Down South; or an Englishman's Experience at the Seat of the American War*, vol. 1, p. 311.
2. Wise, p. 330.
3. Cooke, *Wearing*, p. 93.
4. *O. R.*, vol. 19, p. 772.
5. Mrs. Chesnut, p. 63.
6. *O. R.*, vol. 10, p. 397.
7. *O. R.*, vol. 2, p. 907.
8. *O. R.*, vol. 2, p. 492.
9. *O. R.*, vol. 19, p. 955.
10. *O. R.*, vol. 108, p. 689.
11. Roman, vol. 1, p. 347.
12. Major Giles P. Cooke.
13. *O. R.*, vol. 19, p. 918.
14. Cooke, *Wearing*, p. 86.
15. Mrs. Chesnut, p. 99.
16. *O. R.*, vol. 5, p. 920.
17. *O. R.*, vol. 5, p. 945.
18. *B. and L.*, vol. 1, p. 223.
19. *B. and L.*, vol. 1, p. 220.
20. Roman, vol. 1, p. 88.
21. *O. R.*, vol. 25, p. 440.
22. *B. and L.*, vol. 1, p. 277.
23. Pollard, *Lee*, p. 255.
24. *O. R.*, vol. 19, p. 911.
25. *O. R.*, vol. 19, p. 825.
26. *O. R.*, vol. 19, p. 918.
27. Morris Schaff, *The Spirit of Old West Point*, p. 196.
28. *O. R.*, vol. 19, p. 910.
29. William P. Johnston, *Life of General Albert Sidney Johnston*, p. 549.
30. Roman, vol. 1, p. 414.
31. Roman, vol. II, p. 2.
32. Roman, vol. 1, p. 4.
33. Roman, vol. 1, p. 5.

34. *O. R.*, vol. II, p. 405.
35. *O. R.*, vol. 19, p. 773.
36. Cooke, *Wearing*, p. 92.
37. *O. R.*, vol. 99, p. 1031.
38. Cooke, *Wearing*, p. 91.
39. *O. R.*, vol. 10, p. 353.
40. *O. R.*, vol. 19, p. 603.
41. *O. R.*, vol. 2, p. 514.
42. Pollard, *Lee*, p. 268.
43. Fremantle, p. 33.
44. *O. R.*, vol. 19, p. 895.
45. G. T. Beauregard, *Commentary on the Campaign and Battle of Manassas*, p. 150.
46. *O. R.*, vol. 19, p. 955.
47. *O. R.*, vol. 110, p. 804.
48. G. T. Beauregard, *Commentary on the Campaign and Battle of Manassas*, p. 37.
49. E. Grasset, *La Guerre de la Sécession*, vol. II, p. 199.
50. *O. R.*, vol. 2, p. 511.
51. *O. R.*, vol 2, p. 508. In *Rise and Fall* Davis printed "dwelling," which is certainly more civil than "driveling."
52. *B. and L.*, vol. I, p. 223.

CHAPTER V

1. Kohler, p. 71.
2. Butler, p. 8.
3. Butler, p. 424.
4. *U.S.*, vol. v, p. 63.
5. Wise, p. 401.
6. W. E. Dodd, *Jefferson Davis*, p. 343.
7. Kohler, p. 79.
8. London *Times*, May 9, 1884.
9. Wise, p. 176.
10. *Globe*, 1857–58, pt. I, p. 1070.
11. *Globe*, 1857–58, pt. I, p. 1071.
12. *Globe*, 35th Congress, 1st Sess., vol. I, p. 87.
13. *Globe*, 35th Congress, 1st Sess., vol. I, p. 157.
14. *Globe*, 35th Congress, 1st Sess., vol. I, p. 700.
15. *A Generation of Judges*, by their Reporter, p. 202.
16. *A Generation of Judges*, p. 199.
17. E. H. Coleridge, *Life and Correspondence of John Duke, Lord Coleridge*, vol. II, p. 327.

18. London *Times*, quoted in Butler, p. 439.
19. *Journals of the Confederate Congress*, March 5, 1862.
20. *Works* (ed. Ford), vol. IX, p. 362.
21. To Mason, in Richardson, vol. II, p. 616.
22. T. C. De Leon, *Four Years in Rebel Capitals*, p. 276.
23. William H. Russell, in *North American Review*, vol. 166, p. 373, quoted in Kohler.
24. *O. R.*, vol. 5, p. 883.
25. *O. R.*, vol. 4, p. 453.
26. In Butler, p. 426.
27. Butler, p. 332.
28. *Diary*, August 10, 1861.
29. Diary, April 18, 1862.
30. *S. H. S. P.*, vol. VI, p. 186.
31. *O. R.*, vol. 8, p. 699.
32. Mrs. Davis, in Butler, p. 245.
33. *S. H. S. P.*, vol. XIX, p. 384.
34. *The Letters of Charles Lamb* (Ainger, 1896), vol. I, p. 258.
35. E. L. Pierce, *Memoirs and Letters of Charles Sumner*, vol. III, p. 391.
36. William H. Russell, *My Diary, North and South*, p. 175.
37. Butler, p. 174.
38. *The Green Bag*, vol. X, p. 396.
39. *Davis*, p. 151.
40. Jones, *Diary*, May 22, 1861.
41. Butler, p. 61.
42. *O. R.*, vol. 110, p. 198.
43. *O. R.*, vol. 4, p. 474.
44. Kohler, p. 52.
45. Kohler, p. 82.
46. Butler, p. 405.
47. *Globe*, 1857–58, pt. II, p. 2782.
48. *Globe*, 1857–58, pt. II, p. 2823.
49. London *Times*, July 2, 1883.
50. William H. Russell, *My Diary, North and South*, p. 175.
51. Butler, p. 64.
52. Fremantle, p. 213.
53. Butler, p. 335.
54. *S. H. S. P.*, vol. XIX, p. 384.
55. *O. R.*, vol. 5, p. 955.
56. Butler, p. 228.
57. *O. R.*, vol. 7, p. 785.
58. *S. H. S. P.*, vol. XXXII, p. 170.
59. Moore's *Rebellion Record*, vol. XI, p. 82.

60. Richardson, vol. II, p. 619.
61. Virginia Mason, *The Public Life and Diplomatic Correspondence of James Murray Mason*, p. 542.
62. Virginia Mason, *Life of Mason*, p. 404.
63. *Rise and Fall*, vol. I, p. 242.

CHAPTER VI

1. Johnston and Browne, p. 294.
2. Johnston and Browne, p. 81.
3. *Diary*, p. 107.
4. Johnston and Browne, p. 77.
5. Richard Taylor, *Destruction and Reconstruction*, p. 30.
6. Cleveland, p. 6.
7. *Diary*, p. 550.
8. Johnston and Browne, p. 83.
9. *Diary*, p. 146.
10. Johnston and Browne, p. 82.
11. Johnston and Browne, p. 342.
12. Johnston and Browne, p. 73.
13. Johnston and Browne, p. 262.
14. Johnston and Browne, p. 263.
15. Johnston and Browne, p. 451.
16. *Ibid.*
17. Johnston and Browne, p. 439.
18. *Diary*, p. 472.
19. Johnston and Browne, p. 288.
20. *Diary*, p. 43.
21. *Diary*, p. 326.
22. Dobbin to Cobb, January 15, 1848, *Toombs Correspondence.*
23. *Diary*, p. 10.
24. *Diary*, p. 253.
25. Johnston and Browne, p. 90.
26. *Diary*, p. 139.
27. *Diary*, p. 58.
28. Johnston and Browne, p. 40.
29. *Diary*, p. 474.
30. Johnston and Browne, p. 438.
31. *Diary*, p. 473.
32. Cleveland, p. 795.
33. *Diary*, p. 96.
34. *Diary*, p. 42.

35. *War Between the States*, vol. II, p. 625.
36. To J. Henley Smith, October 13, 1860, *Toombs Correspondence.*
37. Phillips, p. 228.
38. *War Between the States*, vol. II, p. 625.
39. Johnston and Browne, p. 448.
40. To Thomas W. Thomas, December 12, 1856, *Toombs Correspondence.*
41. To Crittenden, February 6, 1849, *Toombs Correspondence.*
42. Cleveland, p. 452.
43. *Diary*, p. 380.
44. *Diary*, p. 14.
45. *Diary*, p. 383.
46. *Diary*, p. 385.
47. *Diary*, p. 311.
48. Johnston and Browne, p. 298.
49. *Diary*, p. 61.
50. *Diary*, p. 48.
51. To editor of Augusta *Chronicle and Sentinel*, January 28, 1852, *Toombs Correspondence.*
52. Johnston and Browne, p. 239.
53. To J. Henley Smith, February 24, 1860, *Toombs Correspondence.*
54. Richard Taylor, *Destruction and Reconstruction*, p. 29.
55. Johnston and Browne, p. 104.

CHAPTER VII

1. Richardson, vol. II, p. 152.
2. Mrs. Davis, vol. I, p. 410.
3. Stephens, *Diary*, p. 427.
4. Reed, p. 237.
5. Stovall, p. 28.
6. C. J. Woodbury, in *Overland Monthly*, Series 2, vol. 7, p. 125.
7. To Stephens, December 15, 1865, *Toombs Correspondence.*
8. Stovall, p. 104.
9. Stovall, p. 57.
10. Stovall, p. 53.
11. *Globe*, April 25, 1856.
12. Stovall, p. 198.
13. Stovall, p. 188.
14. Stovall, p. 192.
15. Stovall, p. 90.
16. Stovall, p. 191.
17. *Globe*, April 25, 1856.

18. *Globe*, April 27, 1858.
19. Stovall, p. 71.
20. Stovall, p. 72.
21. *Globe*, May 27, 1856.
22. *Ibid.*
23. Richard Taylor, *Destruction and Reconstruction*, p. 215.
24. Stovall, p. 19.
25. Stovall, p. 321.
26. Mrs. Chesnut, February 19, 1861.
27. Communicated by Mrs. F. M. Colston, from personal recollection.
28. James D. Waddell, *Linton Stephens*, p. 387.
29. Mrs. Davis, vol. I, p. 411.
30. Stovall, p. 330.
31. Stephens, *Diary*, p. 426.
32. To Stephens, May 17, 1862, *Toombs Correspondence.*
33. Stovall, p. 357.
34. Reed, p. 280.
35. Johnston and Browne, p. 218.
36. To Thomas W. Thomas, May 1, 1848, *Toombs Correspondence.*
37. Gabriel Toombs to Stephens, July 3, 1861, *Toombs Correspondence.*
38. Stovall, p. 372.
39. Stovall, p. 312.
40. Stovall, p. 355.
41. Stovall, p. 185.
42. *Toombs Correspondence.*
43. *Diary*, p. 427.
44. *Diary*, p. 426.
45. *U.S.*, vol. II, p. 91.
46. Stovall, p. 18.
47. Stovall, p. 19.
48. Reed, p. 281.
49. To Rhett, Collins, and others, May 10, 1860, *Toombs Correspondence.*
50. *U.S.*, vol. II, p. 89.
51. *U.S.*, vol. II, p. 353.
52. To Crittenden, January 3, 1849, *Toombs Correspondence.*
53. *Diary*, p. 55.
54. William P. Trent, *Southern Statesmen of the Old Régime*, p. 235.
55. Savannah *Republican*, quoted in Rhodes, *U.S.*, vol. III, p. 213.
56. Charleston *Mercury*, quoted in Rhodes, *U.S.*, vol. III, p. 214.
57. Stovall, p. 226.
58. To Crittenden, February 9, 1849, *Toombs Correspondence.*
59. Stovall, p. 242.
60. C. J. Woodbury, in *Overland Monthly*, Series 2, vol. VII, p. 125.

61. Jones, *Diary*, May 22, 1861.
62. Mrs. Chesnut, p. 108.
63. Stovall, p. 242.
64. To G. Hill and others, June 11, 1862, *Toombs Correspondence.*
65. Quoted by C. J. Woodbury, in *Overland Monthly*, Series 2, vol. VII, p. 126.
66. Stovall, p. 264.
67. Stovall, p. 269.
68. Stovall, p. 243.
69. To Stephens, September, 1861 (day uncertain), *Toombs Correspondence.*
70. To Stephens, September 22, 1861, *Toombs Correspondence.*
71. To Stephens, July 14, 1862, *Toombs Correspondence.*
72. Stovall, p. 262.
73. *M. to A.*, p. 161.
74. Toombs to Stephens, August 22, 1862, *Toombs Correspondence.*
75. Stovall, p. 254.
76. *B. and L.*, vol. II, p. 525.
77. Mrs. Chesnut, p. 171.
78. Stovall, p. 302.
79. Stovall, p. 325.
80. Stovall, p. 320.
81. To Stephens, November 19, 1870, *Toombs Correspondence.*
82. Stovall, p. 342.
83. Stovall, p. 349.
84. Stovall, p. 374.
85. Stovall, p. 375.
86. Stovall, p. 314.
87. *S. H. S. P.*, vol. XIV, p. 303.

CHAPTER VIII

1. Kell, p. 149.
2. J. Russell Soley, *The Blockade and the Cruisers*, p. 229.
3. *Atlantic Monthly*, vol. XXX, p. 95.
4. Semmes, *Mexican War*, p. 80.
5. Semmes, *Mexican War*, p. 82.
6. *O. R. N.*, vol. I, p. 88.
7. W. H. Rideing, *Many Celebrities and a Few Others*, p. 2.
8. Sinclair, p. 275.
9. Johnston and Browne, p. 433.
10. Sinclair, p. 55.

11. *O. R. N.*, vol. I, p. 811.
12. *Executive Documents, Forty-first Congress, Alabama Claims*, vol. III, p. 200.
13. *Atlantic Monthly*, vol. XXX, p. 150.
14. *O. R. N.*, vol. I, p. 758.
15. Sinclair, p. 40. *Executive Documents, Forty-first Congress, Alabama Claims*, vol. III, p. 212; vol. IV, p. 184, *et seq.*
16. *O. R. N.*, p. 816.
17. Sinclair, p. 167.
18. *Executive Documents, Forty-first Congress, Alabama Claims*, vol. III, p. 75.
19. *O. R. N.*, vol. II, p. 562.
20. *Service Afloat*, p. 343.
21. Kell, p. 249.
22. *Service Afloat*, p. 497.
23. *O. R. N.*, vol. II, p. 741.
24. *O. R. N.*, vol. II, p. 745.
25. *O. R. N.*, vol. II, p. 739.
26. *O. R. N.*, vol. I, p. 719.
27. *O. R. N.*, vol. I, p. 719.
28. *O. R. N.*, vol. II, p. 737.
29. *O. R. N.*, vol. II, p. 768.
30. *O. R. N.*, vol. I, p. 715.
31. *O. R. N.*, vol. II, p. 757.
32. *O. R. N.*, vol. II, p. 768.
33. January 26, 1861, *Toombs Correspondence.*
34. *O. R. N.*, vol. II, p. 775.
35. *O. R. N.*, vol. II, p. 764.
36. *Service Afloat*, p. 301.
37. Kell, p. 276.
38. *Service Afloat*, p. 760.
39. *O. R. N.*, vol. II, p. 728.
40. *Service Afloat*, p. 212.
41. *Southern Magazine*, November, 1877, quoted in Kell, p. 279.

INDEX

INDEX

Adams, John Quincy, diary of, 124; wrote verses to A. H. Stephens, 164.

Alabama, the, 221, 222, 223; built by stealth, 224; her crew largely ruffians, 224; her career, 224; her usefulness, 225; not a fighting ship, 225, 226; testimony of prisoners, 233, 234.

Alexander, General E. P., his judgment of Johnston, 4; of Stuart, 44.

Alfriend, F. N., on Benjamin, 138, 144, 145.

Allan, Colonel William, cited, 85.

Anderson, Colonel Archer, his portrayal of Johnston, 24.

Antietam, Toombs's magnificent defense of the bridge at, 209.

Badeau, General Adam, his Life of Grant, 99.

Baker, E. D., demolishes Benjamin in debate on secession, 147.

Bartlett, General Joseph J., 53.

Battine, Captain Cecil, his estimate of Stuart, 44.

Bayard, Thomas F., on Benjamin, 139.

Beauregard, General P. G. T., 19, 118; chronology, 94; born in French Louisiana, 95; his appearance and some of his characteristics, 95, 96; contrasted with Napoleon, 95, 96; had French talents of speech, 97; his "beauty and booty" proclamation, 97; his vanity, 96, 98, 101; naïve letters of, 99; adopts ingenious method of self laudation, 99; Colonel Roman's biography of, 99, 100; his own book on first battle of Bull Run, 100, 105, 113; contrasted with Stuart, 101; had little sense of humor, 101; Cooke's comment on his smile, 101; relations with Davis unpleasant, 102–104; casts slurs upon other generals, 105, 117; contention with Joseph E. Johnston, 105; his conduct during the actual course of the war, 106; his superintendency at West Point, 107; love of country, 107, 108; meeting with A. S. Johnston at Corinth, 108; offers plans for Bragg's use, 108; anecdotes of childhood, 109; at Drewry's Bluff, 110, 118; as a commander, 110; letter about General Ripley, 110, 111; personal relations with officers and soldiers, 111; worshiped in Louisiana, 111, 112; attitude of soldiers and officers toward, 112; his vivid imagination, 113, 114, 117–120; always ready with advice and schemes, 114–120; strategic qualities, 115; a captain in Mexico, 115; offers plan to War Department to end the war, 116; an indefatigable dreamer, 117–120; exclaims against Johnston's conservatism, 118; his weaknesses, 118, 119; Davis's sharp comment, 119.

Benjamin, Judah P., not admired by Johnston, 14; a Jew, 95, 123; chronology, 122; born a British subject, 123; became U.S. Senator, seceded with his state, and died a London barrister, 123; his view of biography, 123, 124; his reputation, 124, 125; known best as author of *Benjamin on Sales*, 125;

connection with St. Albans raid and the attempt to burn New York, 125, 131; his oratory, 126, 127; self-educated, 127; his income, 127, 128; success at the English Bar, 128; tributes to, 128, 129, 139; political aspects of his career, 129; his offices in the Confederate Government, 129, 130; censured by Congress for Roanoke Island affair, 130; advanced by Davis, 130; contrasted with Cavour, 132; prediction in regard to North America, 133; his hope of European recognition, 133; an admirable man of business, 133, 134; knew how to handle men, 135; his devotion to President Davis, 135, 136; contrasted with Lee, 137; trouble with other generals, 137; personal characteristics, 138, 139; his smile, 139, 140; some kindly deeds of, 140; attitude towards life, 140, 141; had no religion, 141; buried in Paris with Catholic rites, 141; quick tempered, 142; his "spat" with Davis, 142, 143; fond of games, 144; a lover of good living, 144, 145; affectionate toward relatives, 145, 146; relations with his wife, 145, 146; contrasted with Lincoln, 146, 147; his real attitude towards the Confederacy, 147–149; compares Gladstone and Disraeli, 147; Gilmore's description of, 148; of mediocre ability, 150; contrasted with Alexander H. Stephens, 180.

Bigelow, Major John, Jr., 45.

Blaine, J. G., on Benjamin, 128.

Bolles, Robert A., explains why Semmes was not prosecuted, 221; his defense of "the pirate Semmes," 231, 232.

Bragg, General Braxton, superseded by Johnston, 3, 4; Johnston's confidence in, 28; his regard for Johnston, 29; relations with Longstreet, 75, 76.

Brooks, Preston, his assault on Charles Sumner, 194.

Brown, John, capture of, 36.

Buckner, General S. B., letter from Longstreet, quoted, 76.

Bull Run, Johnston in control at, 3; the name "unrefined," 97; a brilliant victory, 98; Beauregard's book on, 100, 105; contention between Beauregard and Johnston about, 105, 106; two armed mobs at, 252.

Burnside, General Ambrose E., 253.

Burton, Robert, his *Anatomy of Melancholy*, 160.

Butler, Benjamin F., 128.

Butler, Professor Pierce, biographer of Benjamin, 124, 128.

Byron, Lord, 160, 245.

Cavour, Count, 132, 133.

Chancellorsville, Stuart at, 45, 60.

Chesney, Colonel C. C., his estimate of Johnston, 5.

Chesnut, Mrs. Mary B., 9; quoted in regard to Johnston, 31; on Beauregard's vanity, 102; explains failure of Toombs as Secretary of State, 208; sums up career of Toombs, 212, 213.

Cicero, as a pleader, 126; a confirmed intellectualist, 173.

Clarendon, Earl of, on the Earl of Essex, 26, 27.

Cobb, Howell, letter of Semmes to, 241.

Cocke, General Philip St. George, 219.

Coleridge, Lord, his tribute to Benjamin, 128.

Colston, Captain F. M., on Stuart's scrupulousness, 59.

Cone, Judge, his affair with Alexander H. Stephens, 175.

Cooke, Major Giles P., Beauregard's aide, 111.

Cooke, John Esten, on Stuart at Chancellorsville, 45; pen pictures of Stuart, 50, 56; his account of Beauregard's social relations, 96; his comment on Beauregard's smile, 101; describes Beauregard's relations with officers, 111.
Cooke, General Philip St. George, 219.
Cooper, General Samuel, his rank in the Confederate army, 10.
Cox, General J. D., an admirer of Johnston, 4, 25, 26.
Crittenden, John J., Toombs's friendship for, 198.

Dalgetty, Captain Dugald, 97.
D'Artagnan, 96, 113.
Davis, Jefferson, his hopes of Johnston's success, 3; growing unfriendliness between them, 7, 8, 10; placed Johnston fourth in Confederate army, 10; had his own ideas of military policy, 11; writes sharply to Johnston, 11, 12; characterizes letter of Johnston as insubordinate, 14; more diplomatic than Johnston, 17; his later utterances more savage than Johnston's, 19; his patriotism, 20; contrasted with Lincoln, 22, 147; on Stuart, 45; snubs Longstreet, 80; unpleasant relations with Beauregard, 102, 103; writes sharply to Beauregard, 119; shows confidence in Benjamin, 130; a patriotic idealist in purpose, 135; objects to advice, 135; "spat" with Benjamin, 143; complimentary to Benjamin, 150; opposed by Stephens, 154; comments on, by Stephens, 163, 171; criticism of, 207, 211.
Davis, Mrs. Jefferson, writes Life of her husband, 81; writes of Benjamin, 135, 136, 142, 144, 145; her portrait of Robert Toombs, 185, 186, 196.
Deerhound, the, English yacht that rescued Semmes, 229, 240.
de Sévigné, Madame, her comment on the historical novels of her day, 52.
Dodd, W. E., calls Benjamin "hated Jew," 125.
Drewry's Bluff, General Whiting at, 110; Beauregard's plans not carried out at, 118.
Dumas, Alexandre, 96.

Early, General J. A., explains criticism of Longstreet, 84.
Emerson, Ralph Waldo, on self-confidence, 68.
Enobarbus, profound doctrine of, in regard to women, 56.
Ewell, General Richard S., 14, 105, 256.

Fair Oaks, 3; Johnston struck down by a shell at, 6, 23.
Fernando de Noronha, 237.
Floyd, General John B., 112.
Fort Loudon, Longstreet and McLaws at, 78, 79.
Fort Warren, A. H. Stephens imprisoned in, 163, 165.
Fremantle, A. J. L., 6; quoted, 13, 14, 26; his description of Stuart's movements, 42; on Longstreet, 65, 67, 71.

Garnett, Judge Theodore S, writes of Stuart's discipline, 41.
Gettysburg, battle of, Longstreet's connection with, 66, 67, 73, 74, 78, 83, 256, 257; the climax of an inevitable struggle, 249; Lee and Meade in command at, 254; position of opposing forces, 255; the first day, 255, 256; the second day, 256, 257; Pickett's great charge, 257–259; consequences of, 259, 260.
Gilmore, J. R., describes Benjamin, 148.

Gordon, General J. B., says Johnston was not ambitious, 26; and Longstreet, 88.
Grant, General U. S., 104, 117, 119, 120; on Johnston, 5.
Grasset, E., his characterization of Beauregard, 118.

Hampton, General Wade, tribute of Longstreet to, 88.
Hampton Roads Peace Commission, 130.
Hancock, General Winfield S., 256, 260.
Hardee, General William J., 76.
Harper's Ferry, Johnston's first command at, 3; capture of John Brown at, 35, 36; Jackson and McLaws at, 85.
Hatteras, the, sunk by the Alabama, 226.
Hill, General A. P., 45; his proposed duel with Longstreet, 84.
Hill, General D. H., his difficulty with Toombs, 212.
Hood, General John B., supersedes Johnston, 4, 14, 19.
Hooker, General Joseph, 116, 253.
Hugo, Victor, 98.

Imagination, value of, to a commander, 117.

Jackson, Andrew, youthful interview of A. H. Stephens with, 179, 180.
Jackson (T. J.), Stonewall, criticized by Johnston, 13, 14; his estimate of Longstreet, 44; contrasted with Stuart, 50; Stuart's jest at his expense, 53; his passionate affection for Lee, 71; his imagination, 117; had trouble with Benjamin, 137; and Lee, 252–254.
James, Sir Henry, praises Benjamin, 128, 129.
Jefferson, Thomas, quoted as to burning London, 132.
Jenkins, General Albert G., death of, 91.
Johnson, Dr. Samuel, quoted, 22; dialogue between him and Adam Smith, 143.
Johnston, General Albert Sidney, 120; his rank in the Confederate Army, 10; his meeting with Beauregard at Corinth, 108.
Johnston, General Joseph E., chronology, 2; his distinguished service, 3, 4; rank in Confederate Army, 3, 10; often wounded, 3, 6, 8, 9, 17, 23, 36, 37; his relations with Davis, 3, 7, 8, 10–20; superseded by Hood, 4, 14, 19; restored, 4; unsurpassed in retreat and defense, 4, 5; opinions of, expressed by Cox, Alexander, Longstreet, Pollard, 4; by Chesney, Grant, Young, Sherman, Ropes, 5; his wife's understanding of, 6; his ill luck, 7, 9, 10, 23; criticizes Lee, Jackson, and other generals, 13, 14; writes an "insubordinate" letter to Davis, 14, 15; but seeks to be obedient and respectful, 17, 18; an admirable writer, 20; his book, 20, 22, 31; loose in statement, 21; over-sensitive, 22, 26; had many attractive qualities, 23, 25; his bravery, 23; afraid of kerosene lamps, 23, 24; honest and upright, 24, 25; candidate for Congress after the war, 25; cared nothing for display, 26; his warmth of nature, 27, 28, 29; praises Stuart, Longstreet, Bragg, and Lee, 27, 28; adored his wife, 29; was loved and trusted by officers and soldiers, 29, 30; a magnetic leader, 30, 31; his opinion of Stuart, 44; contention between him and Beauregard about first battle of Bull Run, 105.
Johnston, Mrs. Joseph E., 6, 29.

Jones, Aaron, Beauregard's orderly, 110.
Jones, J. B., his estimate of Stuart, 41; his distrust of Benjamin, 136, 139, 140.

Kearsarge, the, destroys the Alabama, 226.
Kell, Lieutenant John M., devotion of sailors to, 235.
Knoxville expedition, Longstreet in charge of, 78, 79.

Lamb, Charles, quoted, 138; his description of Coleridge, 220.
Law, General E. M., and Longstreet, 78, 79.
Lay, Bishop Henry C., 5.
Lee, General Fitzhugh, on Stuart at West Point, 35; a favorite of Stuart, 41; his characterization of Stuart's voice, 47; his picture of Stuart, 50.
Lee, General Robert E., 111, 117; wounded but once, 6; with Johnston on voyage to Mexico, 7; his original rank in the Confederate army, 10; criticized by Johnston, 13; on Johnston's sensitiveness, 22; Johnston's letter to Wigfall about, 28; an officer's comment on, 31; his high opinion of Stuart, 42, 44, 45, 46; too lofty for vanity, 50; his severe taste, 51; retort to Stuart, 58; writes to Stuart after Chancellorsville, 60; affection for Longstreet, 70; Jackson's praise of, 71; disregards Longstreet's advice, 72–74; takes blame for failure at Gettysburg, 74, 102; generosity toward Longstreet, 78; his personal appearance, 86; his kindness to Beauregard, 118; his tact, 137; his praise of Toombs, 209; typified all that was best in the South, 253; some characteristics of, 253, 254.
Lee, General S. D., 16.
Leopardi, Giacomo, Alexander H. Stephens contrasted with, 160, 162, 165.
Lincoln, Abraham, 86, 87, 104; contrasted with Benjamin, 146, 147; his correspondence with Alexander H. Stephens, 171; his eulogy of Stephens, 178.
Longstreet, General James, on Johnston, 4, 30; praised by Johnston, 27, 28; his estimate of Stuart, 44; chronology, 64; of mixed blood, 65; his appearance and characteristics, 65, 66; a superb fighter, 66; at Gettysburg, 66, 67, 73, 74, 78, 83, 256, 257; his recklessness, 67; his defects, 68, 83–87; his stolid self-confidence, 68–70, 81; his love of Lee, 71; his attitude as Lee's subordinate, 71, 72, 73, 74; objects to the campaign into Pennsylvania, 73; sent to the West, 74; his attitude toward Bragg, 75; writes to Buckner about Bragg, 76; offers advice to Davis, 76, 77; his dealings with subordinates in the West, 77–80; in charge of Knoxville expedition, 78; snubbed by Davis, 76, 77, 80; suggests "impressing" all the gold in the country, 81; conduct after the war, 81, 82; a practical American, 82; attitude toward Lee after the war, 83, 84, 86; his cruel language towards Early, 84, 85; remarks about Jackson and Virginia, 85; appeal at outbreak of Spanish War, 86; reference to Lincoln, 87; genuinely patriotic, 87; his sympathy for noncombatants, 87, 88; relations with his men, 88–90; becomes a Roman Catholic, 90–92.
Longstreet, Mrs. James, writes Life of her husband, 81, 82; quotes him, 86; comments on General Hampton, 88.

Mackall, W. W., letter to Johnston, quoted, 15, 16; on Longstreet, 75.
MacTurk, Captain, joyous comment of, 13.
Maffitt, John N., saying attributed by him to Semmes, 246.
Mahan, Admiral A. T., as a young midshipman begged permission to pursue Semmes, 226.
Maranham, the Federal Consul at, 244, 245.
Martinique, 237.
McClellan, General George B., 47, 115, 252.
McClellan, Major H. B., incident of General Stuart, 39.
McCulloch, General Ben, harsh telegram of Benjamin to, 137.
McLaws, General Lafayette, his criticism of Longstreet, at Knoxville, 78; charges against, 79, 80; at Harper's Ferry, 85.
Meade, General George G., succeeds Hooker at Gettysburg, 254; personal characteristics of, 254, 255.
Mosby, General John S., a favorite of Stuart, 41; writes of Stuart's gayety and power of endurance, 48.

Napoleon, 51, 95, 96, 113, 117.
Navy, the Union, played significant part in the war, 252.
New York, attempted burning of, 125, 131.
North, the, contrast with the South before the war, 249, 250.

"Old Beeswax," a nickname for Semmes, 245.

Palfrey, General F. W., his opinion of Johnston's accuracy, 21.
Patterson, General Robert, outmanœuvred by Johnston, 3; proposed scheme of Beauregard against, 115.
Pemberton, General John C., 14, 16.
Pepys, Samuel, diary of, 124.
Phillips, Ulrich B., characterization of A. H. Stephens, 173.
Pickens, Governor F. W., writes to Beauregard, 112.
Pickett, General George E., at Gettysburg, 257, 258, 259.
Pickett, Mrs. George E., remark of an officer to, in regard to Johnston, 31.
Plutarch, cited, 220.
Poe, Orlando M., and General Stuart, 54.
Pollard, E. A., on Johnston, 4, 5; describes Longstreet's appearance, 65; on Beauregard, 112; notes Benjamin's smile, 139.
Pollock, Sir Frederick, praises Benjamin, 139.
Public opinion, power of, 191.

Rabelais, 196.
Randolph, General George W., admired by Johnston, 14.
Reed, Colonel John C., an admirer of Toombs, 186.
Reynolds, General John F., 255.
Rhodes, James Ford, contrasts Johnston with Lee, 22; compares Davis and Lincoln, 22; on Benjamin, 125, 131; comments on Robert Toombs, 200; on Toombs's bill in connection with Kansas struggle, 202, 203.
Rideing, W. H., on Semmes, 227.
Ripley, General Roswell S., Beauregard's accusations of, 110, 111.
Roanoke Island, 130.
Robbins, Lieutenant W. T., 52.
Robertson, General J. B., and Longstreet, 78, 79.
Roman, Colonel Alfred, his biography of Beauregard, 99, 100.
Ropes, John Codman, on Johnston, 5.
Russell, William H., on Benjamin, 139.
Ryan, Lieutenant George, 70.

St. Albans, raid on, 125, 131.
Schaff, General Morris, tells of Beauregard at West Point, 107.
Scheibert, J., on General Stuart, 38, 44; his account of Stuart's planning, 43; quotes General von Schmidt's opinion of Stuart, 44.
Scott, General Winfield, 6, 115; and Toombs, 195.
Seddon, J. A., 22, 107; letter of Stuart to, 40.
Sedgwick, General John, his estimate of Stuart, 36.
Semmes, Raphael, considered as a pirate, 220; on the composition of pirate crews, 222, 223; his defense of his methods, 225; sank the Hatteras, 226; defeated by the Kearsarge, 226; the real Semmes, 227; early life, 227; personal appearance and characteristics, 227; a Douglas man, 228; kept log-book of his cruises, 228; his legal lore, 229; his sincerity, 229; wrote book on Mexican War, 229, 230; his treatment of prisoners, 230, 231; the prisoners' view, 231, 234; his treatment of his crew, 232, 233; had confidence of his sailors, 234, 235; incident told by Lieutenant Kell, 235; much attached to his wife and children, 235, 236; literary in tastes, 236; his diary records love of nature, 236, 237; deeply religious, 238, 239; his courage and patriotism, 240; letter to Howell Cobb, 241; defended by Sinclair, 242; pursued with scorn and abuse, 242, 243; reply to Mrs. Kell, 243; his speech often belied his real feeling, 243; quotation from his war diary, 244; coarse streak shows in some of his writing, 244, 245; "Old Beeswax," 245, 246; his words on the sinking of the Alabama, 246.
Seven Pines, Johnston's one aggressive battle, 4; Johnston wounded at, 8.
Sherman, General W. T., on Johnston, 5, 117.
Shiloh, Beauregard at, 100, 118, 119.
Slidell, John, comment on Benjamin, 138.
Sinclair, Lieutenant Arthur, 27; comments of, on the Alabama, 223; tells of treatment of prisoners, 230; of discipline of crew, 233; defends utterances of Semmes, 242.
Smith, General Kirby, his feeling toward Johnston, 29, 30.
Soley, Professor J. Russell, defends Confederate privateers, and cruisers, 221; on the defeat of the Alabama, 226.
South, the, conditions in, contrasted with those in the North before the war, 249, 250.
Speer, Judge Emory, and Longstreet, 88.
Stephens, Alexander H., chronology, 152; character and career of, involve contradictions, 153, 154; his physique, 153, 155; distinctive traits, 153, 175, 176; a logical defender of slavery, 153, 154, 179; bitterly opposed secession, 154, 165, 178; imprisoned at Fort Warren, 154, 163; extracts from his diary, 154, 166, 168; opposed to the conduct of the Government, 154; devotion of Negroes to, 154, 164; his health, 155; Dick Taylor's diatribe on, 156; contrast between physical lack and spiritual strength, 156, 157; quoted in regard to himself, 157, 158, 159, 160, 161, 162; contrasted with Voltaire, 158; constitutionally melancholy, 159; sensitive as to his appearance, 159, 160; his physical and spiritual courage, 160; his religious life, 161, 162, 176, 177; his home, Liberty Hall, open to all,

162; rich in social qualities, 163; comments on Davis, 163, 206; generally beloved, 163, 164; never married, 165; his affection for his native state, 165, 166; contrasted with Toombs, 166, 167, 188, 189; his love for his family, 167, 168; tenderness toward animals, 168, 169; his dog Rio, 168; constantly helping other men, 169, 170; his tolerance, 171; a deductive thinker, 172; his vanity compared with Cicero's, 173; modest, but self-confident, 174; his affair with Judge Cone, 175; as a lawyer, 176, 177; as a politician, 177, 178, 180; Lincoln's eulogy of, 178; depended on his convictions, 178, 179; caustic remark of Richard Taylor about, 179; youthful interview with President Jackson, 179, 180; attitude after the war, 180; an idealist, 180; on Robert Toombs, 206; on Semmes, 228.

Stephens, Linton, half-brother of A. H. Stephens, 159; their mutual devotion, 167, 168; quoted in regard to Toombs, 196.

Stevens, General Clement H., on general feeling of army towards Johnston, 30, 31.

Stiles, Robert, estimate of Johnston, 28, 29; his account of behavior of officers at time of Longstreet's wound, 90.

Stuart, General J. E. B., praised by Johnston, 27; chronology, 34; a fighter by nature, 35, 36, 46; distinguishing characteristics, 35; an exceptional horseman, 35, 48; his account of the capture of John Brown, 36; wounded but once, 37; his naïveté, 38; won love of his men, 38; his love for and care of his men, 39, 40; sends characteristic letter to Secretary Seddon, 40; his discipline, 41; his self-control, 42; Lee's tribute to, 42, 44, 45; careful in planning, 43; opinions of other generals about him, 44; considered for command of Jackson's corps, 44, 45; at Chancellorsville, 45; his exuberant cheerfulness, 46, 47; his resourcefulness, 47, 48; his voice like music, 47; magnificent physique, 48; single handed capture of forty-four Union soldiers, 49; quotes Horace, 50; Fitzhugh Lee's picture of, 50; Cooke's picture, 50, 51; his golden spurs, 51; his flowery style, 51, 52; jests at Jackson's expense, 53; has fun with his adversaries, 53, 54; his West Point nickname, 54; his taste in music, 54, 55; fond of dancing, 55; his attitude toward women, 56–58; married at twenty-two, 58; of high moral character, 58, 59; his religion, 59, 60; a strict observer of Sunday, 59, 60; died at thirty, 60; answers aspersions of General Trimble, 61, 62; his best epitaph, 62; contrasted with Beauregard, 101.

Sully, Chancellor, 100, 147.

Sumner, Charles, on Benjamin, 139; assault by Brooks on, 194.

Sumter, career of the, 223.

Sweeney, "Bob," Stuart's banjo-player, 55.

Talleyrand, 124, 147.

Taney, Roger Brooke, Benjamin's compliment to, 126.

Taylor, General Richard, on health of Alexander H. Stephens, 156; caustic remark by, about Stephens, 179.

Toombs, Gabriel, his tribute to his brother Robert, 198.

Toombs, Robert, contrasted with A. H. Stephens, 166, 188, 189; chronology, 184; a Georgian estimate of, 185; his physique impressive, 185; Mrs. Davis's portrait of, 185, 186; a fighter, 186, 187, 194, 215; as a speaker, 186, 187, 191, 192;

as a lawyer, 187, 200; a believer in Revolution, 188; his feeling about Mexico, 188; hated the party system, 189; his view of war, 189; an individualist, 189, 190, 215; indifferent to popularity, 190; deplored rise of the money power, 191; on public opinion, 191; power given by his temperament, 192; contest over the speakership of the House (1849), 193; defended slavery in Tremont Temple (1856), 193, 203; his testimony in regard to Brooks's assault on Sumner, 194; had sense of humor and a shrewd wit, 195; his story of the red-headed man, 195, 196; a brilliant and fascinating talker, 196; fond of nature, 197; his treatment of his slaves, 197; his taste for alcohol, 197; ready to entertain everybody, 197; tribute of his brother, 198; his religious experience, 198, 199, 215; affection for his wife, 199; letters to her, 199; a good man of business, 200; his honesty, 200, 201; "violent in speech, but safe in counsel," 201; supported Clay and Webster, 202; his part in the Kansas struggle, 202, 203; opposed immediate secession, 204; his attitude toward the attack on Sumter, 205; mentioned for presidency of Confederacy, 205, 206; lacked necessary qualities for that office, 206, 207; made secretary of state, 207; his failure, 208; refused to become secretary of war, 208; his ambitions, 209; his bravery, 209; praised by Lee at Antietam, 209; beloved by his men, 210; lacked self-discipline, 210, 212; hated West Point, 211; his opinion of J. E. Johnston, 211; his feeling toward Davis, 211; disobeys orders at Second Bull Run, 211, 212; has trouble with D. H. Hill, 212; Longstreet's opinion of, 212; a Chesterfield with ladies, 213; his course after returning from Europe, 213, 214; helps form new constitution for Georgia, 214, 215; an unreconstructed rebel, 215.

Trimble, General, underrated cavalry, 40; his aspersions of Stuart, 61, 62.

Truth of history, the, 106.

Vallandigham, Clement L., 116.

Van Dorn, General Earl, dispatch from Beauregard to, 109.

Voltaire, Alexander H. Stephens contrasted with, 158, 177.

Von Borcke, H., quoted, 37.

Von Schmidt, General, his opinion of Stuart, 44.

Waddell, James D., his life of Linton Stephens, 168.

War, the, between the North and South, indispensable, 251; some results of, 259, 260; some lessons learned from, 260, 261.

Webster, Daniel, anecdote of, 141.

West, the great, question of its place in struggle between North and South, 250, 251.

West Point, Davis and Johnston said to have been hostile at, 8; Stuart's characteristics at, 35; Beauregard's superintendency at, 107; hated by Toombs, 211.

Whiting, General W. H. C., 110.

Whitmore, William, his pamphlet, *The Cavalier Dismounted*, 196.

Wigfall, General Louis T., letter from Johnston to, about Lee, 28.

Williamsburg, Johnston at, 3.

Winslow, Commodore John A., commander of the Kearsarge, 243.

Wise, John S., on Beauregard's admiration for women, 96; uncomplimentary to Benjamin, 125, 130, 138.

Young, J. R., 5.

A CATALOG OF SELECTED

DOVER BOOKS

IN ALL FIELDS OF INTEREST

A CATALOG OF SELECTED DOVER BOOKS IN ALL FIELDS OF INTEREST

CONCERNING THE SPIRITUAL IN ART, Wassily Kandinsky. Pioneering work by father of abstract art. Thoughts on color theory, nature of art. Analysis of earlier masters. 12 illustrations. 80pp. of text. 5⅜ x 8½. 23411-8

ANIMALS: 1,419 Copyright-Free Illustrations of Mammals, Birds, Fish, Insects, etc., Jim Harter (ed.). Clear wood engravings present, in extremely lifelike poses, over 1,000 species of animals. One of the most extensive pictorial sourcebooks of its kind. Captions. Index. 284pp. 9 x 12. 23766-4

CELTIC ART: The Methods of Construction, George Bain. Simple geometric techniques for making Celtic interlacements, spirals, Kells-type initials, animals, humans, etc. Over 500 illustrations. 160pp. 9 x 12. (Available in U.S. only.) 22923-8

AN ATLAS OF ANATOMY FOR ARTISTS, Fritz Schider. Most thorough reference work on art anatomy in the world. Hundreds of illustrations, including selections from works by Vesalius, Leonardo, Goya, Ingres, Michelangelo, others. 593 illustrations. 192pp. 7⅛ x 10¼. 20241-0

CELTIC HAND STROKE-BY-STROKE (Irish Half-Uncial from "The Book of Kells"): An Arthur Baker Calligraphy Manual, Arthur Baker. Complete guide to creating each letter of the alphabet in distinctive Celtic manner. Covers hand position, strokes, pens, inks, paper, more. Illustrated. 48pp. 8¼ x 11. 24336-2

EASY ORIGAMI, John Montroll. Charming collection of 32 projects (hat, cup, pelican, piano, swan, many more) specially designed for the novice origami hobbyist. Clearly illustrated easy-to-follow instructions insure that even beginning papercrafters will achieve successful results. 48pp. 8¼ x 11. 27298-2

THE COMPLETE BOOK OF BIRDHOUSE CONSTRUCTION FOR WOODWORKERS, Scott D. Campbell. Detailed instructions, illustrations, tables. Also data on bird habitat and instinct patterns. Bibliography. 3 tables. 63 illustrations in 15 figures. 48pp. 5¼ x 8½. 24407-5

BLOOMINGDALE'S ILLUSTRATED 1886 CATALOG: Fashions, Dry Goods and Housewares, Bloomingdale Brothers. Famed merchants' extremely rare catalog depicting about 1,700 products: clothing, housewares, firearms, dry goods, jewelry, more. Invaluable for dating, identifying vintage items. Also, copyright-free graphics for artists, designers. Co-published with Henry Ford Museum & Greenfield Village. 160pp. 8¼ x 11. 25780-0

HISTORIC COSTUME IN PICTURES, Braun & Schneider. Over 1,450 costumed figures in clearly detailed engravings–from dawn of civilization to end of 19th century. Captions. Many folk costumes. 256pp. 8⅜ x 11¾. 23150-X

STICKLEY CRAFTSMAN FURNITURE CATALOGS, Gustav Stickley and L. & J. G. Stickley. Beautiful, functional furniture in two authentic catalogs from 1910. 594 illustrations, including 277 photos, show settles, rockers, armchairs, reclining chairs, bookcases, desks, tables. 183pp. 6½ x 9¼. 23838-5

AMERICAN LOCOMOTIVES IN HISTORIC PHOTOGRAPHS: 1858 to 1949, Ron Ziel (ed.). A rare collection of 126 meticulously detailed official photographs, called "builder portraits," of American locomotives that majestically chronicle the rise of steam locomotive power in America. Introduction. Detailed captions. xi+ 129pp. 9 x 12. 27393-8

AMERICA'S LIGHTHOUSES: An Illustrated History, Francis Ross Holland, Jr. Delightfully written, profusely illustrated fact-filled survey of over 200 American lighthouses since 1716. History, anecdotes, technological advances, more. 240pp. 8 x 10¾. 25576-X

TOWARDS A NEW ARCHITECTURE, Le Corbusier. Pioneering manifesto by founder of "International School." Technical and aesthetic theories, views of industry, economics, relation of form to function, "mass-production split" and much more. Profusely illustrated. 320pp. 6⅛ x 9¼. (Available in U.S. only.) 25023-7

HOW THE OTHER HALF LIVES, Jacob Riis. Famous journalistic record, exposing poverty and degradation of New York slums around 1900, by major social reformer. 100 striking and influential photographs. 233pp. 10 x 7⅞. 22012-5

FRUIT KEY AND TWIG KEY TO TREES AND SHRUBS, William M. Harlow. One of the handiest and most widely used identification aids. Fruit key covers 120 deciduous and evergreen species; twig key 160 deciduous species. Easily used. Over 300 photographs. 126pp. 5⅜ x 8½. 20511-8

COMMON BIRD SONGS, Dr. Donald J. Borror. Songs of 60 most common U.S. birds: robins, sparrows, cardinals, bluejays, finches, more–arranged in order of increasing complexity. Up to 9 variations of songs of each species.
Cassette and manual 99911-4

ORCHIDS AS HOUSE PLANTS, Rebecca Tyson Northen. Grow cattleyas and many other kinds of orchids–in a window, in a case, or under artificial light. 63 illustrations. 148pp. 5⅜ x 8½. 23261-1

MONSTER MAZES, Dave Phillips. Masterful mazes at four levels of difficulty. Avoid deadly perils and evil creatures to find magical treasures. Solutions for all 32 exciting illustrated puzzles. 48pp. 8¼ x 11. 26005-4

MOZART'S DON GIOVANNI (DOVER OPERA LIBRETTO SERIES), Wolfgang Amadeus Mozart. Introduced and translated by Ellen H. Bleiler. Standard Italian libretto, with complete English translation. Convenient and thoroughly portable–an ideal companion for reading along with a recording or the performance itself. Introduction. List of characters. Plot summary. 121pp. 5¼ x 8½. 24944-1

TECHNICAL MANUAL AND DICTIONARY OF CLASSICAL BALLET, Gail Grant. Defines, explains, comments on steps, movements, poses and concepts. 15-page pictorial section. Basic book for student, viewer. 127pp. 5⅜ x 8½. 21843-0

THE CLARINET AND CLARINET PLAYING, David Pino. Lively, comprehensive work features suggestions about technique, musicianship, and musical interpretation, as well as guidelines for teaching, making your own reeds, and preparing for public performance. Includes an intriguing look at clarinet history. "A godsend," *The Clarinet,* Journal of the International Clarinet Society. Appendixes. 7 illus. 320pp. 5⅜ x 8½. 40270-3

HOLLYWOOD GLAMOR PORTRAITS, John Kobal (ed.). 145 photos from 1926-49. Harlow, Gable, Bogart, Bacall; 94 stars in all. Full background on photographers, technical aspects. 160pp. 8⅜ x 11¼. 23352-9

THE ANNOTATED CASEY AT THE BAT: A Collection of Ballads about the Mighty Casey/Third, Revised Edition, Martin Gardner (ed.). Amusing sequels and parodies of one of America's best-loved poems: Casey's Revenge, Why Casey Whiffed, Casey's Sister at the Bat, others. 256pp. 5⅜ x 8½. 28598-7

THE RAVEN AND OTHER FAVORITE POEMS, Edgar Allan Poe. Over 40 of the author's most memorable poems: "The Bells," "Ulalume," "Israfel," "To Helen," "The Conqueror Worm," "Eldorado," "Annabel Lee," many more. Alphabetic lists of titles and first lines. 64pp. 5$\frac{3}{16}$ x 8¼. 26685-0

PERSONAL MEMOIRS OF U. S. GRANT, Ulysses Simpson Grant. Intelligent, deeply moving firsthand account of Civil War campaigns, considered by many the finest military memoirs ever written. Includes letters, historic photographs, maps and more. 528pp. 6⅛ x 9¼. 28587-1

ANCIENT EGYPTIAN MATERIALS AND INDUSTRIES, A. Lucas and J. Harris. Fascinating, comprehensive, thoroughly documented text describes this ancient civilization's vast resources and the processes that incorporated them in daily life, including the use of animal products, building materials, cosmetics, perfumes and incense, fibers, glazed ware, glass and its manufacture, materials used in the mummification process, and much more. 544pp. 6⅛ x 9¼. (Available in U.S. only.) 40446-3

RUSSIAN STORIES/RUSSKIE RASSKAZY: A Dual-Language Book, edited by Gleb Struve. Twelve tales by such masters as Chekhov, Tolstoy, Dostoevsky, Pushkin, others. Excellent word-for-word English translations on facing pages, plus teaching and study aids, Russian/English vocabulary, biographical/critical introductions, more. 416pp. 5⅜ x 8½. 26244-8

PHILADELPHIA THEN AND NOW: 60 Sites Photographed in the Past and Present, Kenneth Finkel and Susan Oyama. Rare photographs of City Hall, Logan Square, Independence Hall, Betsy Ross House, other landmarks juxtaposed with contemporary views. Captures changing face of historic city. Introduction. Captions. 128pp. 8¼ x 11. 25790-8

AIA ARCHITECTURAL GUIDE TO NASSAU AND SUFFOLK COUNTIES, LONG ISLAND, The American Institute of Architects, Long Island Chapter, and the Society for the Preservation of Long Island Antiquities. Comprehensive, well-researched and generously illustrated volume brings to life over three centuries of Long Island's great architectural heritage. More than 240 photographs with authoritative, extensively detailed captions. 176pp. 8¼ x 11. 26946-9

NORTH AMERICAN INDIAN LIFE: Customs and Traditions of 23 Tribes, Elsie Clews Parsons (ed.). 27 fictionalized essays by noted anthropologists examine religion, customs, government, additional facets of life among the Winnebago, Crow, Zuni, Eskimo, other tribes. 480pp. 6⅛ x 9¼. 27377-6

FRANK LLOYD WRIGHT'S DANA HOUSE, Donald Hoffmann. Pictorial essay of residential masterpiece with over 160 interior and exterior photos, plans, elevations, sketches and studies. 128pp. 9¼ x 10¾. 29120-0

THE MALE AND FEMALE FIGURE IN MOTION: 60 Classic Photographic Sequences, Eadweard Muybridge. 60 true-action photographs of men and women walking, running, climbing, bending, turning, etc., reproduced from rare 19th-century masterpiece. vi + 121pp. 9 x 12. 24745-7

1001 QUESTIONS ANSWERED ABOUT THE SEASHORE, N. J. Berrill and Jacquelyn Berrill. Queries answered about dolphins, sea snails, sponges, starfish, fishes, shore birds, many others. Covers appearance, breeding, growth, feeding, much more. 305pp. 5¼ x 8¼. 23366-9

ATTRACTING BIRDS TO YOUR YARD, William J. Weber. Easy-to-follow guide offers advice on how to attract the greatest diversity of birds: birdhouses, feeders, water and waterers, much more. 96pp. $5\frac{3}{16}$ x 8¼. 28927-3

MEDICINAL AND OTHER USES OF NORTH AMERICAN PLANTS: A Historical Survey with Special Reference to the Eastern Indian Tribes, Charlotte Erichsen-Brown. Chronological historical citations document 500 years of usage of plants, trees, shrubs native to eastern Canada, northeastern U.S. Also complete identifying information. 343 illustrations. 544pp. 6½ x 9¼. 25951-X

STORYBOOK MAZES, Dave Phillips. 23 stories and mazes on two-page spreads: Wizard of Oz, Treasure Island, Robin Hood, etc. Solutions. 64pp. 8¼ x 11. 23628-5

AMERICAN NEGRO SONGS: 230 Folk Songs and Spirituals, Religious and Secular, John W. Work. This authoritative study traces the African influences of songs sung and played by black Americans at work, in church, and as entertainment. The author discusses the lyric significance of such songs as "Swing Low, Sweet Chariot," "John Henry," and others and offers the words and music for 230 songs. Bibliography. Index of Song Titles. 272pp. 6½ x 9¼. 40271-1

MOVIE-STAR PORTRAITS OF THE FORTIES, John Kobal (ed.). 163 glamor, studio photos of 106 stars of the 1940s: Rita Hayworth, Ava Gardner, Marlon Brando, Clark Gable, many more. 176pp. 8⅜ x 11¼. 23546-7

BENCHLEY LOST AND FOUND, Robert Benchley. Finest humor from early 30s, about pet peeves, child psychologists, post office and others. Mostly unavailable elsewhere. 73 illustrations by Peter Arno and others. 183pp. 5⅜ x 8½. 22410-4

YEKL and THE IMPORTED BRIDEGROOM AND OTHER STORIES OF YIDDISH NEW YORK, Abraham Cahan. Film Hester Street based on *Yekl* (1896). Novel, other stories among first about Jewish immigrants on N.Y.'s East Side. 240pp. 5⅜ x 8½. 22427-9

SELECTED POEMS, Walt Whitman. Generous sampling from *Leaves of Grass*. Twenty-four poems include "I Hear America Singing," "Song of the Open Road," "I Sing the Body Electric," "When Lilacs Last in the Dooryard Bloom'd," "O Captain! My Captain!"–all reprinted from an authoritative edition. Lists of titles and first lines. 128pp. $5\frac{3}{16}$ x 8¼. 26878-0

THE BEST TALES OF HOFFMANN, E. T. A. Hoffmann. 10 of Hoffmann's most important stories: "Nutcracker and the King of Mice," "The Golden Flowerpot," etc. 458pp. 5⅜ x 8½. 21793-0

FROM FETISH TO GOD IN ANCIENT EGYPT, E. A. Wallis Budge. Rich detailed survey of Egyptian conception of "God" and gods, magic, cult of animals, Osiris, more. Also, superb English translations of hymns and legends. 240 illustrations. 545pp. 5⅜ x 8½. 25803-3

FRENCH STORIES/CONTES FRANÇAIS: A Dual-Language Book, Wallace Fowlie. Ten stories by French masters, Voltaire to Camus: "Micromegas" by Voltaire; "The Atheist's Mass" by Balzac; "Minuet" by de Maupassant; "The Guest" by Camus, six more. Excellent English translations on facing pages. Also French-English vocabulary list, exercises, more. 352pp. 5⅜ x 8½. 26443-2

CHICAGO AT THE TURN OF THE CENTURY IN PHOTOGRAPHS: 122 Historic Views from the Collections of the Chicago Historical Society, Larry A. Viskochil. Rare large-format prints offer detailed views of City Hall, State Street, the Loop, Hull House, Union Station, many other landmarks, circa 1904-1913. Introduction. Captions. Maps. 144pp. 9⅜ x 12¼. 24656-6

OLD BROOKLYN IN EARLY PHOTOGRAPHS, 1865-1929, William Lee Younger. Luna Park, Gravesend race track, construction of Grand Army Plaza, moving of Hotel Brighton, etc. 157 previously unpublished photographs. 165pp. 8⅞ x 11¾. 23587-4

THE MYTHS OF THE NORTH AMERICAN INDIANS, Lewis Spence. Rich anthology of the myths and legends of the Algonquins, Iroquois, Pawnees and Sioux, prefaced by an extensive historical and ethnological commentary. 36 illustrations. 480pp. 5⅜ x 8½. 25967-6

AN ENCYCLOPEDIA OF BATTLES: Accounts of Over 1,560 Battles from 1479 B.C. to the Present, David Eggenberger. Essential details of every major battle in recorded history from the first battle of Megiddo in 1479 B.C. to Grenada in 1984. List of Battle Maps. New Appendix covering the years 1967-1984. Index. 99 illustrations. 544pp. 6½ x 9¼. 24913-1

SAILING ALONE AROUND THE WORLD, Captain Joshua Slocum. First man to sail around the world, alone, in small boat. One of great feats of seamanship told in delightful manner. 67 illustrations. 294pp. 5⅜ x 8½. 20326-3

ANARCHISM AND OTHER ESSAYS, Emma Goldman. Powerful, penetrating, prophetic essays on direct action, role of minorities, prison reform, puritan hypocrisy, violence, etc. 271pp. 5⅜ x 8½. 22484-8

MYTHS OF THE HINDUS AND BUDDHISTS, Ananda K. Coomaraswamy and Sister Nivedita. Great stories of the epics; deeds of Krishna, Shiva, taken from puranas, Vedas, folk tales; etc. 32 illustrations. 400pp. 5⅜ x 8½. 21759-0

THE TRAUMA OF BIRTH, Otto Rank. Rank's controversial thesis that anxiety neurosis is caused by profound psychological trauma which occurs at birth. 256pp. 5⅜ x 8½. 27974-X

A THEOLOGICO-POLITICAL TREATISE, Benedict Spinoza. Also contains unfinished Political Treatise. Great classic on religious liberty, theory of government on common consent. R. Elwes translation. Total of 421pp. 5⅜ x 8½. 20249-6

MY BONDAGE AND MY FREEDOM, Frederick Douglass. Born a slave, Douglass became outspoken force in antislavery movement. The best of Douglass' autobiographies. Graphic description of slave life. 464pp. 5⅜ x 8½. 22457-0

FOLLOWING THE EQUATOR: A Journey Around the World, Mark Twain. Fascinating humorous account of 1897 voyage to Hawaii, Australia, India, New Zealand, etc. Ironic, bemused reports on peoples, customs, climate, flora and fauna, politics, much more. 197 illustrations. 720pp. 5⅜ x 8½. 26113-1

THE PEOPLE CALLED SHAKERS, Edward D. Andrews. Definitive study of Shakers: origins, beliefs, practices, dances, social organization, furniture and crafts, etc. 33 illustrations. 351pp. 5⅜ x 8½. 21081-2

THE MYTHS OF GREECE AND ROME, H. A. Guerber. A classic of mythology, generously illustrated, long prized for its simple, graphic, accurate retelling of the principal myths of Greece and Rome, and for its commentary on their origins and significance. With 64 illustrations by Michelangelo, Raphael, Titian, Rubens, Canova, Bernini and others. 480pp. 5⅜ x 8½. 27584-1

PSYCHOLOGY OF MUSIC, Carl E. Seashore. Classic work discusses music as a medium from psychological viewpoint. Clear treatment of physical acoustics, auditory apparatus, sound perception, development of musical skills, nature of musical feeling, host of other topics. 88 figures. 408pp. 5⅜ x 8½. 21851-1

THE PHILOSOPHY OF HISTORY, Georg W. Hegel. Great classic of Western thought develops concept that history is not chance but rational process, the evolution of freedom. 457pp. 5⅜ x 8½. 20112-0

THE BOOK OF TEA, Kakuzo Okakura. Minor classic of the Orient: entertaining, charming explanation, interpretation of traditional Japanese culture in terms of tea ceremony. 94pp. 5⅜ x 8½. 20070-1

LIFE IN ANCIENT EGYPT, Adolf Erman. Fullest, most thorough, detailed older account with much not in more recent books, domestic life, religion, magic, medicine, commerce, much more. Many illustrations reproduce tomb paintings, carvings, hieroglyphs, etc. 597pp. 5⅜ x 8½. 22632-8

SUNDIALS, Their Theory and Construction, Albert Waugh. Far and away the best, most thorough coverage of ideas, mathematics concerned, types, construction, adjusting anywhere. Simple, nontechnical treatment allows even children to build several of these dials. Over 100 illustrations. 230pp. 5⅜ x 8½. 22947-5

THEORETICAL HYDRODYNAMICS, L. M. Milne-Thomson. Classic exposition of the mathematical theory of fluid motion, applicable to both hydrodynamics and aerodynamics. Over 600 exercises. 768pp. 6⅛ x 9¼. 68970-0

SONGS OF EXPERIENCE: Facsimile Reproduction with 26 Plates in Full Color, William Blake. 26 full-color plates from a rare 1826 edition. Includes "The Tyger," "London," "Holy Thursday," and other poems. Printed text of poems. 48pp. 5¼ x 7. 24636-1

OLD-TIME VIGNETTES IN FULL COLOR, Carol Belanger Grafton (ed.). Over 390 charming, often sentimental illustrations, selected from archives of Victorian graphics–pretty women posing, children playing, food, flowers, kittens and puppies, smiling cherubs, birds and butterflies, much more. All copyright-free. 48pp. 9¼ x 12¼. 27269-9

PERSPECTIVE FOR ARTISTS, Rex Vicat Cole. Depth, perspective of sky and sea, shadows, much more, not usually covered. 391 diagrams, 81 reproductions of drawings and paintings. 279pp. 5⅜ x 8½. 22487-2

DRAWING THE LIVING FIGURE, Joseph Sheppard. Innovative approach to artistic anatomy focuses on specifics of surface anatomy, rather than muscles and bones. Over 170 drawings of live models in front, back and side views, and in widely varying poses. Accompanying diagrams. 177 illustrations. Introduction. Index. 144pp. 8⅜ x11¼. 26723-7

GOTHIC AND OLD ENGLISH ALPHABETS: 100 Complete Fonts, Dan X. Solo. Add power, elegance to posters, signs, other graphics with 100 stunning copyright-free alphabets: Blackstone, Dolbey, Germania, 97 more–including many lower-case, numerals, punctuation marks. 104pp. 8⅛ x 11. 24695-7

HOW TO DO BEADWORK, Mary White. Fundamental book on craft from simple projects to five-bead chains and woven works. 106 illustrations. 142pp. 5⅜ x 8. 20697-1

THE BOOK OF WOOD CARVING, Charles Marshall Sayers. Finest book for beginners discusses fundamentals and offers 34 designs. "Absolutely first rate . . . well thought out and well executed."–E. J. Tangerman. 118pp. 7¾ x 10⅝. 23654-4

ILLUSTRATED CATALOG OF CIVIL WAR MILITARY GOODS: Union Army Weapons, Insignia, Uniform Accessories, and Other Equipment, Schuyler, Hartley, and Graham. Rare, profusely illustrated 1846 catalog includes Union Army uniform and dress regulations, arms and ammunition, coats, insignia, flags, swords, rifles, etc. 226 illustrations. 160pp. 9 x 12. 24939-5

WOMEN'S FASHIONS OF THE EARLY 1900s: An Unabridged Republication of "New York Fashions, 1909," National Cloak & Suit Co. Rare catalog of mail-order fashions documents women's and children's clothing styles shortly after the turn of the century. Captions offer full descriptions, prices. Invaluable resource for fashion, costume historians. Approximately 725 illustrations. 128pp. 8⅜ x 11¼. 27276-1

THE 1912 AND 1915 GUSTAV STICKLEY FURNITURE CATALOGS, Gustav Stickley. With over 200 detailed illustrations and descriptions, these two catalogs are essential reading and reference materials and identification guides for Stickley furniture. Captions cite materials, dimensions and prices. 112pp. 6½ x 9¼. 26676-1

EARLY AMERICAN LOCOMOTIVES, John H. White, Jr. Finest locomotive engravings from early 19th century: historical (1804–74), main-line (after 1870), special, foreign, etc. 147 plates. 142pp. 11⅜ x 8¼. 22772-3

THE TALL SHIPS OF TODAY IN PHOTOGRAPHS, Frank O. Braynard. Lavishly illustrated tribute to nearly 100 majestic contemporary sailing vessels: Amerigo Vespucci, Clearwater, Constitution, Eagle, Mayflower, Sea Cloud, Victory, many more. Authoritative captions provide statistics, background on each ship. 190 black-and-white photographs and illustrations. Introduction. 128pp. 8⅞ x 11¾. 27163-3

LITTLE BOOK OF EARLY AMERICAN CRAFTS AND TRADES, Peter Stockham (ed.). 1807 children's book explains crafts and trades: baker, hatter, cooper, potter, and many others. 23 copperplate illustrations. 140pp. 4⅝ x 6. 23336-7

VICTORIAN FASHIONS AND COSTUMES FROM HARPER'S BAZAR, 1867–1898, Stella Blum (ed.). Day costumes, evening wear, sports clothes, shoes, hats, other accessories in over 1,000 detailed engravings. 320pp. 9⅜ x 12¼. 22990-4

GUSTAV STICKLEY, THE CRAFTSMAN, Mary Ann Smith. Superb study surveys broad scope of Stickley's achievement, especially in architecture. Design philosophy, rise and fall of the Craftsman empire, descriptions and floor plans for many Craftsman houses, more. 86 black-and-white halftones. 31 line illustrations. Introduction 208pp. 6½ x 9¼. 27210-9

THE LONG ISLAND RAIL ROAD IN EARLY PHOTOGRAPHS, Ron Ziel. Over 220 rare photos, informative text document origin (1844) and development of rail service on Long Island. Vintage views of early trains, locomotives, stations, passengers, crews, much more. Captions. 8⅞ x 11¾. 26301-0

VOYAGE OF THE LIBERDADE, Joshua Slocum. Great 19th-century mariner's thrilling, first-hand account of the wreck of his ship off South America, the 35-foot boat he built from the wreckage, and its remarkable voyage home. 128pp. 5⅜ x 8½. 40022-0

TEN BOOKS ON ARCHITECTURE, Vitruvius. The most important book ever written on architecture. Early Roman aesthetics, technology, classical orders, site selection, all other aspects. Morgan translation. 331pp. 5⅜ x 8½. 20645-9

THE HUMAN FIGURE IN MOTION, Eadweard Muybridge. More than 4,500 stopped-action photos, in action series, showing undraped men, women, children jumping, lying down, throwing, sitting, wrestling, carrying, etc. 390pp. 7⅞ x 10⅝. 20204-6 Clothbd.

TREES OF THE EASTERN AND CENTRAL UNITED STATES AND CANADA, William M. Harlow. Best one-volume guide to 140 trees. Full descriptions, woodlore, range, etc. Over 600 illustrations. Handy size. 288pp. 4½ x 6⅜. 20395-6

SONGS OF WESTERN BIRDS, Dr. Donald J. Borror. Complete song and call repertoire of 60 western species, including flycatchers, juncoes, cactus wrens, many more–includes fully illustrated booklet. Cassette and manual 99913-0

GROWING AND USING HERBS AND SPICES, Milo Miloradovich. Versatile handbook provides all the information needed for cultivation and use of all the herbs and spices available in North America. 4 illustrations. Index. Glossary. 236pp. 5⅜ x 8½. 25058-X

BIG BOOK OF MAZES AND LABYRINTHS, Walter Shepherd. 50 mazes and labyrinths in all–classical, solid, ripple, and more–in one great volume. Perfect inexpensive puzzler for clever youngsters. Full solutions. 112pp. 8⅛ x 11. 22951-3

PIANO TUNING, J. Cree Fischer. Clearest, best book for beginner, amateur. Simple repairs, raising dropped notes, tuning by easy method of flattened fifths. No previous skills needed. 4 illustrations. 201pp. 5⅜ x 8½. 23267-0

HINTS TO SINGERS, Lillian Nordica. Selecting the right teacher, developing confidence, overcoming stage fright, and many other important skills receive thoughtful discussion in this indispensible guide, written by a world-famous diva of four decades' experience. 96pp. 5⅜ x 8½. 40094-8

THE COMPLETE NONSENSE OF EDWARD LEAR, Edward Lear. All nonsense limericks, zany alphabets, Owl and Pussycat, songs, nonsense botany, etc., illustrated by Lear. Total of 320pp. 5⅜ x 8½. (Available in U.S. only.) 20167-8

VICTORIAN PARLOUR POETRY: An Annotated Anthology, Michael R. Turner. 117 gems by Longfellow, Tennyson, Browning, many lesser-known poets. "The Village Blacksmith," "Curfew Must Not Ring Tonight," "Only a Baby Small," dozens more, often difficult to find elsewhere. Index of poets, titles, first lines. xxiii + 325pp. 5⅜ x 8¼. 27044-0

DUBLINERS, James Joyce. Fifteen stories offer vivid, tightly focused observations of the lives of Dublin's poorer classes. At least one, "The Dead," is considered a masterpiece. Reprinted complete and unabridged from standard edition. 160pp. 5$\frac{3}{16}$ x 8¼. 26870-5

GREAT WEIRD TALES: 14 Stories by Lovecraft, Blackwood, Machen and Others, S. T. Joshi (ed.). 14 spellbinding tales, including "The Sin Eater," by Fiona McLeod, "The Eye Above the Mantel," by Frank Belknap Long, as well as renowned works by R. H. Barlow, Lord Dunsany, Arthur Machen, W. C. Morrow and eight other masters of the genre. 256pp. 5⅜ x 8½. (Available in U.S. only.) 40436-6

THE BOOK OF THE SACRED MAGIC OF ABRAMELIN THE MAGE, translated by S. MacGregor Mathers. Medieval manuscript of ceremonial magic. Basic document in Aleister Crowley, Golden Dawn groups. 268pp. 5⅜ x 8½. 23211-5

NEW RUSSIAN-ENGLISH AND ENGLISH-RUSSIAN DICTIONARY, M. A. O'Brien. This is a remarkably handy Russian dictionary, containing a surprising amount of information, including over 70,000 entries. 366pp. 4½ x 6⅛. 20208-9

HISTORIC HOMES OF THE AMERICAN PRESIDENTS, Second, Revised Edition, Irvin Haas. A traveler's guide to American Presidential homes, most open to the public, depicting and describing homes occupied by every American President from George Washington to George Bush. With visiting hours, admission charges, travel routes. 175 photographs. Index. 160pp. 8¼ x 11. 26751-2

NEW YORK IN THE FORTIES, Andreas Feininger. 162 brilliant photographs by the well-known photographer, formerly with *Life* magazine. Commuters, shoppers, Times Square at night, much else from city at its peak. Captions by John von Hartz. 181pp. 9¼ x 10¾. 23585-8

INDIAN SIGN LANGUAGE, William Tomkins. Over 525 signs developed by Sioux and other tribes. Written instructions and diagrams. Also 290 pictographs. 111pp. 6⅛ x 9¼. 22029-X

ANATOMY: A Complete Guide for Artists, Joseph Sheppard. A master of figure drawing shows artists how to render human anatomy convincingly. Over 460 illustrations. 224pp. 8⅜ x 11¼. 27279-6

MEDIEVAL CALLIGRAPHY: Its History and Technique, Marc Drogin. Spirited history, comprehensive instruction manual covers 13 styles (ca. 4th century through 15th). Excellent photographs; directions for duplicating medieval techniques with modern tools. 224pp. 8⅜ x 11¼. 26142-5

DRIED FLOWERS: How to Prepare Them, Sarah Whitlock and Martha Rankin. Complete instructions on how to use silica gel, meal and borax, perlite aggregate, sand and borax, glycerine and water to create attractive permanent flower arrangements. 12 illustrations. 32pp. 5⅜ x 8½. 21802-3

EASY-TO-MAKE BIRD FEEDERS FOR WOODWORKERS, Scott D. Campbell. Detailed, simple-to-use guide for designing, constructing, caring for and using feeders. Text, illustrations for 12 classic and contemporary designs. 96pp. 5⅜ x 8½. 25847-5

SCOTTISH WONDER TALES FROM MYTH AND LEGEND, Donald A. Mackenzie. 16 lively tales tell of giants rumbling down mountainsides, of a magic wand that turns stone pillars into warriors, of gods and goddesses, evil hags, powerful forces and more. 240pp. 5⅜ x 8½. 29677-6

THE HISTORY OF UNDERCLOTHES, C. Willett Cunnington and Phyllis Cunnington. Fascinating, well-documented survey covering six centuries of English undergarments, enhanced with over 100 illustrations: 12th-century laced-up bodice, footed long drawers (1795), 19th-century bustles, 19th-century corsets for men, Victorian "bust improvers," much more. 272pp. 5⅜ x 8¼. 27124-2

ARTS AND CRAFTS FURNITURE: The Complete Brooks Catalog of 1912, Brooks Manufacturing Co. Photos and detailed descriptions of more than 150 now very collectible furniture designs from the Arts and Crafts movement depict davenports, settees, buffets, desks, tables, chairs, bedsteads, dressers and more, all built of solid, quarter-sawed oak. Invaluable for students and enthusiasts of antiques, Americana and the decorative arts. 80pp. 6½ x 9¼. 27471-3

WILBUR AND ORVILLE: A Biography of the Wright Brothers, Fred Howard. Definitive, crisply written study tells the full story of the brothers' lives and work. A vividly written biography, unparalleled in scope and color, that also captures the spirit of an extraordinary era. 560pp. 6⅛ x 9¼. 40297-5

THE ARTS OF THE SAILOR: Knotting, Splicing and Ropework, Hervey Garrett Smith. Indispensable shipboard reference covers tools, basic knots and useful hitches; handsewing and canvas work, more. Over 100 illustrations. Delightful reading for sea lovers. 256pp. 5⅜ x 8½. 26440-8

FRANK LLOYD WRIGHT'S FALLINGWATER: The House and Its History, Second, Revised Edition, Donald Hoffmann. A total revision–both in text and illustrations–of the standard document on Fallingwater, the boldest, most personal architectural statement of Wright's mature years, updated with valuable new material from the recently opened Frank Lloyd Wright Archives. "Fascinating"–*The New York Times.* 116 illustrations. 128pp. 9¼ x 10¾. 27430-6

PHOTOGRAPHIC SKETCHBOOK OF THE CIVIL WAR, Alexander Gardner. 100 photos taken on field during the Civil War. Famous shots of Manassas Harper's Ferry, Lincoln, Richmond, slave pens, etc. 244pp. 10⅝ x 8¼. 22731-6

FIVE ACRES AND INDEPENDENCE, Maurice G. Kains. Great back-to-the-land classic explains basics of self-sufficient farming. The one book to get. 95 illustrations. 397pp. 5⅜ x 8½. 20974-1

SONGS OF EASTERN BIRDS, Dr. Donald J. Borror. Songs and calls of 60 species most common to eastern U.S.: warblers, woodpeckers, flycatchers, thrushes, larks, many more in high-quality recording. Cassette and manual 99912-2

A MODERN HERBAL, Margaret Grieve. Much the fullest, most exact, most useful compilation of herbal material. Gigantic alphabetical encyclopedia, from aconite to zedoary, gives botanical information, medical properties, folklore, economic uses, much else. Indispensable to serious reader. 161 illustrations. 888pp. 6½ x 9¼. 2-vol. set. (Available in U.S. only.) Vol. I: 22798-7
Vol. II: 22799-5

HIDDEN TREASURE MAZE BOOK, Dave Phillips. Solve 34 challenging mazes accompanied by heroic tales of adventure. Evil dragons, people-eating plants, bloodthirsty giants, many more dangerous adversaries lurk at every twist and turn. 34 mazes, stories, solutions. 48pp. 8¼ x 11. 24566-7

LETTERS OF W. A. MOZART, Wolfgang A. Mozart. Remarkable letters show bawdy wit, humor, imagination, musical insights, contemporary musical world; includes some letters from Leopold Mozart. 276pp. 5⅜ x 8½. 22859-2

BASIC PRINCIPLES OF CLASSICAL BALLET, Agrippina Vaganova. Great Russian theoretician, teacher explains methods for teaching classical ballet. 118 illustrations. 175pp. 5⅜ x 8½. 22036-2

THE JUMPING FROG, Mark Twain. Revenge edition. The original story of The Celebrated Jumping Frog of Calaveras County, a hapless French translation, and Twain's hilarious "retranslation" from the French. 12 illustrations. 66pp. 5⅜ x 8½. 22686-7

BEST REMEMBERED POEMS, Martin Gardner (ed.). The 126 poems in this superb collection of 19th- and 20th-century British and American verse range from Shelley's "To a Skylark" to the impassioned "Renascence" of Edna St. Vincent Millay and to Edward Lear's whimsical "The Owl and the Pussycat." 224pp. 5⅜ x 8½. 27165-X

COMPLETE SONNETS, William Shakespeare. Over 150 exquisite poems deal with love, friendship, the tyranny of time, beauty's evanescence, death and other themes in language of remarkable power, precision and beauty. Glossary of archaic terms. 80pp. 5$\frac{3}{16}$ x 8¼. 26686-9

THE BATTLES THAT CHANGED HISTORY, Fletcher Pratt. Eminent historian profiles 16 crucial conflicts, ancient to modern, that changed the course of civilization. 352pp. 5⅜ x 8½. 41129-X

THE WIT AND HUMOR OF OSCAR WILDE, Alvin Redman (ed.). More than 1,000 ripostes, paradoxes, wisecracks: Work is the curse of the drinking classes; I can resist everything except temptation; etc. 258pp. 5⅜ x 8½. 20602-5

SHAKESPEARE LEXICON AND QUOTATION DICTIONARY, Alexander Schmidt. Full definitions, locations, shades of meaning in every word in plays and poems. More than 50,000 exact quotations. 1,485pp. 6½ x 9¼. 2-vol. set.
Vol. 1: 22726-X
Vol. 2: 22727-8

SELECTED POEMS, Emily Dickinson. Over 100 best-known, best-loved poems by one of America's foremost poets, reprinted from authoritative early editions. No comparable edition at this price. Index of first lines. 64pp. 5$\frac{3}{16}$ x 8¼. 26466-1

THE INSIDIOUS DR. FU-MANCHU, Sax Rohmer. The first of the popular mystery series introduces a pair of English detectives to their archnemesis, the diabolical Dr. Fu-Manchu. Flavorful atmosphere, fast-paced action, and colorful characters enliven this classic of the genre. 208pp. 5$\frac{3}{16}$ x 8¼. 29898-1

THE MALLEUS MALEFICARUM OF KRAMER AND SPRENGER, translated by Montague Summers. Full text of most important witchhunter's "bible," used by both Catholics and Protestants. 278pp. 6⅝ x 10. 22802-9

SPANISH STORIES/CUENTOS ESPAÑOLES: A Dual-Language Book, Angel Flores (ed.). Unique format offers 13 great stories in Spanish by Cervantes, Borges, others. Faithful English translations on facing pages. 352pp. 5⅜ x 8½. 25399-6

GARDEN CITY, LONG ISLAND, IN EARLY PHOTOGRAPHS, 1869–1919, Mildred H. Smith. Handsome treasury of 118 vintage pictures, accompanied by carefully researched captions, document the Garden City Hotel fire (1899), the Vanderbilt Cup Race (1908), the first airmail flight departing from the Nassau Boulevard Aerodrome (1911), and much more. 96pp. 8⅞ x 11¾. 40669-5

OLD QUEENS, N.Y., IN EARLY PHOTOGRAPHS, Vincent F. Seyfried and William Asadorian. Over 160 rare photographs of Maspeth, Jamaica, Jackson Heights, and other areas. Vintage views of DeWitt Clinton mansion, 1939 World's Fair and more. Captions. 192pp. 8⅞ x 11. 26358-4

CAPTURED BY THE INDIANS: 15 Firsthand Accounts, 1750-1870, Frederick Drimmer. Astounding true historical accounts of grisly torture, bloody conflicts, relentless pursuits, miraculous escapes and more, by people who lived to tell the tale. 384pp. 5⅜ x 8½. 24901-8

THE WORLD'S GREAT SPEECHES (Fourth Enlarged Edition), Lewis Copeland, Lawrence W. Lamm, and Stephen J. McKenna. Nearly 300 speeches provide public speakers with a wealth of updated quotes and inspiration–from Pericles' funeral oration and William Jennings Bryan's "Cross of Gold Speech" to Malcolm X's powerful words on the Black Revolution and Earl of Spenser's tribute to his sister, Diana, Princess of Wales. 944pp. 5⅜ x 8⅜. 40903-1

THE BOOK OF THE SWORD, Sir Richard F. Burton. Great Victorian scholar/adventurer's eloquent, erudite history of the "queen of weapons"–from prehistory to early Roman Empire. Evolution and development of early swords, variations (sabre, broadsword, cutlass, scimitar, etc.), much more. 336pp. 6⅛ x 9¼.
25434-8

AUTOBIOGRAPHY: The Story of My Experiments with Truth, Mohandas K. Gandhi. Boyhood, legal studies, purification, the growth of the Satyagraha (nonviolent protest) movement. Critical, inspiring work of the man responsible for the freedom of India. 480pp. 5⅜ x 8½. (Available in U.S. only.) 24593-4

CELTIC MYTHS AND LEGENDS, T. W. Rolleston. Masterful retelling of Irish and Welsh stories and tales. Cuchulain, King Arthur, Deirdre, the Grail, many more. First paperback edition. 58 full-page illustrations. 512pp. 5⅜ x 8½. 26507-2

THE PRINCIPLES OF PSYCHOLOGY, William James. Famous long course complete, unabridged. Stream of thought, time perception, memory, experimental methods; great work decades ahead of its time. 94 figures. 1,391pp. 5⅜ x 8½. 2-vol. set.
Vol. I: 20381-6 Vol. II: 20382-4

THE WORLD AS WILL AND REPRESENTATION, Arthur Schopenhauer. Definitive English translation of Schopenhauer's life work, correcting more than 1,000 errors, omissions in earlier translations. Translated by E. F. J. Payne. Total of 1,269pp. 5⅜ x 8½. 2-vol. set. Vol. 1: 21761-2 Vol. 2: 21762-0

MAGIC AND MYSTERY IN TIBET, Madame Alexandra David-Neel. Experiences among lamas, magicians, sages, sorcerers, Bonpa wizards. A true psychic discovery. 32 illustrations. 321pp. 5⅜ x 8½. (Available in U.S. only.) 22682-4

THE EGYPTIAN BOOK OF THE DEAD, E. A. Wallis Budge. Complete reproduction of Ani's papyrus, finest ever found. Full hieroglyphic text, interlinear transliteration, word-for-word translation, smooth translation. 533pp. 6½ x 9¼. 21866-X

MATHEMATICS FOR THE NONMATHEMATICIAN, Morris Kline. Detailed, college-level treatment of mathematics in cultural and historical context, with numerous exercises. Recommended Reading Lists. Tables. Numerous figures. 641pp. 5⅜ x 8½.
24823-2

PROBABILISTIC METHODS IN THE THEORY OF STRUCTURES, Isaac Elishakoff. Well-written introduction covers the elements of the theory of probability from two or more random variables, the reliability of such multivariable structures, the theory of random function, Monte Carlo methods of treating problems incapable of exact solution, and more. Examples. 502pp. 5⅜ x 8½. 40691-1

THE RIME OF THE ANCIENT MARINER, Gustave Doré, S. T. Coleridge. Doré's finest work; 34 plates capture moods, subtleties of poem. Flawless full-size reproductions printed on facing pages with authoritative text of poem. "Beautiful. Simply beautiful."–*Publisher's Weekly.* 77pp. 9¼ x 12. 22305-1

NORTH AMERICAN INDIAN DESIGNS FOR ARTISTS AND CRAFTSPEOPLE, Eva Wilson. Over 360 authentic copyright-free designs adapted from Navajo blankets, Hopi pottery, Sioux buffalo hides, more. Geometrics, symbolic figures, plant and animal motifs, etc. 128pp. 8⅜ x 11. (Not for sale in the United Kingdom.) 25341-4

SCULPTURE: Principles and Practice, Louis Slobodkin. Step-by-step approach to clay, plaster, metals, stone; classical and modern. 253 drawings, photos. 255pp. 8⅛ x 11.
22960-2

THE INFLUENCE OF SEA POWER UPON HISTORY, 1660–1783, A. T. Mahan. Influential classic of naval history and tactics still used as text in war colleges. First paperback edition. 4 maps. 24 battle plans. 640pp. 5⅜ x 8½. 25509-3

THE STORY OF THE TITANIC AS TOLD BY ITS SURVIVORS, Jack Winocour (ed.). What it was really like. Panic, despair, shocking inefficiency, and a little heroism. More thrilling than any fictional account. 26 illustrations. 320pp. 5⅜ x 8½. 20610-6

FAIRY AND FOLK TALES OF THE IRISH PEASANTRY, William Butler Yeats (ed.). Treasury of 64 tales from the twilight world of Celtic myth and legend: "The Soul Cages," "The Kildare Pooka," "King O'Toole and his Goose," many more. Introduction and Notes by W. B. Yeats. 352pp. 5⅜ x 8½. 26941-8

BUDDHIST MAHAYANA TEXTS, E. B. Cowell and others (eds.). Superb, accurate translations of basic documents in Mahayana Buddhism, highly important in history of religions. The Buddha-karita of Asvaghosha, Larger Sukhavativyuha, more. 448pp. 5⅜ x 8½. 25552-2

ONE TWO THREE . . . INFINITY: Facts and Speculations of Science, George Gamow. Great physicist's fascinating, readable overview of contemporary science: number theory, relativity, fourth dimension, entropy, genes, atomic structure, much more. 128 illustrations. Index. 352pp. 5⅜ x 8½. 25664-2

EXPERIMENTATION AND MEASUREMENT, W. J. Youden. Introductory manual explains laws of measurement in simple terms and offers tips for achieving accuracy and minimizing errors. Mathematics of measurement, use of instruments, experimenting with machines. 1994 edition. Foreword. Preface. Introduction. Epilogue. Selected Readings. Glossary. Index. Tables and figures. 128pp. 5⅜ x 8½. 40451-X

DALÍ ON MODERN ART: The Cuckolds of Antiquated Modern Art, Salvador Dalí. Influential painter skewers modern art and its practitioners. Outrageous evaluations of Picasso, Cézanne, Turner, more. 15 renderings of paintings discussed. 44 calligraphic decorations by Dalí. 96pp. 5⅜ x 8½. (Available in U.S. only.) 29220-7

ANTIQUE PLAYING CARDS: A Pictorial History, Henry René D'Allemagne. Over 900 elaborate, decorative images from rare playing cards (14th–20th centuries): Bacchus, death, dancing dogs, hunting scenes, royal coats of arms, players cheating, much more. 96pp. 9¼ x 12¼. 29265-7

MAKING FURNITURE MASTERPIECES: 30 Projects with Measured Drawings, Franklin H. Gottshall. Step-by-step instructions, illustrations for constructing handsome, useful pieces, among them a Sheraton desk, Chippendale chair, Spanish desk, Queen Anne table and a William and Mary dressing mirror. 224pp. 8⅛ x 11¼. 29338-6

THE FOSSIL BOOK: A Record of Prehistoric Life, Patricia V. Rich et al. Profusely illustrated definitive guide covers everything from single-celled organisms and dinosaurs to birds and mammals and the interplay between climate and man. Over 1,500 illustrations. 760pp. 7½ x 10⅛. 29371-8